ANATOMY OF A GHOST

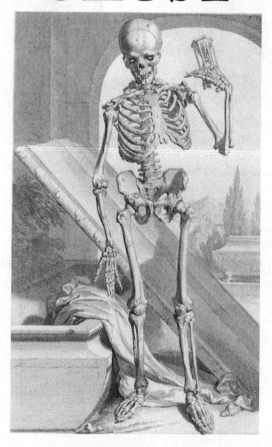

By Robin M. Strom-Mackey

PUBLISHED BY COSMIC PANTHEON PRESS
www.cosmicpantheon.com
PROUDLY PRINTED IN THE USA!

*This book is dedicated to Linda
who has always loved and supported me,*

*and Gene who has always believed in me and
inspired me.*

CHAPTER 1: TABLE OF CONTENTS

INTRODUCTION

Frequently I am asked how I got into paranormal research. As a young girl, I was always fascinated by the macabre. During sleepovers with my friend Heidi we would tell each other ghost stories from our rather limited repertoire. Oh, the delicious scary stories we told one another, working ourselves up to such a fright that we would inevitably have to sleep in her parents' room on the floor. As a teenager I loved spooky movies, and my brother and our friends would stay up all night on Halloween watching back to back horror movies. I was absolutely paralyzed with fear by *The Shining.*

Many years later I'd find that the story was actually based on a real hotel. For me the stories were just that, stories; fascinating, entertaining, blood curdling fun. I never once had an unusual experience. I'm not sure I ever seriously considered that a ghost story was anything but fictional. I have heard it explained that the difference between believers in the paranormal, and non- believers is merely the difference between someone who has experienced the paranormal and someone who has not. I think this is a true observation.

I OWNED A HOUSE IN PENNSYLVANIA

I'd gotten a job as a professor in the Communications Department at the local college in a small town in northern Pennsylvania. We were a younger couple, in our thirties with abundant energy and financial resources at our disposal. This was to be the first home we purchased and we were ecstatic.

We contacted an agent and began the furious hunt for a house. The town was an old one, full of the relics of mansions from the height of the coal mining industry. The coal mines were mainly defunct, but the relics of the golden age were still standing, testimony to better times.

BY ROBIN M. STROM-MACKEY

It had always been a dream of mine to own a stately Victorian mansion and I finally had the opportunity. The two staircases, the grand entry way, the two parlors (one for the men, one for the ladies) the large formal dining room all were as they had always been. The house was a magnificent example of 19th century craftsmanship.

After closing on our new house, we began cleaning the old manse like a horde of banshees set on destruction. We put our two-year-old son down for the night in the first-floor bedroom in a nest of pillows and blankets, away from all the mess and chaos. We ourselves worked late into the night, finally bedding down in the parlor in a couple of sleeping bags.

Exhausted we fell to sleep in minutes. Sometime in the wee hours of the night I awoke abruptly. I opened my eyes and looked up into the face of a small child, the face I took to be that of my tiny son. It was very dark, and I was barely awake, and so I knew only that it was the face of a small child that I was looking at – hovering directly over my face. The child then got up from his kneeling position next to my sleeping bag and before my eyes skipped off down the hall. Now, two-year-olds are precocious and so I thought nothing of it, except for the fact that at two a child doesn't typically have the coordination to skip, that being a later skill they acquire. I do remember thinking, I didn't know he could skip, followed closely by the thought, what in the hell is he up to now? I didn't hear him moving around, which is usually a bad sign when it comes to very small children – or even bigger children truth be told. I called his name a few times, but got absolutely no response. Finally, I dragged my very tired frame out of the sleeping bag to follow him down the hall. I didn't see him about. So I went into the first-floor bedroom where we had put him down in the first place to find him sound asleep in his little nest of pillows and blankets. I remember thinking, "that isn't possible, I just saw him skipping down the hall," followed closely by the thought, "what in the hell did I just see?"

Throughout what turned out to be a short tenure in that beautiful old home I never again saw the child ghost that I believe resided there with us. But I would experience many aural anomalies. My son was and is an early riser. One morning at 5am while in the Mansfield house I distinctly heard him playing in the upstairs hallway outside our bedroom. I inwardly moaned at the hour, wondering why any human being would willingly leave their bed at such a crazy time. Not wanting to get out of bed myself, I yelled at him instead, telling him to go back to bed. When that didn't work, I finally got up and went out to the hall to find...no one there. Confused profoundly I walked across the hall to my son's room to find him in bed and sound asleep.

ANATOMY OF A GHOST

My mother came to visit us and had a similar experience. She heard playing on the back stairs. Worried that her grandson was playing on the stairs and might get hurt, she went to shag him off, only to find nothing. She must have been confused, but she didn't say anything about it to us. It wasn't until a couple of years later when I was talking to her about the child ghost I thought must have lived in the house, that she confessed to having the experience.

As I said before, my son was quite young at the time, and he had a lot of the age appropriate electronic toys. Cars whose headlights would light up and which would make revving noises. Toy horns, keyboards, talking stuffed animals and at least one jack in the box. The toys seemed to start up on their own regularly. It was usually when no one was in the room that I would hear the toys starting, when I would dutifully go into his closet and shut them off. At the time, I simply assumed that they were malfunctioning, or needed new batteries. I do recall that the race car toy seemed to be the one that started on its own the most often. It honestly didn't occur to me that it might be anything but a toy malfunctioning. I did notice that once we moved out of the house it didn't happen.

One night my husband was ill and restless. I knew if I didn't let him have the bed to himself I'd never get any sleep. I decided to bunk down for the night in the back bedroom, the room that had been the servant's bedroom. Our master bedroom was to the front of the house, by the street. It was a boisterous college town, with students out on the streets at all times of the night and day. There were also street lights to the front of the house, so the master bedroom was never really dark or quiet. The back bedroom was very different, dark and muted, with only a shaft of lonely moonlight and the distant ringing of the church bells for company. I told myself that was the difference between the two rooms, tried to convince myself that was the only difference. But as I bedded down for the night I was very uneasy. It felt like the room was somehow out of time, forgotten and unused, and that something or someone equally out-of-time had taken up residence there. I felt distinctly that I was invading someone's space, and I was half convinced that that someone was going to let me know at any time. My eyes darted about the room restlessly, my ears tuned to any nuance, I finally fell into a fitful sleep. I believe I was awake and out of bed before my son the next morning, a true feat for me. Throughout our tenure in the house I never again slept a night in that room.

The reason that this short uneventful episode made it into a book about ghosts is because of how palpable the presence in that room had been. I'd learn years later to seek out those forgotten unused spaces during investigations. Spirits appear to take up residence in the areas of a building not frequented by us. I became an investigator because I was skeptical, because I normally seek out the rational answer first and think paranormal second. I also have only a smidge of the sensitive in me, and tend to be dubious of those that claim a spirit in every closet, attic and or icky basement.

But the night I slept in that back bedroom was one of the creepiest nights I've ever spent.

It was perhaps two or three years later, long after we moved to another state that I was cruising through some channels around Halloween when I discovered a reality TV show about real life ghost hunters that my perspective changed. I realized that average, everyday people could explore the paranormal. And I realized that I wanted to be one of them. I was hooked.

When I began I was far more skeptical than I am now, although I think a heavy dose of skepticism is important. When I began the question was, are ghosts or spirits real? Over time and multiple experiences, I can say that odd things do happen. Now the question has changed to something more like, what *are* ghosts or spirits? Are they the earthbound souls of a human, or are they merely a memory of a person left in the environment after the person has left? Are they creations of the human psyche or hallucinations brought on by environmental factors? Because at the core of that question is the more important question. If ghosts or spirits are real phenomena does that actually prove the existence of the soul surviving death? As you'll find throughout the rest of the book, that question is not as black and white as it right first appear. And therein lies the rub, as Hamlet would say.

INTERPRETING THE PARANORMAL

When it comes to the way in which supernatural events are interpreted has more to do with our cultural or religious upbringing than with the event itself. When you seek out the paranormal you tend to find that which you seek rather sooner than later. I've witnessed many strange thing, and I find it's the way that supernatural events are interpreted that makes all the difference. Having a background in cameras and video, I like to think of our view on the supernatural as a type of lens through which we look.

For example, I once welcomed into the group a gentleman who had a fundamentalist outlook on the paranormal. He had been taught that a person who died, and didn't for some reason follow the beacon of Christ to heaven, must be evil. In his mind they had done something in their life to be forsaken heaven. I asked him honestly to try to suspend judgement, to investigate with me and to explore other possibilities. After all, he had sought my group out asking to investigate.

He said he would try to see the whole subject from a different perspective. And he did make it through two investigations, although we could all tell that his predispositions were eating away at his resolve near the end. After the second investigation, however, he had a cataclysmic melt-down, loudly and mainly incoherently expounding about evil spirits and possession. What I hadn't anticipated was how extreme his fundamental beliefs were when interpreting what was fairly mundane paranormal activity.

I received an email inquiry from a woman once who was terrorized as well. Grandma had passed away it seems, and now she was returning to visit the family. In fact the granddaughter had unwittingly come in contact with Grandma on the stairs of their home, and Grandma had had the temerity to reach out and attempt to touch the girl. I must come and exorcise the house, the frantic woman explained. What else were they to do?

I told her that I don't perform exorcisms or house blessings, I gather evidence and assess a situation, I explained. "But why," I questioned, would you be so frightened of Grandma that you would seek to forcefully oust her from your home by whatever means available?" Instead I suggested she send Grandma thoughts of, "love and light," to steal a phrase from *Eat, Pray, Love,* and then send her on her way. Perceptions again, it comes down to our inherent perceptions.

A NEW TREND IN PARANORMAL TELEVISION

I've noticed over the course of the last couple of years that paranormal reality shows are turning darker in tone. As the American public become desensitized to paranormal activity on television they have started to hunger for more sensational cases. Television shows despite the moniker "reality" are first and foremost a vehicle for entertainment. Their survival depends on the number of viewers – ratings. If the ratings are low, if viewers are going elsewhere then the network can't sell advertising space. It's just as simple as that. Show producers are continually looking for ways to hook and keep their audience entertained. And when it comes to paranormal television shows that means painting paranormal activity as darker and more frightening. Of course this puts distinct pressure on the paranormal investigators involved. Eventually even the most ethical will be faced with the dilemma of whether to fake evidence just to keep the excitement up.

But what is even more disturbing to me is an increase number of cases labeled demonic or evil. My organization is contacted regularly by television producers trying to fill their insatiable need for new and more sensational cases. Here is a snippet of an email I received as an inquiry. Notice the language they use:

> "We're looking for families or individuals whose lives changed because of their experiences with ghosts, demons, or the spiritual world. Perhaps they have contacted investigators to help them understand or cope with the situation. The stories we portray **must escalate** [my emphasis] to a point where no one can ignore the frightening, even threatening occurrences."

And from another email:

> "We are looking for more amazing, unusual and, most of all, terrifying true-life horror stories to feature in the new season...We're interested in hearing about Voodoo, Satanic cults, haunted objects, urban myths (real life Siren encounters),

religion-related hauntings…. The key ingredients for us are: multiple eyewitnesses and engaging characters that felt genuine fear and whose experience developed and escalated over time, ideally with some kind of resolution. For example, being forced from a house by spirits or an exorcism – it's these kind of stories that make really good, exciting television."

Real life siren encounters? Who since Odysseus has had a real-life siren encounter?

While this type of claptrap may "make really good, exciting television," dissemination of this nonsense is incredibly irresponsible, not to mention dangerous. They convince the public, who doesn't have a solid background in paranormal research beyond what they see on TV, that the majority of hauntings are evil in nature. And they also suggest that the activity will likely *escalate* to a point where it can no longer be endured. First, I've read copious volumes and spoke with exceedingly ethical paranormal researchers that have investigated in the field *for years* that have never come across a demonic haunting. That's not to say that it can't happen, but that paranormal activity of this type is exceedingly rare. Second, most of the cases I investigate don't escalate out of control. In fact, normally they act very much like the case I spoke of at the beginning of this chapter. Sometimes the activity increases. Often it will cease for long periods of time. Usually it just appears to be an entity that is trying to get itself noticed, trying to communicate or simply voicing its irritation that you are invading its space. As one of my investigators said, it could just be a spirit who is in a bad mood. Remember it's all about perspective.

STARTLED VS. AFRAID

I've often theorized that the interpretation of a paranormal encounter should be evaluated for the surprise factor. For those who are honest, there is a difference between being startled and being truly frightened. And that's what many encounters cause us to feel – startled. You climb a staircase in an attorney's office during an investigation and a black cat jumps out at you, very nearly causing you to pee your pants (it's happened). You turn and see a dark figure in the hall and you startle. You feel a ghostly touch on your hand and you're startled. You hear a big bang that sounds like a gunshot (as happened in an old fort) and you're startled – perhaps profoundly. These are very startling when they occur, but the fright we feel, that is a valuation we place consciously on the event after it has occurred.

I loved the water all my life. I swam on the swim team, was a lifeguard and taught swimming at the local YMCA. I remember distinctly one child I had in class that refused to dunk her face and head in the water. After many sessions of trying to get my little student to put her face in the water, I finally devised a trick. When the other students were putting their faces in to blow bubbles I gently tripped my little swimmer so that she unceremoniously went under. Now we were in about 3 feet of water at the time, for all of you about to scream child abuse.

The wee lass went under immediately and came up sputtering water. She was startled. Then she did something that I thought was really a statement as to human temperament. She looked at me to gauge my reaction. "Oops, you slipped sweetheart," I said with a big smile, "but hey, you finally got your face wet. Good job!"

"I did! I got my face wet!" she said, all proud and puffed up. For the rest of the lesson she told us all about her amazing courage in facing the big, bad pool of water. Now I'd love to say that she never again had any compunction about putting her face in the water, but that wouldn't be honest. However, I did provide a different perspective on the water, a different perception perhaps. I suspect her fear was probably stemming from a parent with the same fears. Parental fears are subtle but strong, becoming the lens, you grow up looking through.

Consider the granddaughter who saw Grandma in the stairwell, and whose mother wanted Grand-mama forcefully exorcised. Perhaps if mother had ever read any of the literature on After Death Communications the situation might have gone differently.

Think again of the little girl looking to me for my reaction to her dunking. I, myself, have been her. I've had paranormal experiences in my own home that have left me feeling shaken and worse, powerless. When that happened, however, I was lucky enough seek out people who gave me sage advice and told me I wasn't crazy. I can't tell you how many times I've heard that phrase from homeowners and building owners for whom I have done investigations. Mostly they just want to tell you a) they had a startling event, b) they don't know what to make of it, and c) would you please tell them they're not crazy and didn't make the whole thing up? That's a very healthy position to start from.

Throughout the rest of the book we'll look at how the ancients interpreted ghosts, the history of modern day paranormal research and discuss different classifications and theories that paranormal investigators use today. We'll also discuss some of the research being conducted, not by paranormal investigators, but by scientists and medical researchers that may shed some light on the subject as well.

CHAPTER 1: ANCIENT MAN AND GHOST LORE

M an has always had a fascination with the unknown. From the earliest cave dweller to modern man the same mysteries abound, the same questions remain unanswered. Why am I here? Where will I go? Is there anything beyond death?

And what of the mysteries, those things of which that do not fit into the neat category of reality? Those strange phenomena that occur just at the periphery of our awareness. The footstep on the stair when no one is around, the dark shape that moves in the empty room. The strange creature that flits behind trees just out of vision in an old forest. The mysteries for which we have no answers, but assail us still.

And ghosts, the supposed return of the dead to visit or perhaps assail the living. What of those? Are they real? Is this evidence that we survive the death of our bodies? I can say unequivocally that every culture as far back as we have written history, has a history of ghost stories, a tradition, usually oral, that recounts the culture's beliefs and fears of ghosts and the supernatural.

Indeed, the oldest recorded ghost story occurs in the city of Athens in ancient Mesopotamia. The story involved the stalwart Athenodorus (74-7 A.D.), a gentleman born in Canana an area within modern day Turkey. A philosopher and teacher of great renown, he had been a student of Posidonius of Rhodes, and became the teacher of Octavian (the later Caesar Augustus).

It isn't Athenodorus' words that are recounted, and passed down through the ages, but those of Pliny the Younger or Gaius Plinius Caecilius Secundus (61-115 A.D.) a Roman letter-writer, who transcribed the story from a surviving eye-witness account (1, 4, 5). In 1746 William Melmouth translated the story from the ancient Greek to modern English. It is probably where the tradition of ghosts rattling chains began, though Dickens would certainly make much of its conceit in his classic *A Christmas Carol*. The following is from Melmouth's treatise (1).

"There was in Athens a house, spacious and open, but with an infamous reputation, as if filled with pestilence. For in the dead of night, a noise like the clashing of iron could be heard. And if one listened carefully, it sounded like the rattling of chains. At first the noise seemed to be at a distance, but then it would approach, nearer, nearer, nearer. Suddenly a phantom would appear, an old man pale and emaciated, with a long beard and hair that appeared driven by the wind. The fetters on his feet and hands rattled as he moved them."

"Any dwellers in the house passed sleepless nights under the most dismal terrors imaginable. The nights without rest led them to a kind of madness, and as the horrors in their minds increased, unto a path toward death. Even in the daytime—when the phantom did not appear – the memory of the nightmare was so strong that it still passed before their eyes. The terror remained when the cause of it was gone."

"Damned as uninhabitable, the house was at last deserted, left to the spectral monster...."

The story begins with Athenodorus, looking to rent a house in ancient Athens. Eventually he came upon just such an abode, a palatial home being let for a remarkably low price. The cheap rent raised his suspicions immediately. He asked around apparently, and was told the reason was because the house was haunted. Being of a stalwart nature, Athenodorus decided to rent the dwelling anyway. In fact, in Melmouth's words Athenodorus was *"eager to take the place"* whether because he was excited by the challenge or thought the haunted house idea was superstitious hogwash and he could get a house for little money.

"It happened that a philosopher named Athenodorus came to Athens at that time. Reading the posted bill, he discovered the dwelling price. The extraordinary cheapness raised his suspicion, yet when he heard the whole story, he was not in the least put off. Indeed he was eager to take the place, and did so immediately.

From the very first evening the ghost, however, made its presence known.

"As evening drew near, Athenodorus had a couch prepared for him in the front section of the house. He asked for a light and his writing materials, and then dismissed his retainers. To keep his mind from being distracted by vain terrors of imaginary noises and apparitions, he directed all his energy toward his writing.

"For a time the night was silent, then came the rattling of fetters. Athenodorus neither lifted up his eyes, nor laid down his pen. Instead he closed his ears by concentrating on his work. But the noise increased and advanced closer till it seemed to be at the door, and at last in the very chamber. Athenodorus looked round and saw the apparition exactly as it had been described to him. It stood before him, beckoning with one finger.

Athenodorus made a sign with his hand that the visitor should wait a little, and bent over his work. The ghost, however, shook the chains over the philosopher's head, beckoning as before. Athenodorus now took up his lamp and followed. The ghost moved slowly, as if held back by his chains. Once it reached the courtyard, it suddenly vanished.

Athenodorus, now deserted, carefully marked the spot with a handful of grass and leaves. The next day he asked the magistrate to have the spot dug up. There they found – intertwined with chains – the bones that were all that remained of a body that had long lain in the ground. Carefully, the skeletal relics were collected and given proper burial, at public expense. The tortured ancient was at rest. And the house in Athens was haunted no more.

Athenodorus' ghost, satisfied finally by being properly buried was never heard from again. This theme runs across many cultures. In the Japanese culture if one died by murder or suicide, and did not receive proper burial it was believed they returned as ghosts. In many African cultures, proper preservation of the body before burial was believed paramount to putting a spirit properly to rest. And if the family lost your body before burial you were likely to come back as a ghost as well. It is well known that the Egyptians had extensive preparations for removing organs properly and mummifying the body.

Anthropologists and historians contend that, with a life much more rooted in spiritualism and superstition, ancient people did not suffer from the nagging question of an afterlife as do we. The question as to whether ghosts exist was not a matter of importance either. They were taught to accept such ideas from birth. That the soul existed, that it survived death in some capacity, that it resided thereafter, all things being equal, in some type of heavenly afterlife, these things were believed literally. The questioning of an after-life, the sometimes-dramatic desire to have proven that souls survive death, the idea that spirits exist, that they are capable of interacting with the living; these are all quandaries of our modern age.

Author and Professor, Joshua J. Mark postulates as I have for years that the dilemma was caused by the one-two punch of the Christian religion, which in many cases forbade a belief in ghosts, and the emergence of scientific zeal that relegated all things unexplainable to the scrapheap of superstition and folklore (8).

A thorough study of afterlife beliefs and ghost lore across cultures or within a culture has already been written by authors more capable than myself. Professor Mark in his article "Ghosts in the Ancient World" notes that looking at the topic of ghost lore across cultures has demonstrated that, while details vary greatly, the overall themes are remarkably similar. I'd like to briefly list those themes that appear consistently across the cultures of ancient people, and then briefly discuss some of the world's more imaginative ghost lore.

Again, as noted, ancient people didn't doubt the existence of an afterlife. One lived, one died, and then one's "soul" lived on in another form. Most argued that the bodiless spirit still needed some type of substance to exist. Thus, the Egyptians put offerings of meat and drink in the tombs of the dead. The Chinese in kind, left offerings of food and drink on the altars honoring dead relatives. A certain take on this concept is seen even in the west where alcoholic beverages are poured as libations at the burial place of a deceased friend or family member.

The ancients further believed irrefutably that a place such as heaven existed, that there was literally spiritual real estate somewhere where the souls continued to live. They further believed that there were immutable laws that governed a) the realm of the dead, b) the journey to said realm, or c) admittance into said realm.

Once residing in the realm of the dead, the dead were supposed to stay there. They weren't supposed to return to the land of the living in order to harass those they had left behind. Many cultures interpreted a returning spirit as a very bad omen, often assuming that the living (in particular the family that survived) were responsible for the unrest of the dead.

Now, to leave "heaven" a spirit needed special dispensation from a God or Gods, and such dispensation was granted only a) for a limited time and b) in order to fulfill some duty, job, obligation or to right some justifiable wrong. There were several broad categories of reasons strong enough to warrant a weekend pass. They were: improper funeral rites, lack of burial (or cremation), death by drowning where the body was not recovered, death by battle where the body was not recovered, murder in which the body was never found, to provide a true account of events – such as a murder, to avenge a murder or resolve unfinished business (8). How a person's remains were prepared and or disposed is an important theme throughout. Recall the story of poor Athenodorus and his nightly specter for example.

The Afterlife Quality-Of-Life was controlled by three major factors: whether or not the person had led a good and just existence; how their remains were prepared and or disposed; how the deceased was remembered by the living – usually in particular by family members.

Certainly, no Christian hasn't heard of the Day of Reckoning when God will judge the soul's virtues and sins, as an entrance requirement to heaven. The Jewish tradition shares a similar belief that on the day of the Apocalypse God will raise all the dead from their graves and make a final determination. Egyptians believed that the soul travelled to The Hall of Justice where Osiris and a panel of 42 Judges judged the soul. There the heart of the deceased was weighed literally on a scale against a white feather of truth. Should the heart weigh more than the feather, it was determined that it had been weighted down with foul deeds. Those of light heart were granted an afterlife in the Field of Reeds. Those with heavy hearts had their hearts thrown to the ground where they were consumed by monsters. The only culture I've found that didn't rely on a judgement of past deeds were the early Germanic or Norse people, who did believe in an afterlife, but an afterlife to which everyone was invited.

CHINESE GHOST LORE

While all cultures have ghost stories, not all of the interpret stories of the dead in the same way. The Chinese culture is one rich in lore about spirits of all varieties. For the Chinese, the dead are all around them, all the time. Communication or contact with a spirit is thus inevitable and desirable. So important was the practice of honoring the dead that ancestral worship became the mainstay of their national faith. The Chinese would erect small shrines in their homes, performing daily obeisance to their dearly departed.

Because many of the spirits are believed to be benign or even loving, ghost stories of the Chinese often share certain themes. When the death of a child was imminent it was often the custom for a mother to go out to the garden and call the child's name, in order to call back the wandering spirit. There are also many stories of ghostly mothers returning from the grave to succor a grieving child.

For the Chinese spirits are endowed with a purpose or task. They may be sent to restore stolen treasure, or right a wrong, or provide a virtuous path in the face of hardship. For the Chinese, duty and honor are vaunted ideals, and certainly their beloved spirits are beacons of those virtues.

That is not to say that all spirits are good, in Chinese folklore. The way to determine whether a spirit meant you harm or help was easy. Departed loved ones gave their sage advice via dreams. A spirit that had died in battle, had been drowned, been murdered or died in some way that they were denied proper burial, these spirits would appear only at night and only be seen by torch light (8). Similarly, the spirit of a person who committed suicide or was wicked became inevitably a very unhappy soul as he witnessed first-hand a complete reversal of fortune. The wicked spirit would hear his family curse him, instead of praise him, see his children grow up to be corrupt, his wife contracts a horrible disease, his money turn to debt, his land sold, his house inhabited by strangers and his last desires forgotten. Perhaps at the end one last friend might stroke his coffin and shed a tear, while wearing a cold grin. And thus, was the price of a wicked existence (2).

While the beloved family spirit was welcome, wandering spirits in the Chinese culture were something to be feared. These were spirits whose life had been taken from them, or who had been improperly respected by family. A strong theme in Chinese literature is that of the wronged spirit who returned to seek justice from the guilty (2). The Chinese believed that an angry spirit could return only with special dispensation from heaven, and that its return to torment the living was therefore justified. Confucius referred to these as Hungry Ghosts. The culture is rich with descriptions of angry, Hungry Ghosts tormenting the living with poltergeist type activity of a most frightening nature (8).

JAPANESE GHOST LORE

The Japanese culture is resplendent with ghosts and spirits as well. The Japanese believe that within us all is a powerful presence called a reikon which is released after death. The yurei is the Japanese ghost, both feared and honored by people. And as far back as the beginnings of a written Japanese history, stories of the yurei have been recounted.

The yurei found their golden age during the Endo period (1603-1868) perhaps the Japanese equivalent of the spiritualist movement of the west. Despite the fact that it appears the telling of ghost stories was banned at the time, the Japanese developed a game called the *Hyakumonogatari Kaidankai*. Players would sit in a circle with 100 lit candles, and each would tell a ghost story in succession as the candles were slowly snuffed out. In order to assuage their insatiable appetite for stories every elderly grandparent was interviewed, every ancient edifice ransacked for clues of the yurei.

The yurei are portrayed as beautiful young women of unearthly pale, white skin, as if drained of all blood. Their long blue-black hair hangs loose and disheveled. The yurei floats around in a white kimono, the garb in which she was buried, and she has no feet.

Author Zack Davisson, contends that while the ghostly ideal of white skin, black hair, white kimono was a national tradition, the fact that yurei are drawn without feet is due to the influence of the famous naturalist painter Maruyama Ōkyo (6).

Apparently the artist was enamored with a lovely geisha lady, who died very young. How or in what manner the life of the lady was cut short is not detailed. However, shortly after her death the painter awoke one night to see his beloved hovering near the foot of his bed. She stayed in this manner for a number of moments, and then she disappeared. The painter, sprang from his bed immediately and started painting the ghost in the image still fresh in his mind. Ōkyo was considered at the time the most accurate naturalist painter, and it was believed that if he painted something it was a reliable reproduction of the original. Thus, when he painted his masterpiece 'The Ghost of Oyuki" the yurei's likeness became the national idea of a ghost (6).

Like their Chinese neighbors, many ghost stories in Japan are about righting wrongs or fulfilling obligations. The word for an obligation in Japanese is *on*, and many of the yurei return because they have not fulfilled their duty. For example there is a story of a young lady who had failed in her responsibility to guard a set of precious plates, assigned by a samurai who did not take the failure lightly. While the samurai was gone, one of the plates was either broken or stolen. Upon returning and finding one of his precious treasures destroyed he killed the young lady, throwing body down a well. It is said her yurei returns to count plates, trying to fulfill her *on*, but always coming up one plate short (**7**).

CELEBRATION OF THE DEAD

Unlike our western culture, for the Japanese, summer is the time to tell ghost stories, especially as the Obon Festival approaches during which ancestors are honored. Occurring on either the 13th day or 15th day of the seventh month (apparently the festival varies by region), it is the evening that Buddhists believe that the spirits of ancestors return to visit with family. The Japanese hang paper lanterns in front of their house to guide the family spirits to the door, perform Obon dances called obon odori, and graves are visited with food offerings left at graves, family altars and temples. At the end of the festival the lanterns are placed onto the water (rivers, lakes or ocean) where they float away guiding the spirits back to mysterious shores (**9**).

The Chinese have a similar summer festival which falls always on the 15th day of the seventh month at which time people put out food and gifts in order to entice spirits to stay in the land of the dead where they are felt to belong. Actually the entire seventh month is considered the Ghost Month, a time when the veil between the worlds of living and dead is considered to be thin, and thus easily breached. Notice the similarities in theme with the Celtic celebration of Samhain, and the Mesoamerican Day of the Dead celebration (8).

THE DEAD OF EGYPT

No one can deny that one of the most supernaturally predisposed culture was that of the ancient Egyptians with their elaborate traditions of mummification and their monolithic pyramids filled with treasure built to shelter the pharaohs in their never-ending afterlife.

For the Egyptian's no human was merely physical, but consisted of several elements. Each human had a body or physical presence as well as a shadow, a double, a soul, a heart, a spirit, a name, a power and a spiritual body. After death the shadow departed, and could only be brought back with a mystical ceremony. There were subtleties to the different entities that are hard to describe with our western terms such as soul.

The double or ka (the double or image or character) of the deceased lived with the body in the tomb, or didn't if ceremonies were not performed properly. So it was the Ka that was the immortal dweller of the tomb, and was believed to be the one to inhabit the statue of the deceased. A statue closely resembling the deceased was thoughtfully left for that purpose. So important to keeping the double satisfied that special priests, called priests of the ka were called in to minister to the ka, and there was a special room of the tomb set aside for the ka, called the house of the ka (**3**). But it was the ka, who if not properly maintained became a wandering spirit after death. Apparently, the ka had an insatiable appetite and needed to be fed with offerings of meat and drink. Should the offerings not be performed, the ka might depart the tomb in search of food. Apparently, the ka did not have a refined palette and would consume any dung or filthy water it came across.

The ba (or soul) resided in heaven with Osiris or Ra. It can return to the tomb at will, however, and could also partake of the offerings of food and drink that were left for the ka. It could assume a material or semi-material form sometimes.

At times, the ba and ka might become united, into a being that was called the Akh or khu or akhu, which was an enlightened being. Earlier Egyptians believed that only Pharaoh could achieve this union, but later interpretations declared that people of higher moral character could as well. To become an akh or enlightened spirit one must be judged just. These souls were allowed to live among the gods or among the pole stars which never set. However, the akh spirit could interact with the living as well, and it was the akh that returned as an unhappy spirit to harass the living. If proper burial rites had been neglected or if someone close to the akh had sinned against him or her, then the akh could return briefly to the Earth to seek restitution. The accused had to seek forgiveness directly to the akh, in order to be forgiven. If this didn't work, then a priest was called in order to determine judgement in the matter.

Found in a tomb from the New Kingdom, a widower's letter to his deceased wife is an exemplary example of the dilemma between the living and the dead (**8**). Apparently, after the wife had died, the widower had found himself besieged by misfortune. Assuming his deceased wife was at the bottom of the mischief he wrote her a heartfelt letter listing his kindnesses and begging her to cease her wicked deeds.

> *What wicked thing have I done to thee that I should have come to this evil pass? What have I done to thee? But what thou hast done to me is to have laid hands on me although I did nothing wicked to thee. From the time I lived with thee as thy husband down to today, what have I done to thee that I need hide? When thou didst sicken of the illness which thou hadst, I caused a master-physician to be fetched...I spent eight months without eating and drinking like a man. I wept exceedingly together with my household in front of my street-quarter. I gave linen clothes to wrap thee and left no benefit undone that had to be performed for thee. And now, behold, I have spent three years alone without entering into a house, though it is not right that one like me should have to do it. This have I done for thy sake. But, behold, thou dost not know good from bad (**8**).*

GHOSTS OF INDIA

India's spirit culture is similar to the Confucius' "Hungry Ghosts" of China. The Indians call their angry spirits bhoots, and although bhoots appear as normal human beings there is one way one dead giveaway (couldn't resist) they appear with their feet on backwards. Bhoots could change their appearance without warning, however, perhaps masking their true identity. The backwards feet were thought to symbolize that something had gone terribly wrong, the spirit in essence was in an unnatural state. The strange backward-footed ghost was thought to indicate that the person had died before their allotted time. Because bhoots had died before enjoying their life to the fullest, they were feared for their desire to possess the life of a living person. Possession of a living body or perhaps even more fearful, spirit reanimation of dead flesh were serious concerns. Scholars believe the fear of the dead reviving led to the practice of cremation. Following Indian ritual, the burning of the body in concert with the burning of certain spices, intertwined with the use of amulets and prayers would protect the living from the body-hungry dead (8).

The churail was another particularly dangerous Indian spirit. These were the spirits of women that died in childbirth. Remember that before modern science roughly 50% of women died in childbirth, making the threat of churail especially daunting. These churails were crossroads ghosts. They waited at quiet intersections and turnings of a lane. They offered friendship to travelers. Especially dangerous to young women, the churail would seek to steal the children of the living or try to repossess the body of the living woman. Male travelers were in danger as well, as the churail would attempt to seduce the man, and then kill him.

Luckily, there was a time limit on what a churail could accomplish. Once her allotted time on Earth had been reached, she was called back to reenter the stream of reincarnation. The Indian transmigration of souls dictated that what the spirit did while in the body would determine whether they moved up or down in the spiritual hierarchy toward the next incarnation.

It seems that not every soul returned as it should leaving whole regions as having the taint to being haunted – giving a whole new meaning to the term ghost town. One such area is the abandoned Dudley Town in the backwoods of Connecticut, reportedly so haunted that all the living inhabitants left. In India the most famous of these is the abandoned fort city of Bhangarh Fort Ruins, Rajasthan built under the Mughal Empire in 1573 A.D. There are completely disparate stories about how the city became abandoned and then haunted. One involves an unhappy hermit who didn't mind the building in the fort city until it starting casting shadows on his hermitage at which time he blighted the city by knocking down overnight all of the upper stories of the buildings, after which the inhabitants left quickly.

In another fanciful tale, the evil wizard Baba Balnath (who was apparently pretty icky) fell in lust with the young and beautiful princess (aren't they always a princess?) Ratnavi. Knowing himself icky and not deserving of the princess's attentions he brewed a potion to attract two unlike objects together and gave it to Ratnavi under the pretense that it was perfume. Ratnavi, being savvy as well as lovely, knew the "perfume" to be a ruse and broke the bottle on a giant boulder. It appears the boulder did indeed find Baba Balnath attractive, crushing him. According to one version of the legend, Baba Balnath, in his dying gasps then cursed Ratnavi and the entire city. And in at least one version of the story, the inhabitants of the town fled in one night never to return. My goodness, the Indian race are one of great creativity, and their women of great pluck. It may simply be a tourist attraction with a checkered past; however, to this day there are throughout the city reports of disembodied voices, lights seen, footsteps heard and laughter reported around the city (8). Such is the reputation of the old fort-city that a sign stands in front of the gate warning that all visitors must depart before nightfall, because those that remain within the environs of the city disappear, never to be seen again.

CELTIC FOLKLORE AND THE DEAD

The Halloween celebration has its roots soundly in the Celtic tradition of Samhain. In northern Europe, including the regions of Ireland, Scotland and Wales, the period of Samhain (pronounced either as sou-when or sow-when) meaning literally summers end, running from October 31st to November 2nd. It was as much a harvest festival as a remembrance of the dead, when crops were brought in and stored and animals slaughtered for the long winter ahead. It was also a time when it was believed that the veil between the worlds of the living and the dead was very thin, so thin in fact that those who were dead could cross back to walk again among the living. The Celts were eons ahead of Einstein in the fact that they saw time not as linear but as something mutable and changeable. Actually the Celts considered time as cyclical, with the year revolving like a wheel. Samhain was the end of one cycle and the beginning of the next.

Certainly for an agrarian society this symbolism is obvious, summer being the time of growth and bounty, winter being a time of stark survival, with fall being the changeover between the two. A poor harvest meant not enough stores were put aside for the winter, which foretold a long cold spell with not enough to eat. This undoubtedly meant sickness and even death within the community. Thus the harvest season took on its own spiritual significance with the path between life and death at times an unnervingly thin line.

During the Samhain observances cattle were slaughtered and the bones burned in "bone fires" later "bon fires." During this time the dead walked freely, and locals prepared meals that were favored among the departed. The Dead whose motives were sometimes feared, were free to walk about at Samhain. Fearing that an angry spirit might find them, the Celts took to wearing masks to cover their identity. Therein lies the root of the tradition of wearing costumes at Halloween.

The Romans eventually defeated and subjugated most of the Celtic people in the first century A.D. imposing the Christian religion on the indigenous peoples. The Church found it easier in many cases to shuffle many pagan traditions into the fold of Christian holidays, thus making the pill of Christianity that much easier to swallow. Samhain became Hallowmas or Allhallows, which in turn became All Soul's Day, and eventually All Saint's Day when Christians were to pray for the release of sinners who had become foundered in purgatory. Notice with each evolution how much more Christian the holiday became (8).

CELTIC GHOSTS AND FAIRIES

Speaking of angry spirits, departed sinners, according to the Irish, may end up as part of an evil spirit band called the sluagh (pronounced sloo-ah) meaning host in Gaelic. Also known under other monikers such as the Under folk, The Wild Hunt or the Host of Unforgiven Dead, these spirits are thought to take to the air in dangerous flocks, like a murder of crows, moving in stealthily to steal the souls of the dying. While categorized as Sidhe or fairies, they are also considered to be the errant souls of the dead, the vilest of evil, unrepentant souls, truly a band of the damned set free to terrorize mortals. Do note, when discussing Celtic folklore, it becomes extremely difficult to distinguish between ghosts and fairy lore, particularly in Ireland, as all supernatural happenings seem to end up being attributed to the wee folk (14).

During the day the Sluagh hide in dark and forgotten places, but take to the skies at night looking like a moving band of abnormally large black ravens, moving in waves from the west. The flapping of wings, a screeching sound of many throats and a dark, moving cloud-like mass are what a victim sees, if one is unlucky enough to be out in a secluded place when the Host is on the move. It is said that the Host is more feared than Death, as the Sluagh know no loyalties and abide by no laws of nature. So fearful of the Host are many Irish residents that they keep their west side windows and doors shut and shuttered if they have someone who is sick or dying residing within.

The host is capable of stealing the souls of living, healthy individuals under certain circumstances as well, and in fact especially relish the delight. Those that are depressed or seeking death, or those that unwittingly call the Host to them (such as saying sluagh out loud) can gain their attention. Once a member of the Hunt a soul is trapped, denied rest, the ability to make restitution, or entrance into heaven. They become a prisoner of the dark band, stealing souls for eternity.

If one were to come across a member of The Host during daylight hours there are tell-tale signs of their membership. Even when in human form, they are said to be more birdlike than human, being scrawny, bony and haggard appearance, with thin, fang-like teeth and a mouth that resembles a beak. Sparse, wispy dark hair hangs limply from their leathery heads, and their hands and feet appear more claw like than human. They wear their dark, sinewy wings close to the body so it appears they are wearing a black cape wrapped tightly about them (**14**).

While the Sluagh are particularly an Irish and Scottish legend, similar folklore of roaming soul-stealing black ravens can be found throughout much of central Europe as well, including Germany, France, Czechoslovakia, Poland and in Scandinavian and Russian cultures. The black horde that rides the winds is sometimes seen as an omen of war, plague or disaster. And consider as well the black raven in regards to the vampiric tradition, the bird as precursor of death and damnation.

BANSHEE

The Banshee is a supernatural being within the wraith category, meaning they are spirits that appear to herald a death (**11**). The name is derived from the words bean (meaning female) and sidhe (meaning fairy). Thus banshees are always described as being female spirits, though it is disputed whether banshees are derived from fairies or are the souls of the departed. It is long established, however, that banshees are family spirits, attaching themselves with a single bloodline whether because of family obligations or because of a personal grudge. Banshees attach themselves to long-standing Irish families staying with one particular family line until the very last member is deceased, following the family even into obscurity and poverty. According to Sir Walter Scott, they attach themselves only to families of Milesian stock, and not to families of the later arriving Saxons or Normans, or later settlers to the Emerald Isle.

If a banshee attaches because of familial loyalty, upon the dying of a family member the banshee will lovingly keen low and melodically as if inviting the ill person to accompany her to the next realm. The O'Reardon family has just such a family banshee, who appears as a beautiful young lady sent to croon the sick one welcomingly to the other side (**11**).

Sometimes, however a banshee is attached for motives other than loyalty. A noble family in the Mayo County has just such an angry spirit wraith attached to their family tree. Supposedly, the banshee was a young lady "deceived" and later murdered by the male head of the clan. As she lay dying she cursed the murdering deceiver and all his kin, vowing to seek vengeance on the family throughout the ages. She remains an enemy of the clan through the ages appearing when a member is passing away, screaming and keening a horrific, strident death wail which terrorizes everyone within hearing distance (**11**).

Banshees are usually thought to old women although sometimes beautiful young women, usually draped in gray or white draping garments, perhaps a long, grey cloak over a gown. They're always described as having long-flowing, disheveled hair which hangs down over thin, bony shoulders. Her eyes may be red and swollen looking, as if from weeping (**12**). She is often heard but not seen, with her wail sounding very much like the soft wailing of the mournful wind. Sometimes as evening approaches the banshee may be spotted as well. While she may not appear visible to the living, she is always discernible to the one for whom she waits.

The Scottish Highlands also have a Banshee tradition. There she is known, however, as bean-nighe (meaning little washer by the ford). She is known as the washer woman because she is seen at the side of a river or waterway, washing the blood from the clothes of the person who is about to die (**11**). Unlike her comely Irish cousin, the bean-nighe is described as ugly and evil with having one nostril, big buck teeth, gargantuan, pendulous breasts and red-webbed feet.

NORDIC GHOSTS

Per Nordic Mythology ghosts aren't wispy, ethereal shadowy figures, but rock-solid flesh eating undead monsters with strong similarities in the folklore to Eastern European Vampiric lore. The dead in Scandinavian countries are buried in graves or underground barrows – although burial practices vary and have at times changed, for example with the emergence of Christianity. The great warriors of old, however, were said to be buried in a howe or barrow, which was a hollowed out cave lined with stone, and timbers for a ceiling, the whole covered over with earth. Once interred in the barrow the dead person was thought to live a type of half-life, the dead flesh becoming animated, acquiring power and supernatural skills. They continue in this type of pseudo-life, usually dangerous only if disturbed.

The undead are known by different names, according to their different proclivities. The haugbui (meaning howe or barrow) lived on, usually fairly peacefully within its hill-side or underground barrow. Usually found in Norwegian sagas, the haugbui stayed within close proximity of its tomb. Not being of the traveling variety, the haugbui rarely caused the living misery, unless disturbed. It was customary to bury, especially among warriors or warlords, riches such as weapons or armor as well as the family's gold or silver stores. Such treasure attracted grave robbers, both in folklore and reality, who would invariably meet the inhabitant of the barrow much to their horror. The haugbui would gain strength and size in their undead state, and the attacked interloper would find himself in mortal combat with the haugbui, as the foolish Grettir learns.

Grettir took all the treasure and carried it towards the rope, but as he was making his way through the barrow he was seized fast by someone. He let go of the treasure and turned to attack, and they set on each other mercilessly, so that everything in their way was thrown out of place. The mound-dweller attacked vigorously, and for a while Grettir had to give way, but finally he realized that this was not a good time to spare himself. Then they both fought desperately, and moved towards the horse bones, where they had a fierce struggle for a long time. Now the one and now the other was forced to his knees, but in the end the mound-dweller fell backwards, and there was a great crash. Then Audun ran away from the rope, thinking that Grettir must be dead …. *(16)*

Being of flesh, however, the haugbui could be defeated in hand to hand combat, and even "killed" by being decapitated and then having a stake pierced through the heart, notice again the similarity to vampiric lore. Cold iron, as in many cultures, could slow a haugbui down, but not defeat it entirely. Sometimes it could be slew with a sword, usually the haugbui's own sword buried in the barrow with him. To do this also required the hero to perform acrobatics leaping between the head and the body of the corpse before it hit the ground. To keep the haugbui dead one had to burn the body and throw the ashes into the sea. Only then was one assured the haugbui was finally vanquished.

The draugr or aptrgangr (literally "after-goer" or one who walks after death) was a different matter. These corpses might show "restlessness on the road to burial," or wander out after being buried. Icelandic sagas are rich in stories of the draugr, literally the walking, flesh-eating corpse of the dead – think George R.R. Martin's walking undead from *A Song of Fire and Ice*, and you wouldn't be far off. The descriptions of the undead are similar to Martin's description as well. They are either described as *hel-blár,* which means either black or blue as death, think congealed blood, or as corpse-pale *ná-folr* (15). While residing in their barrow the corpse was said to grow in size and to become quite heavy, but this growth was not due to gases from decay, nor did the dead body become corrupt, but appears to have remained fresh even years after bodily death. The draugr was said to emit a foul stench, however, a combination of rotting flesh and soil. Aside from large size the being was also believed to gain in strength, sometimes supernatural strength with the ability to rip flesh from a body with claws and teeth and to crush bones with their very hands (15).

Aside from sheer size and strength, the draugr also acquired supernatural abilities. They could under certain circumstances predict the future, control the weather or shape-shift. Draugrs could change shape into many forms including taking on the form of a great, flayed bull, a broken-backed grey horse without tail or ears or a heavy cat which would sit on the chest of a victim becoming steadily heavier until crushing them. Despite being corporeal, draugrs could defy physics, able to melt down and move through solid rock and earth (15).

Those that died at sea might become an even more hideous draugr. These creatures could hunt the living on land or in the water. They could disguise themselves as moss covered rocks to deceive the unwary. They were even more horrible in appearance. They were said to not possess a human head, but rather some hideous facsimile of a human head created by seaweed through which their glowing malevolent eyes showed through. And instead of clothing, they were covered only in oilskins. The draugrs often banded together, building wooden boats in which they sailed the coasts of Sweden, Denmark, Iceland and Norway, hunting unwary sailors (83).

THE DEAD AT MIDWINTER

The northern Scandinavian countries have a dearth of sunlight during the long winter months, eventually being plunged into several weeks of endless night at the time of midwinter. It is not surprising, that this the period of time when the dead were thought to be able to cross the barrier into the land of the living. The Undead were thought to begin their attacks in the fall, but that their strength intensified as the winter deepened.

The draugr appear to need the dark to move in, and could even cloak themselves in semi-darkness or create an opaque mist in order to mask their movements during the day. During the night the draugr moved in and out of shadows, or were half-glimpsed in the open when dark clouds obscured the moon. One might catch a glimpse as the moon emerged, as if the light hit bare bone, but this was only visible for a second before the creature fled back to the black recesses of the night.

THE DEAD AND THE LIVING

Because the dead were thought to live on in their bodies, they were believed to feel the same sensations as the living. Thus they could feel hunger, in fact intense, insatiable hunger for meat, attacking mercilessly any living creature that came across their paths. They also felt cold, thirst and loneliness for kin, leaving them envious of the living. Thus it was feared that the dead would leave their frigid barrows to seek out the creature comforts which they were missing.

To prevent the dead from returning to their former abodes the Scandinavians devised rituals. In some of the more backwoods locales residents would prepare a body by driving pins through the soles of their feet to prevent them from walking, and tying the big toes of the feet together to prevent the legs from being separated. An open scissors was laid across the chest of the corpse and pieces of straw might be lain crosswise under the death shroud, in the sign of the cross. After the body was taken from the home all pots and pans were turned upside down, and the chairs upon which the coffin had sat were turned over.

Some homes even had a corpse-door a bricked up opening that could be torn down to remove a coffin and then re-bricked after the body was removed. The dead were carried out feet first, so the ghost could not see where it was going, and thus could not return.

GHOST LORE AND WESTERN CULTURE

Researching the ghost lore of different cultures is a fascinating endeavor. There are striking similarities in themes. The idea of the dead seeking retribution or revenge or simply seeking to satisfy their envious desires on the living is a constant. From the backward-footed bhoot of India, to the Hungry Ghosts of China to the flesh-shredding draugr of the Nordic cultures, certainly there is a long tradition of frightening beings with ulterior motives.

There is also a theme that appears across the spectrum, and that is that a ghost that doesn't stay where it should, whether it be an earthen barrow, an Egyptian crypt, or simply in the "heavenly realm" must basically be up to no good. This is true of the more traditionalist Christians as well; those who believe that a soul should either go to heaven or hell, thus any spirit left hanging around must needs be evil. The Asian cultures seem to have the most conciliatory relationship with their dead. The Chinese, in particular, with their ancestral worship and their acceptance that the dead as residing among them, seem to be the most at peace with the departed. However, there never seems to be total reconciliation for the dead always want to be among the living, and the living would always rather they keep their distance.

All of the folklore speak of a period of the year when the dead are able to walk more freely among the living, a time for greater caution among the living. For the Asian cultures this time falls in the seventh month of the year. For the Norse this period is during the darkest time of the year – near the midwinter solstice. For the Celts Samhain or the end of the harvest is the time for greatest care. For those of us in the west this corresponds with the fall celebration of Halloween.

Most, but not all, cultures seem to have some idea of a day of reckoning for the dead when their good deeds are weighed against their sins, with some type of tallying being the final outcome.

Why spend so much time talking about ancient cultural beliefs on ghosts? Because all things old become new again. As I was writing this book I kept being drawn to this chapter, remembering parallels to the ancients' beliefs. We often think of people in the past, prior to the scientific age as being simple or stupid. However, nothing could be further from the truth. Consider the fact that the atom was first theorized in 400 B.C. by the philosopher Leucippus and Democritus who described the most fundamental building blocks of matter, and concluded that all physical phenomena was explainable by understanding the properties and behavior of these tiny but fundamental particles. Aristotle and his supporters sadly disagreed, and so the theory was buried. It wouldn't be until Einstein that they would be proven correct. What I'm trying to prove here is that while the ancients may have lacked the vocabulary and scientific education to describe their universe, they certainly did not the lack the vision or the knowledge.

So what is our western ghost tradition? This is difficult to determine for a number of reasons. First, the scientific revolution and the almost reverent belief that science trumps all has relegated many of our beliefs to the trash heap of base superstition, embarrassing to even consider. Centuries of Christianity has further driven the wedge between culture and religion. Many of the culture's pagan traditions have survived, but only in a watered down, sanitized form.

Third, the intermingling of so many cultures in the U.S. has made the whole subject a leviathan of monstrous proportions. We have shared or stolen from the Eastern European vampiric tradition and the undead walking of the Norse. We have the ethereal ghosts of the East, along with the evil demons of the bible. We have Big foot, UFO's, Mothmen, the men in black, black dogs, black shadows, wraiths, fairies, demons, angels, ghosts of the living, of the dead, out of body experiences, near death experiences, battlefield ghosts, crisis apparitions, vengeful spirits, helpful spirits, nature spirits...more certainly than one person in any one book could possibly categorize or make sense of.

Perhaps it was this voluminous spiritual vacuum that caused the spiritualist revolution of the late 1800's. We are a people who don't know what to believe, or whether to believe at all. I would argue we're seeing a resurgence of the same in our modern culture. Remember that for ancient cultures there was no quandary of an after-life, it was simply a given. For Americans, the question is not so cut and dried.

I remember I stood up to introduce myself in front of a class once. Told to give my name and occupation and tell a little about myself, I stood up and boldly told my classmates that I was a proud paranormal investigator. I was shocked by the reaction of about half the class who outwardly exclaimed that there was no such thing as a ghost, and the rest of the group who were as silent as the grave on the subject. I learned a valuable lesson that day; choose your audience carefully. Do consider, however, that in polls of spiritual beliefs around 50% of the American population admits to believing in ghosts and the supernatural, despite scientific and religious teachings. Taken into consideration of the cultural bias, this is a stunning statistic. And it demonstrates some very fundamental questions:

First, people, no matter what they're taught, still experience ghosts and a variety of things paranormal. According to a Pew Research survey one in five Americans report having experienced a ghost (18%), and 29% of Americans believe they've been in contact with a departed loved one. Around a third of the population believe that a spirit could return from the dead, and about that many also believe in the possibility of a haunted house. Belief in the paranormal diminishes with the amount of church services one attends, with the smallest percent of paranormal belief resting with evangelicals **(17)**. Aside from religion, there are no barriers to experiencing the paranormal. Education level, socioeconomic level, neither appear to make any difference. Gender remains a divider, with more women (33%) than men (26%) believing.

Second, people don't know what to believe about the things they experience, perhaps because they've been taught not to believe in them at all. Because we have no formal cultural teachings on the matter, such experiences are all the more inexplicable.

Third, everyone lives and dies. We all lose loved ones. Eventually we all face the same demise. And so for everyone the fundamental questions will eventually become important. Why am I here? Where do I go? Is there anything beyond this life? Does it have meaning? Will I someday see my loved ones again? No matter how hard of heart someone may be, these remain the universal questions.

CHAPTER 2: SPIRITUALIST MOVEMENT

I t is often the case in history that movements seem to begin all at once, as if the stars are finally aligned and events are in in motion that cause the momentous event. When Darwin was rushing to finish his treatise, *On the Origin of Species* in 1859, he was doing so in hopes of beating another gentleman to publication, someone who had come to the same conclusions as had he. Had ornithologist, Alfred Russell Wallace published his theory on natural selection first it would have been his name that every school age child knew and Darwin's name one had to Google. It's probably no accident that Darwin and Wallace came to their conclusions around 1850, as the philosophical movement of the day stressed empiricism.

The Scientific Revolution was winding down in the late 18th century, though it's discoveries in anatomy, physics, biology and mathematics were still the wonders of the age. The industrial revolution was still chugging along. Certainly it must have seemed that between good science and strong engineering there was no problem in the world that couldn't be solved. Positivism was the emerging philosophical theory gaining support starting around 1840. It was a movement that stressed that knowledge should be founded on natural phenomena, by studying properties and relations thereof. It stressed that one should use one's sensory experience to gather data, interpreting this data using one's reason and logic to come to all authoritative knowledge, and stressed that the only valid knowledge (truth, reality) must be derived using this system. Information gathered with our senses is known as empirical evidence, and thus empiricism was the knowledge gleaned (16).

Positivism affected societal views as well. According to the movement, society, like science operated under general, natural laws that could be studied empirically. Introspection, intuitive knowledge, metaphysics, theology, all these touchy-feely philosophies that could neither be observed, tested or proven, these held no value. Basically positivism relegated society to a science experiment. Thus, the author of the movement, philosopher Auguste Comte discredited all the world's mysteries with the stroke of a pen – or more likely a typewriter (invented in 1714).

THE FOX SISTERS

And into this sterile environment entered two of the must unsuspecting characters, a couple of scantily-educated teenagers from a tiny town in upstate New York, the Fox sisters. Margaretta (Maggie), Catherine (Kate) were living in a shabby rental home in Hydesville, New York. The late children of middle-aged parents. Maggie (**15**) and Kate (**12**) probably would have lived an obscure life had it not been for the events of March 1848. The family went to bed one evening but found that sleep alluded them. Strange sounds started to occur all over the house. Sounds like furniture being moved or dragged, gave way to banging that seemed to shake the house. When the Foxes tried to investigate the noises they began to escalate and change to booming, rapping and tapping sounds without origin.

This went on for over a week, with the family enduring the nocturnal noises without cease. And then Kate and Maggie made a momentous discovery. They found that they could communicate with the spirit(s). Kate would clap her hands and a rapping sound could be heard in reply. On March 31st, an eager Mrs. Fox ran off to the neighbors, exclaiming the miracle that was going on in their house, and soon eager neighbors were stopping by.

With the help of an ingenious neighbor, Kate worked out a system of the alphabet to aid communication. The corresponding raps told her the spirit was that of a peddler by the name of Charles Rosa, who reported having been murdered by a previous owner of the house, John Bell. The spirit reported that Bell had buried his body in the basement. Nosing around in the cellar did reveal a bone with some hair attached that a local doctor confirmed was from a human skull. That was the full extent of evidence found, however.

The Fox home quickly became notorious in the little community for supernatural phenomena, and the sisters as the prime communicators with the spirit. Theirs might have remained simply a local sensation, but a small-town journalist, Mr. E.E. Lewis of Canandaigua, New York interviewed several of the eyewitnesses and wrote a pamphlet about the sisters. A copy of the pamphlet caught the attention of Leah Fox Fish, an older sister of Maggie and Kate who had left home to marry Mr. Fish, who had ended up being a dead fish. Leah, who at the time was living in Rochester, New York had been supporting herself by giving music lessons after her husband decamped, but when she learned of her sisters' foray into the macabre she seized upon the business opportunity.

Apparently, Leah was something of a business genius, because Maggie and Kate were very quickly performing for packed houses, with intense media coverage. Their demonstrations grew to include objects moving, tables levitating, and spirit communication with Ben Franklin. Attempts to discredit the sisters as frauds proved futile, and at one time they were even invited to stay at the mansion of Horace Greeley, editor of the New York Tribune. The Fox sisters inspired a new generation of psychic mediums, and by 1852 it was estimated that more than 30,000 would-be psychics had hung out shingles.

The pressure of stardom apparently weighed heavily on both Maggie and Kate. Both were drinking heavily by the late 1850's. Disillusioned, Maggie tried to opt out of the duo, but family pressure made her stay. In 1857 Leah abandoned her golden geese, marrying a wealthy businessman and retiring from the public scene. Kate continued performing on her own, and in 1861 was even said to have started manifesting the spirits of the dead as part of her act. She married Henry Jencken, an Englishman in 1872 and stopped performing. Her first son, Ferdinand, was heralded as a talented psychic from the age of three, and was performing automatic writing by the age of five.

Then in 1888, with spiritualism waning across the country, the sisters did something totally unexpected, they went on stage and announced that they were frauds. They demonstrated how they had created the rapping's and tapping noises by clicking their big toes and their knees, and how Kate had given Maggie body cues. For a shocked audience they even demonstrated how they had done it. In 1891 Maggie recanted her earlier confession. All three sisters died within a short time of each other; Leah in 1890, Kate in 1892 and Maggie in 1893. Their deaths unfortunately left more questions unanswered than answered.

Many writing on the beginning of the spiritualist movement have taken the sister's confession at face value and denounced them as frauds. Others have speculated that the sisters' early performances were probably demonstrations of psychokinesis, and that the sisters may have been quite gifted.

Psychokinesis manifesting in poltergeist type activity such as the rapping, tapping, dragging and banging sounds is usually believed to be manifested by adolescents, especially female adolescents. It is thought that the ability decreases with age. Thus the sisters might have needed to resort to trickery to keep the seats sold. Undoubtedly their acumen at subterfuge would have developed over time, to a point where perhaps even they didn't know where talent ended and the lies began. All that's really known about the Fox sisters is that they began a movement that quickly took on a life of its own.

In a strange aside, after the sisters' deaths, the house in Hydesville, New York now derelict and vacant once again became the subject of the local papers. Local children were playing in the cellar when one of the walls collapsed. A gentlemen apparently heard the screams and helped pull the children to safety. Afterwards it was determined that the wall had been a false wall, behind which was discovered the remains of a body and what appeared to be a peddler's box. Part of the man's skull was missing. Sadly, this proof of the sister's veracity came too late.

MEDIUMS OF THE SPIRITUALIST MOVEMENT

Once the spiritualist movement began it very quickly grew. New "mediums" were popping up everywhere, most of them charlatans seeking either fame or money, or both. It was the era of the séance when it became very posh for those in society to host such an event, often followed by dinner and drinks. In other words, the séance was a type of private entertainment for the believers, the merely curious or even the fiercest skeptics. Heads of state, royalty, scientists, and authors, many of the wealthiest, most powerful leaders of the age attended such events, as did common folk. First Lady, Mary Todd Lincoln became an avid fan of the Spiritualist Movement, holding séances at the White House, some of which Abraham Lincoln attended.

Nearly all the mediums insisted on holding their séances in the dark. Working in the murky light they were then able to produce all manner of devices, often hidden on their person, or rigged about the room, as evidence of spirit communication. Taps, raps, levitating furniture, the sounds of instruments, floating instruments, strange lights, moving objects, ghostly hand and ectoplasm were all part of the show.

Ectoplasm requires a moment of discussion. It was reputed to be a type of ethereal mist-like substance that would materialize from the medium's orifices, during séances and was supposed to signify the coalescence of a spirit brought forth by a medium. It would appear during séances from the nose, mouth, ears and in one case the vagina of mediums. It was debunked as a concoction of newsprint, gauze, lace and probably some snot or other bodily fluids expulsed at just the right moment.

Many of the mediums of the age weren't satisfied to try their high-jinx out in the open, even in a dark room, but insisted on calling forth the spirits from inside a wooden cabinet. Once in the cabinet with a drape drawn all manner of strange things started occurring. We all know of the great (Erich Weisz) Houdini, the world's most preeminent magician. During the spiritualist revolution he also became one of the staunchest medium skeptics, making it his personal mission to reveal and expose the machinations of the age's most infamous mediums.

MINA MARGUERITE (MARGERY) STINSON

One of the era's most brazen charlatans is without a doubt Mina Marguerite (Margery) Stinson (1888-1941). Stinson appears to have been one of those beings that always sought the road of higher celebrity. She married a grocer by the name of Earl Rand, while working as a secretary at a Boston church. The life of grocer's wife was apparently not enticing, because soon enough she deserted Rand for a wealthy older man, Dr. Le Roe Goddard Crandon whom she met for a medical procedure. Crandon, who was 15 years her senior appears to have been indulgent in nature, and soon took up all things spiritualist in support of his wife. The couple had guests over for nights of table tipping and  spirit communication. It wasn't long after that Stinson began to exhibit mediumistic talents. Another medium with whom Stinson became acquainted encouraged her, telling Stinson that she was a powerful psychic and had the spirit of a laughing boy inside her. Emboldened Stinson soon claimed that she could channel her deceased brother Walter. He had died in 1911.

Gardner Murphy, William McDougall and a group of Harvard professors examined Stinson in 1923, but found no evidence to support her claims. Undeterred, a year later she entered a contest sponsored by Scientific American Magazine. The magazine contest offered $2500 to any contest participant who could, under testing, prove psychic mediumship. J. Malcolm Bird dubbed Stinson "Margery" to protect her identity, although the anonymity was quickly blown. Margery became Stinson's stage name for the rest of her career. Although Margery was clearly a fraud, she quickly had the all-male panel of judges on her side. She would often show up to séances in the nude, and was known to pull ectoplasm from her vagina. Her flirtatious manner with the men didn't hurt her either. When it became clear that the $2500 would be rewarded to Margery, Houdini who was on tour, cancelled shows to return to the judging. Houdini was so adamant that "Margery" was a fraud that he attempted to sabotage some of the experiments. She would eventually get caught red handed, when she claimed that fingerprints left in wax were those of her deceased brother Walter. They were found, instead to be those of her dentist.

EUSAPIA PALLADINO

Born in 1854 near Bari in southern Italy, Palladino was of poor peasant stock. Her father was murdered, leaving Palladino an orphan at the age of twelve. It was reported by those who knew her as a child that strange things happened to her and around her even then. Supposedly strange rapping sounds and discarnate whispering were heard, while unseen hands were said to rip her blankets off at night. Relatives eventually shipped her off to Naples to fill a position as a nursemaid.

The position did not last long, however, as the family was not pleased with the odd paranormal phenomena that occurred when she was there. Reportedly, they also might have taken offense at her slovenly demeanor. Palladino stubbornly refused to bathe, comb her hair or learn to read. She left the post and moved in with family members who introduced her to séances. From the first moment she sat at the séance table she appeared to have remarkable talents, the table was said to come up off one leg and then to levitate completely off the floor.

Having discovered a new talent did not convince Palladino to immediately take up a new profession, to her relatives' chagrin. They tried to capitalize on her by encouraging her to do paid séances out of the house. She refused and moved out shortly after to take a job as a laundress. Not long after she met and married Raphael Delgaiz a shop owner. After working for a short time in Delgaiz's store she left him as well, deciding to pursue a career as a professional medium.

She began giving séances in Naples, Italy and probably would have a remained an obscure unknown, had she not caught the attention of Doctor Ercole Chiaia. Chiaia's personal interest in spiritualism led him to publish a letter to the famed criminologist and psychiatrist Cesare Lombroso, imploring Lombroso to investigate Palladino's abilities. He wrote:

> *"She is 30 years old and very ignorant; her appearance is neither fascinating nor endowed with the power which modern criminologists call irresistible; but when she wishes, be it day or night, she can divert a curious group for an hour or so with the most surprising phenomena. Either bound to a seat or firmly held by the hands of the curious, she attracts to her the articles of furniture which surround her, lifts them up, holds them suspended in the air like Mahomet's coffin, and makes them come down again with undulatory movements, as if they were obeying her will. She increases their height or lessens it according to*

her pleasure. She raps or taps upon the walls, the ceiling, the floor, with fine rhythm and cadence. In response to the requests of the spectators something like flashes of electricity shoots forth from her body, and envelops her or enwraps the spectators of their marvelous scenes. She draws upon cards that you hold out, everything that you want — figures, signatures, numbers, sentences, by just stretching out her hand toward the indicated place.

"If you place in the corner of the room a vessel containing a layer of soft clay, you will find after some moments the imprint in it of a small or large hand, the image of a face (front view or profile) from which a plaster cast can be taken. In this way portraits of a face at different angles have been preserved, and those who desire so can thus make serious and important studies.

"This woman rises in the air, no matter what hands tie her down. She seems to lie upon empty air, as on a couch, contrary to all the laws of gravity; she plays on musical instruments — organs, bells, tambourines — as if they had been touched by her hands or moved by the breath of invisible gnomes. This woman at times can increase her stature by more than four inches.

"She is like an India rubber doll, like an automaton of a new kind; she takes strange forms. How many legs and arms has she? We do not know. While her limbs are being held by incredulous spectators, we see other limbs coming into view, without her knowing where they come from. Her shoes are too small to fit these witch-feet of hers, and this particular circumstance gives rise to the intervention of a mysterious power (22)".

It would be two years before Lambroso was able to follow up on the invitation to sit with Palladino. However, her mercurial career and fame as one of the strongest physical mediums of her era began its ascension. During her career she was studied by many paranormal researchers who were at times appalled and at other times amazed by the results. At one point the Society of Psychical Research withdrew their support for Palladino entirely labeling her as a fraud. Years later they were made to rescind their condemnation. Palladino's was a terribly controversial figure for many reasons.

Her crudeness and lack of education or social graces made her a poor fit for the polished scientific community. When threatened or restrained she had an irascible stubborn streak, and her performances at séances would become desultory. Add to this the fact that she often came out of her trances sexually aroused and had to be restrained from crawling onto the laps of male sitters, this during the Victorian era when such behavior was anathema. And then there was the fact that given any opportunity, any lapse in attention by her observers and Palladino would cheat. Palladino always cheated.

Sometimes her tricks were simple and easy to detect. For example, although she might have sitters holding her feet and hands she would often thrash about during séances so that no one knew where here limbs were. At other times her tricks were more subtle and much harder to detect. Paranormal researchers eventually accepted the fact that part of the show was always faked. Yet, much of the phenomena she produced such as the faces and hand prints in the clay and the ability to move objects and lift furniture even when tied in a chair were simply impossible to explain – even by some of the greatest psychical researchers of her time.

The constant scrutiny and attention took a toll on her, and she started to show her age with a sagging face and exhaustion after séances. And her health was also failing and her powers diminishing. Tired and bitter after a failed trip to the U.S. where she felt she was treated as a freakish sideshow instead of a talented medium, she withdrew from the public eye in 1910, and died in May 1910.

D.D. HOME

During this period D.D. Home made his reputation as perhaps the most gifted medium of his era. A few things separated Home from his medium colleagues. For one thing he never insisted on holding his séances in darkness, he never balked at skeptics that would examine his sessions for fraud, he was never publicly caught or denounced for fraud, and he never accepted payment for his séances. The last point is astounding, as Home was the invited guest of most of the royalty of Europe at one time or another.

He reportedly conducted séances for the Czar of Russia, the king of France, the king of Naples, the queen of Holland, the king of Bavaria and the German emperor, just to name a few! He met and married his first wife, Alexandrina de Kroll, the sister-in-law to Count Koucheleff-Besborodka while in Rome. He had Alexandre Dumas as a groomsman, and Count Alexis Tolstoy the writer and Count Bobrinsky, a chamberlain to the emperor, as

invited guests to the affair. And yet he lived most of his life on the brink of poverty, relying on the largesse of devotees, roaming from one country to another as his welcome wore out.

Daniel Douglas Home (pronounced Hume) was of rather questionable descent. According to a footnote in Home's own autobiographical book *Incidents in My Life* (1863) his father was the "natural son" of

Alexander, the tenth earl of Home, and his mother a lass of the Highlands, who claimed to be descended from the Brahan clan, descendants of Kenneth MacKenzie. From birth, Home was said to have special powers, being able to rock his own cradle. During his childhood, Home was considered to be of nervous disposition and poor health, and was at times not expected to live to adulthood (**19**).

He passed his early childhood in Portobello, Scotland, but moved at the age of nine to the U.S. where he was adopted by a childless aunt, a Mrs. McNeill Cook. He lived for a time in Greeneville, Connecticut and Troy, New York. Reportedly he was a sensitive child with a keen memory and strong observation skills. He had his first vision at the age of 13, when a deceased school mate named Edwin visited him in his home in Troy. Four years would pass before his second vision when Home predicted to the hour, his mother's death. When strange rapping's and tapping's started occurring around the house, his aunt first attempted to have Home exorcised and then finally evicted from his home (**19, 20**).

Aside from being able to speak with spirits via a spirit guide, he was able to produce rapping sounds on command, strange lights and spectral hands. One ghostly hand appeared at a séance with Napoleon III which was able to sign his name on a piece of paper producing the signature of Napoleon I (**20**). Home was able to call forth music on ghostly guitars and move objects about the room. Later he was able to elongate his body as much as 11 inches to a height of 6 ½ feet, and then to shrink to five feet while onlookers saw his shoes disappear under his trousers. He often had onlookers hold his frame to prove that he wasn't faking it, and he allowed those present to measure the differences, all again in a lighted room to disprove fakery.

At the age of 19 he developed the ability to levitate, at first bobbing up and down a few feet off the ground before gently floating up to the ceiling (**21**). He later was able to hone his skills and onlookers swore that he could fly. Home swore his abilities were made possible with the aid of friendly spirits, the most frequent of which was Bryan (**19**).

Home was as much loved as despised. He was criticized as being temperamental, with bouts of anxiety and depression, and to have homosexual leanings. Home was also described as vain though somewhat simple, with the ability to brush off even the most vicious of denunciations. He was sometimes fawned over, other times denounced, sometimes within the same family. Elizabeth Barrett Browning, for example, was a fierce supporter of Home. Her husband Robert Browning...not so much. Browning wrote and published the scathing poem Mr. Sludge the Medium, which denounced Home as a fraud and a joke.

> NOW, don't, sir! Don't expose me!
> Just this once! This was the first and only time, I'll swear, —
> Look at me, —see, I kneel, —the only time,

I swear, I ever cheated,—yes, by the soul
Of Her who hears—(your sainted mother, sir!)

Hume himself disdained contact with other mediums with whom he felt he had nothing to learn. The only medium with whom he had a friendship, ironically, was Kate Fox. His gifts were at times considered sinister. The Italian populace found him particularly loathsome, accusing him of witch craft and sorcery.

When Alexandrina de Kroll died in 1862, the family attempted to withhold Home's inheritance. Home was forced to wage a long legal battle, during which time he had no steady income. He tried to become a student of sculpture, going to Rome for a time to study. He was forced to leave the city after a somewhat extended scuffle with the Papacy who accused Home of sorcery. He then emigrated briefly to the U.S. to attempt his hand as stage orator but left before long to return to Europe. Throughout his career there were at least two attempts on his life, and he took knife wounds to the abdomen and the hand. Certainly it is hard to imagine a psychic that was as famous or as infamous, as punished as rewarded (**20**).

Ill health eventually forced Home to retire. He married a second time, to a wealthy Russian widow, Julie de Gloumeline and declined public séances thereafter. He traveled for the rest of his life, dying of tuberculosis while in Auteuil, France in 1886 (**19**).

During a time when skeptics were actively attempting to disprove psychic mediums, there was never any substantial evidence revealed to prove Home a fraud. Certainly skeptics suggested trickery, often after his death when fraud could not be proven one way or another, and yet some of the sharpest minds couldn't figure out how he produced his great feats.

He agreed to be the subject of an experiment with psychical researcher Sir William Crooke. Crookes could detect no foul play and announced Home's abilities as true. The skeptical Frank Podmore grudgingly admitted that, "Home was never publicly exposed as an imposter; there is no evidence of any weight that he was even privately detected in trickery." Although Podmore does not concede that Home had mediumistic abilities, he neither refuted his abilities either. Even the great Houdini couldn't figure out how he produced the results he did. Whether truly a medium of outstanding abilities or a very clever conjurer is still disputed. He remains therefore, the greatest medium of the age (**19, 20**).

THE WANING OF THE SPIRITUALIST AGE

Spiritualism while declining in the later years of the 19th century, would see a resurgence after the Civil War and World War I, both periods when wholesale slaughter left unmitigated loss and longing. With a belief in spiritualism the bereaved didn't have to consider the dead gone forever, but only a "psychic call" away. For those in grief, spiritualism became a lifeline. The movement was so powerful in its attraction that it eventually led to the creation of new religious denominations such as the Apostolic Church the Pentecostal faith - with its many offshoots. Being able to speak in tongues and be possessed by the Holy Spirit; in other words the combined allure of spirit communication and religious fervor was intoxicating to many, and still is today. Still, spiritualism was evolving. The age of the physical medium with levitating tables and ectoplasm was finished, tarnished beyond repair. The age of the mental medium, such as Leonora Piper emerged, mediums far less concerned with fanfare, but bigger on message.

LEONORA PIPER – THE ONE WHITE CROW

Leonora Piper was for psychical researchers the real deal without the theatrics. A simple housewife not seeking attention or fame, Piper still produced outstanding results even under the closest scrutiny. Born Leonora (sometimes misspelled as Leonore in some texts) Simmonds in Nashua, New Hampshire in June of 1859. She had a relatively routine childhood with very little sign of the talent that would emerge later in life. However, two episodes from her childhood did stand out. The first occurred when Leonora was eight years old. She was playing in her family's garden when she suddenly felt a sharp blow to her right ear and then a long drawn out sibilant s sound, somewhat like what one would experience if a tuning fork were held next to the ear. The sibilant sound eventually resolved itself into an s sound. And then the child distinctly heard the words, "Aunt Sara, not dead, but with you still." The terrified child quickly ran to her mother who was stunned by the story, but had the common sense to write down the message with the date and time. In an era without cell phones and computers, it took the family several days to receive the news that Aunt Sara had passed away, at the exact time and day that Leonora had received the visitation.

A few weeks later she complained to her mother that she could not sleep in her bedroom, "because of the bright light in the room and all the faces in it." She also said that her bed wouldn't stop rocking. She apparently had other, occasional experiences such as these, although perhaps not of the same magnitude. She married William Piper of Boston at the age of 22 years. Not long after, for no stated reason, she sought out the advice of a blind, clairvoyant by the name of J. R. Cocke, who had gained some notoriety for his medical diagnoses and cures. At the first visit with Cocke she apparently fell into a short trance.

At the second meeting which was held to affect medical cures and help mediums to develop latent skills, Cocke placed his hand atop Piper's head, she saw a, flood of light in which many strange faced appeared." Entranced, Piper got up from her chair and walked over to a table, picked up a pencil and began writing on a piece of paper. She wrote out a rapid message and then gave it to another sitter at the meeting. The recipient of the written message was the notable jurist, Judge Frost of Cambridge. Frost would later state that the written message was the most remarkable message he had ever received. It was from his deceased son.

DISCOVERED BY THE SOCIETY OF PSYCHICAL RESEARCH

News of the episode spread quickly and soon Piper was receiving far more attention than the shy housewife could stand. Not seeking notoriety or fame, Piper would only give sittings for family or friends. For some reason, however, she agreed to give a sitting for a particular society woman upon request. Mrs. Eliza Gibbens had heard about the psychic through servant gossip and requested a sitting. She and her daughter, Alice Gibbens James were so convinced by Piper's talent and veracity that they convinced Alice's husband to attend a sitting. William James, psychical researcher, founder of the U.S. Society for Psychical Research and famous psychologist, agreed to a sitting with Piper mainly to disprove her abilities. He was so taken with Piper that he took control of all her sittings for the next 18-months in order to study her more closely.

TRANCE MEDIUM

Piper was mainly a trance medium, meaning that during sittings the psychic would appear to go into a trance during which time a control personality would seem to talk through her, controlling communication between whatever spirits were present and the sitters. During the early 18-month experiment with James, Piper's exclusive control was reputedly a French doctor by the name of Phinuit, known during sittings as "Finne" or "Finnett," apparently inherited from her sittings with Cocke. Phinuit's personality came through in a deep gruff voice, much different than that of Piper's, and he appeared to hold reign over the medium from 1884-1892. The difficulty with Phinuit, as with most of the control personalities, is that he didn't appear to link to any actual person, deceased or otherwise. Often what the controls said about themselves was odd, inaccurate or unreliable, and it was speculated that the controls weren't actual discarnate spirits but an offshoot of the medium's own. In the case of Phinuit he neither appeared to know much French nor have a wide knowledge of medicine. Later a George Pelham, supposedly killed in an accident, made his appearance, manifesting his personality in automatic writing sessions. Piper would often speak and write simultaneously while in trance.

In 1897 the Imperator group took over as Piper's controls. The personality of Phinuit disappeared and so too did many of the difficulties Piper had had in the past. She now appeared to slip into trance far more easily and the communication channels appeared to be stronger with fewer interruptions from what the Imperator Group described as earth-bound spirits of lesser intelligence whom they were able to keep from "using the light" and "foreign elements." The sittings themselves became more dignified and took on an almost quasi-religious tone. James pointed out that there were distinct personality characteristics that were obvious among the group and that the sittings now revealed many of the deepest secrets of the sitters. James experimented with hypnotizing Piper and concluded that her hypnotic state vastly different from her trance state. Piper also practiced psychometry at sittings, by gleaning knowledge of past owners by holding objects they had once possessed. Unlike the other mediums discussed in this chapter, Piper was not a physical medium. She had but one odd talent, she could withdraw the scent of a flower, and cause flowers to wither in a short time.

At the end of James' 18-month control over the medium he wrote an article for *Proceedings* the journal of the American Society of Psychical Research (1890, vol. 6, pt. 17). In the article James wrote, "And I repeat again what I said before that, taking everything that I know of Mrs. Piper into account the result is to make me feel absolutely certain as I am of any personal fact in the world that she knows things in her trances which she cannot possibly have heard in her waking state, and that the definite philosophy of her trances is yet to be found....If you wish to upset the conclusion that all crows are black, there is no need to seek demonstration that no crows are black; it is sufficient to produce one white crow; a single one is sufficient." Piper, James believed Piper was the "one white crow"(21, 25).

James' written support for the medium would garner much hostility from the scientific world, and cost him professionally, however he never deviated from what he believed, that Piper was his one white crow. When he was called away from the Piper experiment he enlisted the help of his colleagues in the Society of Psychical Research (SPR) to pick up where he had left off. Richard Hodgson was well known for his work exposing such mediums as Eusapia Pallodino and Helena Petrovna Blavatsky for trickery. He arrived in the United States with the sole purpose of catching up Piper as well. Under Hodgson's control Piper had her most famous period. Hodgson was a task master at controlling the flow of information to Piper. Sittings were held on the first three days of the week, during which time Piper was not allowed to view the newspaper. The names of sitters were kept a secret from Piper, introduced only as "Smith." The sittings were arranged so that random visitors could attend, making it impossible for Piper to know anything about them. Hodgson hired a private detective that followed Piper everywhere she went monitoring to whom she spoke and reporting back any information exchanged.

PIPER IN ENGLAND

In November of 1889 Hodgson even elected to remove Piper to England, one of two trips to England Piper underwent with the Society of Psychical Research. She stayed for a time with F.W.H. Myers – one of the British founders of the SPR. Hodgson chose Piper's servants, and changed them out occasionally. In a country where Piper had never been, where she had no former acquaintances, friends or knowledge, and under strict controls and constant observation the medium continued to astound.

Hodgson concluded that Piper's brand of mediumship was unique. He noted that Piper was often dead wrong on minutiae that false mediums would have gotten right. For example, she was often vague on dates, was better with first names than surnames, and spent more time discussing the sitters, diagnosing their diseases, describing their idiosyncrasies and personalities.

At the end of the experiment Hodgson met with James, William R. Newbold of Pennsylvania University, Walter Leaf and Sir Oliver Lodge, after which James wrote in the Psychological Review, "Dr. Hodgson considers that the hypothesis of fraud cannot be seriously maintained. I agree with him absolutely. The medium has been under observation, much of the time under close observation, as to most of the conditions of her life by a large number of persons, eager, many of them to pounce upon any suspicious circumstance for (nearly) fifteen years. During that time not only has there not been one single suspicious circumstance remarked, not one suggestion has ever been made from any quarter which might tend to positively explain how the medium, living the apparent life she leads, could possibly collect information about so many sitters by natural means (25)."

THE EXPERIMENT, PIPER'S SECOND TRIP TO ENGLAND

In 1906 Piper received an invitation by Mary Lodge, Sir Oliver Lodge's wife, inviting Piper to return to England to conduct an experiment. Self-taught in automatic writing the Classic's Lecturer Margaret Verrall was to partake from Cambridge, Piper in London. Both women would have supervision. The task was to funnel the

Eleanor "Nora" Sidgwick

spirit of F.W.H. Myers or Hodgson (both of whom had since passed away) and to contact Edmund Gurney or Henry Sidgwick (founding members of the SPR) in a long distance communication experiment to prove the existence of life after death.

Mary Lodge

The SPR researcher John Piddington worked with Piper in London. Once the medium was under trance Piddington would ask her to contact Myers and give Myers a message in Latin or Greek. Piper with only a high school education did not speak either language, but the key to the experiment was this, that the spirits of Myers, Gurney and Sidgwick would be fluent in either and thus if actual communication between the three was established, they would understand the instructions and respond as directed to Verrall in Cambridge. If the message survived the language barrier and arrived to Verrall as it should, the researchers concluded, then some type of intelligence after death would be proven.

The first message was sent via Piper's spirit control "Rector" in December 1906. Piddington began with an introduction in Latin signaling to Myers that they had been receiving his messages in various forms for some time. Then Piddington told Rector to convey to Myers that they wished him to receive messages from Piper and to convey his answers to Verrall, with the stipulation that at the end of his message Myers should attach some type of code word or symbol of his choice to prove that it was definitely him.

A couple of weeks went by during which time Piper's Rector informed Piddington that, we have in part understood and conveyed your message to your friend Myers and he is delighted to receive it so far as he has been able to receive it." In January 1907 Rector assured Piddington that "Hodgson is helping Myers with his translation."

Margaret Verrall

In January Piddington had a better idea and told Rector to convey to Myers that he was to end his first message to Verrall with a drawn circle with a triangle in it. That night Verrall through automatic writing wrote the message: *"Justice hold the scales. That gives the words but an anagram would be better. Tell him that –rats, star, tars and so on. Try this, it has been tried before. RTATS. Rearrange these five letters or again t-e-a-r-s…stare."* Thus Myers appeared to be giving advice to Piddington posthumously!

Five days later Verrall wrote" Aster *[a star]…the world's wonder, And all a wonder and a wild desire/the very wings of her…but it is all much the same thing –the winged desire, the hope that leaves the earth for the sky…Abt Vogler for earth, too hard that found itself or lost itself – in the sky. That is what I want, On the broken sounds, threads."* Verrall drew a circle and a triangle at the end.

On February 11th Rector delivered a message from Myers with clues for Piddington as to how to interpret the Verrall message. Hope, star and the poet Browning were all important clues, he said. The widow, Nora Sidgwick broke the code. Myers who had been a lover of poetry was alluding to a poem by Browning entitled "Abt Vogler" about a musician (and ironically had appeared in the same volume of poetry as "Mr. Sludge the Medium").

*"And the emulous heaven yearned down, made effort
to reach the earth,*

*As the earth had done her best, in my passion to scale
the sky;*

*Novel splendours burst forth, grew familiar and dwelt
with mine, Not a point nor peak but found and fixed
its wandering star."*
Robert Browning

Later Verrall wrote down a message from Myers saying that he was concerned that Rector did not understand about the name of the poem, and that Myers was anxious on this account. While entranced, some weeks later, Piper wrote out the words "Abt Vogler." Verrall wrote at another sitting:

"Now, Dear Mrs. Sidgwick, in future have no doubt or fear of the so called death as there is none, as there is certainly intelligent life beyond it." Myers conveyed that he had used the Browning poem as it most aptly conveyed his life, wandering the stars. He conveyed that he had much more to say but the communication was extremely difficult, that getting even one small thought across the divide accurately was frustrating in the extreme.

Piddington in the meantime was obsessed with the anagrams that had come across in the earlier writing. Myers had indicated that Hodgson had been asked to help with the translation and the response. Piddington wrote Harry James in Boston, James was caretaker for Hodgson's papers. Piddington asked James for anything that Hodgson had written that had to do with anagrams. In one of Hodgson's boxes James found a scrawled sheet of paper in Hodgson's handwriting which he promptly mailed to London. It was a practice anagram reading:

John George Piddington

RATES
STARE
TEARS
TEARS
TARE
ARE ST
ST ARE
A REST

REST A
STAR
TARS
RATS
ARTS
TRAS

"I confess that when this came into my hands I felt as I suppose people do who have seen a ghost," Piddington would later admit.

INCONCLUSIVE EVIDENCE

There was never a debate among the researchers that studied Piper's gift that her psychic abilities were beyond reproach. What gave the researchers cause for debate were the inconsistencies of the material she brought forth. The theory of telepathy or the ability to glean information from a living person was being bandied about by the researchers as a possible explanation to explaining spirits. If the researchers could prove the theory of telepathy as real then telepathy might explain people experiencing spirits. Thus the idea was that a person that witnessed a crisis apparition for example, was not actually communicating with the soul of a dead person, but were experiencing instead a veridical hallucination, veridical meaning truthful or coinciding with reality – thus a truthful hallucination. Piper appeared to have telepathic abilities in abundance, being able to describe characteristics of sitters she didn't know with shocking accuracy. She also had psychometric gifts, being able to telepathically describe the history of people when holding the objects they once owned.

Her control personalities were another problem. At times they came forward with astounding details that Piper could not possibly have known prior to a sitting. At other times the controls were simply wrong, and then sometimes they appeared to babble on inanely. Worse, not one of the controls could be convincingly matched to an actual person. Obviously the burning question at the heart of the research was whether Piper could actually communicate with the souls of the deceased? This for Sidgwick, Myers and James who had lost a young son, this was the actual heart of the issue, and the one answer that appeared the most elusive. There were times that there was no other explanation than that Piper was speaking with a spirit. Take this obscure case; at a sitting conducted by Piper, a spirit seemed to break in who identified himself as Hugh. Hugh was actually the deceased husband to an English woman named Edith Mary Barber. Edith Barber had sat for several sittings with Piper in Boston before returning to England, and was not actually present with Hugh during this particular sitting.

A former medical officer in the British Army, Hugh had been assigned for a time to India. At the sitting he recalled a club house in India that he had had gone to with his friend George Dillon, who had been a member at the club. Hugh recounted a situation in which

Dillon had been given an imitation cigar. Upon contacting Edith Barber she confirmed knowing about the club and George Dillon, though neither had been discussed at earlier sittings with Piper, but did not know about the situation with the imitation cigar. Barber actually wrote Dillon who still resided in India, and Dillon wrote back confirming the joke with the imitation cigar.

HODGSON WON OVER TO SURVIVAL

Hodgson, the group's watchdog skeptic, eventually abandoned the telepathy theory in favor of survival after death. Basing his conclusions on his own records of séance reports rather than on quantitative investigation he explained his reasoning in several points. Elucidated in a paper entitled, "A Further Record of Observations of Certain Phenomena of Trance," he submitted to the journal *Proceedings of the Society for Psychical Research* (vol. 13, 1898, pp. 357-412) he explained that: (a) the success of the séance appeared to depend more on the strength of the control speaker than the sitters presents. For example her control Phinuit was a weaker control, the imperator group stronger with trances that were quicker to slip into, deeper, and with better information forthcoming. (b) The information given by a spirit through a control seemed limited to what that person would have known when living, though the sitters were not always similarly limited. (c) Sometimes spirits gave the control information that was *not* known by the sitters, such as the cigar joke incident. Thus the hypothesis that Piper was reading only her sitters was disproven. A base adherence to the telepathy theory would have to suppose that Piper was gleaning information from people not present at the sittings which seems a stretch of the plausible. (d) Often spirits, such as Hugh, would return to later sittings and provide further information, even when the people with whom they were attached were not present. This again, would seem to argue directly against the telepathy theory. (e) The society's experiments with telepathy could not match the rapid dispatch of information that often poured forth during Piper séances (**31**).

Piper continued working with the SPR until her death in 1950, helping to complete decades of unparalleled work in the survival research. She underwent years of observation and control, allowing the SPR to invade her privacy with patience and dignity, never once being caught in even minor fraud or trickery. Because of her incredible graciousness, the SPR could complete reams of careful research, leaving a body of work that have never again been rivaled in either importance or longevity. She was the SPR's best and most talented one white crow.

CHAPTER 3: THE BIRTH OF PARANORMAL RESEARCH

The Spiritualist Age not only created the psychic medium, but also gave birth to paranormal research. Some of the greatest scientific minds of the day devoted their free time, resources, money and devotion studying the question of the existence of life after death, and many of them suffered professionally for their pursuit of a subject considered below scientific attention.

One such was the chemist Sir William Crookes. From 1869-1875 he studied a number of mediums including D.D. Home. Convinced that Home proved the existence of the "psychic force" within the human body, Crookes wrote a paper on the psychic which he tried to have published first in the "Proceedings of the Royal Society of London." It was refused. Crookes then used his considerable force and reputation to have it published in the "Quarterly Journal of Science." Undoubtedly it was a play he lived to regret, because the backlash from the scientific community was fierce and immediate, leaving Crooke's reputation tarnished, his work discredited.

Watching from the sidelines were two scientists who sympathized with Crooke's plight, Professor Henry Sidgwick and F.W.H. (Frederick) Myers. Both thought that the possibility of proving supernatural phenomenon through scientific means was possible. They didn't however know exactly what to do for Crookes and others in the scientific community who might want to study the paranormal further without destruction of their reputation. It was a mutual friend, Sir William F. Barrett (physics professor at the Royal College of Science in Dublin) who proposed forming a society to study psychical research – a term coined by the group – or paranormal phenomenon, using rigorous scientific methodology. Henry Sidgwick, became the organization's first president. His wife Eleanor (Nora) Sidgwick would be one of its founding members, a mathematician and professor in her own right, Nora was one of the earliest champions of women's rights to higher education as well as a tireless psychical researcher (26). Soon thereafter the U.S. chapter of the SPR was opened, the idea carried across the pond by William James, who would become the ASPR president some years later.

The group's first council included Barrett, Edmund Gurney, Balfour Stewart, F.W.H. Myers, and Richard Hutton. Frank Podmore and Richard Hodgson were also among the first members (26). It would later attract other noteworthy followers such as Sir Oliver Lodge, Sigmund Freud, Carl Jung, Sir William Crookes, Sir Arthur Conan Doyle and Mark Twain.

The SPR decided to limit its studies to six areas of research, with committees set up for each area of inquiry. The six committees were to study: hypnotism and clairvoyance; telepathy; mediums; ghosts and hauntings; records and archival research. The idea was to undergo each area of study using scientific methodology, to document precisely, to create painstaking experiments free from the flaws of earlier methods, and therefore to elevate the study of the paranormal to a higher and hopefully irreproachable level of research. The new scientific rigor didn't appeal to everyone involved in the spiritualist community, and the organization with its bloodline of aristocrats and scientists wasn't above snubbing those it felt unworthy of its attention.

THE FOUNDERS OF THE SOCIETY FOR PSYCHICAL RESEARCH

Henry Sidgwick

Sidgwick was a Professor of the Classics at Trinity College Cambridge for 10 years, before switching to moral philosophy. He eventually achieved the Knightsbridge Professorship of Philosophy, the highest honor. His most famous work, The *Methods of Ethics* was hailed as a major work in the field of moral philosophy.

Interestingly, Sidgwick was first compelled to study the supernatural by his cousin and later brother-in-law, Edward White Benson. (Benson would go on to become the Archbishop of Canterbury.) Benson had helped found a Ghost Society at Cambridge, and asked Sidgwick to visit some mediums in his area and report to him. Early on Sidgwick showed a good ability to

Henry Sidgwick

detect mechanical devices and other machinations with which fraudulent mediums tended their trades. Still, he admitted, that he was intrigued by the possibility of something beyond fraud, and that very occasionally he saw a glimmer of something real and yet unexplainable.

Sidgwick would reside as the head of the SPR for the first nine years, and the group that supported and researched with him became known as the Sidgwick group. He was a contributor to the two volume *Phantasm's of the Living*, and involved, at times closely, with the Leonora Piper project. As was everyone involved with Piper, he was at times astounded by the material put forth, and at other times frustrated. The son of a preacher and brother-in-law to the Archbishop of Canterbury, he sought all of his professional career for answers to the world's deeper questions, the study of ethics and theism. He very much wanted to believe that psychical research was pointing toward proving the existence of a soul surviving death, but he couldn't ignore the simpler, "minimum hypothesis" that telepathy was the conclusion. Thus a medium wasn't actually communicating with a spirit, but was simply "reading" the sitters at the séance. So too he feared with crisis apparitions that the people that experienced such were simply experiencing telepathically created hallucinations (what the SPR dubbed veridical hallucinations) and not actually communicating with the departing soul. The disparity in evidence and frustration Sidgwick felt often resulted in black moods, during which time the researcher despaired of ever proving the existence of the soul (**31**).

F.W.H. Myers

The son of an English clergyman, Frederic Myers was a professor of Classics at Cambridge University in England. An essayist and poet, he is known for such works as the poem *St. Paul* and *Essays, Classical and Modern and Science and a Future Life*. As a scholar, Myers was described as a man of "enormous energy" and "great intellectual ability."

He is probably best remembered as a co-founding father of the Society of Psychical Research and was a major contributor to the society for the next twenty years of his life. Myers reportedly experienced an after-death communication with his first wife which fueled Myer's interest in pursuing research in the theory that the human consciousness survived bodily death. At a time when science was proceeding toward stark materialism, a belief in the human soul was seen as basest superstition. Declaring belief in the possibility of the human soul was a daring act of bravery, one likely to besmirch your professional reputation permanently. He wrote a book of essays entitled, *Human Personality and Its Survival of Bodily Death* which became a classic on the subject, in which he tried, in his own words, "to do what can be done to break down that artificial wall between science and superstition." In the book he did a landmark analysis of psychic abilities, trying to prove through scientific research that extrasensory perception is a natural, observable and researchable phenomenon. He carefully analyzed paranormal experiences of people in various states of wakefulness, sleep and hypnotic states. He attempted to apply scientific methods of observation and discussion to discuss the possibility of the survival of the soul. And he attempted to inspire a new generation of researchers to pursue studies in human consciousness (**32**).

Myers wrote in his introduction, "We gradually discovered that the accounts of apparitions at the moment of death--testifying to a supersensory communication between the dying man and the friend who sees him—led on without perceptible break to apparitions occurring after the death of the person seen, but while that death was yet unknown to the percipient, and thus apparently due not to mere brooding memory but to a continued action of that departed spirit. The task next incumbent on us therefore seemed plainly to be the collection and analysis of evidence of this and other types, pointing directly to the survival of man's spirit."

Despite his conclusions in *Human Personality*, Myers like his contemporary Sidgwick continued to have moments of doubt. After countless hours studying mediums and their performances he was in little doubt of the medium's abilities but was in severe doubt of just what that ability entailed. He had attended séances that seemed to insinuate that the dead were speaking through the medium. The medium would adopt a voice that sounded like a dead person, and that voice would list an impressive array of facts about that person's life. At times, however, he'd found that the supposed departed was very much still alive. Sometimes it seemed that the mediums were gathering their information from the minds of the people in the room. Still worse, he conducted case studies, sending in subjects who were instructed to concentrate on fictitious persons. The medium seemed to read the mind of the subject and report through the voice that false identity.

Sadly, Myers concluded that it wasn't simple to determine from whence the information came. In fact the mediums themselves could not determine the source of information, whether from a spirit or the minds of the subjects in the room. After a lifetime's worth of study he wasn't to know the answer to his most troubling question, not at least until he passed over himself.

EDMUND GURNEY

The tall, mercurial, handsome, gentleman-scholar was one of the first three founders of the SPR, along with Henry Sidgwick and Frank Myers. Gurney was educated at Black Heath and Trinity Colleges where he obtained a fellowship. He then studied medicine at Cambridge, devoting himself to physics, chemistry and physiology, though apparently had no intention of ever practicing medicine. Gurney was a gentleman scholar, meaning that he had the money and wherewithal to pursue interests simply because they fascinated him. It also meant that he could devote himself to psychical research, which he did, without  worries about professional reputation or financial limitations. He professed an interest in the paranormal, "looking for an unexplored region of human faculty transcending the normal limitations of sensible knowledge." He intended to approach psychical research through observation and experimentation, with a special interest in the fields of hypnotism and telepathy.

Gurney's crowning achievements was the compilation of the two-volume set of books, *Phantasms of the Living,* sharing credit with Frank Podmore and F.W.H. Myers. Based on years of data collection, the books detailed the phenomenon of crisis apparitions; apparitions of the newly dead that often present themselves to the living either in the last moments of their life or directly following their demise. This work is undoubtedly the most intensive study ever conducted of the phenomena, and it should be noted that Gurney did the bulk of the field work, collecting, analyzing and interviewing the witnesses, and also wrote the bulk of the main text.

Excerpt from: *Phantasms of the Living,* Gurney, E, Myers, F.W.H, Podmore, (1886):

"I sat one evening reading, when on looking up from my book, I distinctly saw a school-friend of mine, to whom I was very much attached, standing near the door I was about to exclaim at the strangeness of her visit when, to my horror, there were no signs of anyone in the room but my mother. I related what I had seen to her, knowing she could not have seen, as she was sitting with her back towards the door, nor did she hear anything unusual, and was greatly amused at my scare, suggesting I had read too much or been dreaming.

A day or so after this strange event, I had news to say my friend was no more. The strange part was that I did not even know she was ill, much less in danger so could not have felt anxious at the time on her account, but may have been thinking of her; that I cannot testify. Her illness was short, and death much unexpected. Her mother told me she spoke of me not long before she died ... She died the same evening and about the same time that I saw her vision, which was the end of October, 1874."

Tragically, not long after publication of Phantasms, Gurney who had suffered from bouts of depression for years was found dead in his hotel room, apparently from suicide. His death was a shocking and tragic loss to his friends and the SPR, and left some stain on the reputation of the organization.

Gurney's theory on spirits was undoubtedly influenced by his painstaking research in crisis apparitions. He believed, however, that when a person experienced an apparition or spirit of a departed person they weren't really experiencing an actual spirit, telepathic communication with the departed. Gurney used the term veridical hallucination (veridical meaning truthful or relating to reality) by which he meant a hallucination which corresponded to an actual event, as when a person witnessed the image of an apparition at the time of the apparition's death.

Gurney believed that the receiver of the message (the person who experienced the apparition) received a telepathic cue. The cue was sent by the dying person often at the moment of crisis, death or near-death experience, when they knowingly or unknowingly sent the message. Think of a telephone answering machine. You arrive home from work to see the light on the machine blinking – the cue. You hit the play button and receive the message – the message sent at the moment of crisis. You're not actually hearing the voice of your loved one, nor are they in the room with you, you're just receiving the pre-recorded message.

Gurney knew his theory was flawed in some respects, as it didn't adequately account for collective phenomena, or several people experiencing the same apparition at the same time. He attempted to explain this very rare phenomena as contagious telepathy.

THE EMERGENCE OF MODERN PARANORMAL RESEARCH

As already noted, the beginning of paranormal research centered on mediums, the endless search for the one white crow in an overwhelming sea of black. It seems a natural progression, if one wishes to research the existence of a soul after death, that one start with psychic mediums, the vessels through which the spirits of the dead were believed to communicate. However, the researchers spent the majority of their time and energy trying to detect fraud, far more time than they did actually investigating the paranormal. And, after defaming so many mediums they hurt not only the reputation of the spiritualist community but also their own.

By the 1920's the SPR was desperately trying to survive. They were disparaged and discredited by the scientific community who viewed any research into the paranormal, even when conducted using scientific methodology, as the most serious of crackpot science. And the SPR had defrauded so many psychics that the spiritualist community now viewed them as the enemy. Frank Myers was sadly implicated in a sex scandal with a medium who was later discredited as a fraud. And Gurney's death had been under questionable circumstances. All of these events had left the SPR with their reputation in tatters (**30**).

It soon became apparent that they had to bring the research into the laboratory, in order to enforce the type of rigor and control necessary to scientific experimentation. Only by focusing on one or two proven psychics, such as Leonora Piper, for extended periods of time and using strict controls, could they hope to glean any valuable data whatsoever. Thus research went in-house, where they set up experiments designed to eliminate (or at least decrease) trickery. They installed restraints on chairs, employed motion sensor photography, recorded transcripts of sessions, invented and tested devices to sense motion and limit psychic interaction with objects; in short employing as many types of control over a séance as their minds could design. It was about this time that Harry Price joined the SPR as a researcher.

HARRY PRICE -FATHER OF MODERN PARANORMAL RESEARCH

Price was born in London in 1881, the son of a grocer and traveling salesman. He saw his first magic show at the age of nine, and thus began a lifelong interest in magic. He became an accomplished amateur conjurer, and amassed a large collection of books on

magic. Such a background became quite valuable to Price when investigating fraudulent psychics. He had his first encounter with the paranormal at the age of 15, when he and a friend decided to spend the night in a reportedly haunted house. During the night both boys heard footsteps coming from a bedroom upstairs and footsteps clearly descending the staircase. Price actually took a photo of the staircase during the episode. But when the print came back it showed only an empty staircase.

Harry Price

Upon finishing his education Price went on to work a number of odd jobs including that of journalist. Then in 1908 Price met Constance Mary Knight, a wealthy heiress whom he wooed and wed, becoming overnight a man of leisure. Not having to work for his daily bread, Price decided to devote himself entirely too paranormal research. Having a penchant for self-promotion, by the time he joined the SPR in 1920 he was already Britain's most famous ghost investigator, having already spent hours in haunted locations and studying psychic mediums.

He quickly made a name for himself within the SPR by exposing **William Hope**, a supposed spirit photographer. Hope's scheme was to take a photograph of a sitter and then develop a print which would show the sitter as well as a dead relative or two in the picture. Price figured out that Hope was acquiring photos of the deceased and exposing his photographic plates beforehand. Thus he'd arrive at the shoot with the images of the deceased already exposed on the plate which he would then use to shoot the photograph. Price could debunk such antics simply. Unbeknownst to Hope, Price would make a quick mark on all the unused plates before the sitting. Hope made a show of using the new plates during the sitting, but actually swapped them out for pre-exposed plates.

Photograph of William Hope

When the plates were developed with the images of the dead relatives, as expected, what they didn't bear was Price's mark. He had caught Hope red-handed.

Price continued with the SPR soon branching into studying a number of psychic mediums and two rather infamous poltergeist cases, one of which involved a talking mongoose! Being somewhat of a genius with mechanical and electronic devices, he invented and built many of his own experimental devices that he used on investigations. Also during this time, Price continued to seek attention for his work. He never worked a case without first alerting the media, and members of the press often accompanied him while he worked.

His self-promotion schemes began to fray his relations with the other SPR members, whose natural inclinations were to distain the son of a middle-class salesman as being less than a gentleman in the first place, and questioned his middle-class education and lack of scientific training. Ironically enough, Price was a wiz with electronics and mechanical devices and invented numerous devices that he used on his investigations. While Price would continue his membership with the SPR until his death, it would remain a love-hate relationship.

In June of 1929 Price conducted a visit to an old house in a sparsely-populated hamlet on the east coast of Britain near the Suffolk border to investigate claims of a haunting. Borley Rectory would become his single focus and greatest achievement in paranormal research, and would consume the next 18 years of his life. Indeed, Price was writing his third book on the subject when he died of a heart attack in 1948. Price created investigative protocols that became the blueprint for many of our modern investigative procedures. And Borley Rectory became the most famous haunted house case in history, making Price both famous and infamous in the paranormal community.

HISTORY OF BORLEY RECTORY

Price, who researched the history of the property, began his chronicle in 1362 when Edward III bestowed the Manor of Borley upon the Benedictine Monks. Much of the history of the property is shrouded in mystery however. During the reign of Henry VIII

many of the country's monasteries were seized, destroyed and denuded. The Waldesgrave family took possession and held the property for some 3oo years. A relative of the Waldesgrave's, Reverend H.D.E. Bull occupied the property from 1832-1892, when he held the position of rector to the church. He built the adjoining rectory (house for his family) a year after his appointment, placing the building, despite warning from the locals, on a plot of land reputedly haunted. He was succeeded by his son Rev. H.F. Bull who stayed on in the manor until 1927. After Bull's death, the rectory remained vacant for a year, until in October 1928 Reverend Guy Eric Smith took the rector position and moved his family into the manor house. Rev. Smith decamped after only one year in the position, plagued by the deteriorating state of the building and the resident ghosts.

The fact that the rectory was haunted was no news. Strange occurrences had been going on for years, but had been "kept quiet" as is the way of things. In 1886 Mrs. E. Byford had left her post as nanny, frightened off the property by ghostly footsteps. Some years later both of Henry Bull's daughters would claim to have witnessed the apparition of a nun who walked across the front lawn in broad daylight with her head bent as if in mourning. The family also reported hearing and seeing a strange array of strange things including: rapping's, footsteps, strange lights, ghostly whispers, objects moving and the sound of carriage and horses.

The paranormal phenomenon unnerved the two young women, but not Rev. Bull who viewed the happenings as smashing good entertainment. Father and son Bull built a summer house on the front lawn where they could sit on the porch smoking cigars after dinner, waiting for a glimpse of the ghostly nun as she made one of her numerous appearances.

Bull shared stories with his friend J. Harley who later gave testimony to Price. The Bulls were not the only ones to see the apparition of the nun. When Price collected local accounts in 1939, 13 people claimed to have witnessed her, including one contractor who reported having spotted the apparition on four separate occasions. Also witnessed by three people was a phantom coach and horses with glittering harness and two people reported seeing the apparition of a headless man, all on the Borley lawns.

Reverend Smith was replaced by the Reverend Lionel Foyster and wife Marianne. The activity became more varied and violent, during the Foyster's 15-month residency, and appeared especially focused on Marianne. Objects appeared and disappeared and moved about, furniture would slide across rooms sometimes violently, strange sounds were heard, windows were broken and doors locked and unlocked themselves unaccountably. Objects and furniture hurled across the room day and night causing Marianne to scramble out of the way in order not to be hurt. One night she was almost suffocated in bed by the mattress. Three other times she found herself hurled forcibly out of bed. The activity was so prevalent that Rev. Foyster started a journal, meaning to publish the manuscript under the title *Fifteen Months in a Haunted House*.

He never did, but later Price would use large excerpts of the manuscript in one of his own books on Borley.

Inexplicably the activity took on a personal nature when the family began to notice messages scrawled on walls by an unknown hand. The messages seemed to be addressed specifically to Marianne, imploring her for help. The confusing messages were often hard to decipher, but included such phrases as "Marianne, please help get," and "Marianne, light mass prayers."

One of the spirit's favorite games was to ring the bells. As in many older homes of the era, a bell system had been installed, the ringing of which would call the servants to service. The bells would often ring around the rectory, despite the fact that the system had been disconnected.

One evening in particular the activity seemed extremely powerful. The Foysters were sitting at the kitchen table with family friend Dom Richard Whitehouse and the family maid Katie with all the windows and doors closed. Suddenly all the bells began ringing in the house. Then as the group sat transfixed, bottles started appearing out of thin air and smashing themselves on the floor. Not long after the shocking display, the Foysters held a séance in the house after which the atmosphere in the house calmed considerably for the space of about a year. While doors were still locked and items still moved across rooms on their own, the activity was not as aggressive in nature.

In 1935, however, the activity began again to escalate toward violence. The Foysters were, not surprisingly, at the end of their tether, and decided to move. The church who ultimately owned the rectory decided to sell the building as it was unfit as a residence for the clergy. Price who had already visited the property twice was offered the building at a price far below fair market value. After some consideration he decided instead to lease the building for one year, with the plan of conducting a one-year, round the clock investigation of the building and grounds, an investigation of such magnitude it had never before or since been attempted.

THE INVESTIGATION

Obviously an investigation of this magnitude required manning. Price ran an advertisement in The Times looking for sound-minded individuals with good observation skills to camp out at the rectory night and day. The advertisement read:

> **HAUNTED HOUSE:** Responsible persons of leisure and intelligence, intrepid, critical and unbiased, are invited to join a Rota of observers in a year's night and day investigation of alleged haunted house in Home Counties. Printed Instructions supplied. Scientific training or ability to operate simple instruments an advantage. House situated in lonely hamlet, so own car is essential. Write Box H.989, The Times, E.C.4.

Price was deluged with applicants, most of whom he felt unsuited to the task. Eventually he managed to choose 40 applicants from the horde. He then wrote the first-ever ghost hunter's handbook detailing the proper way to observe, measure and record paranormal activity. It also contained a list of suggested equipment and supplies the investigators should have on hand during their investigations – the first ghost hunter's kit.

The List Included:
> FELT OVERSHOES
> MEASURING TAPE
> TAPE, ELECTRIC BELLS, LEAD SEALS AND OTHER ITEMS FOR MAKING MOTION DETECTION TOOLS
> MERCURY FOR DETECTING VIBRATIONS
> DRY BATTERIES AND SWITCHES
> CAMERAS
> NOTEBOOKS AND DRAWING PADS
> BALL AND STRING, CHALK
> BASIC FIRST-AID KIT

As in love as we are in this age with our high-tech gizmos much of the equipment on the list would seem archaic. However, many of the objects on the list are rather ingeniously simple, effective items. The tape measure Price reportedly used to measure the width of doorways and walls, looking purportedly for hidden passages and rooms, always as careful to consider the possibility of human trickery as well as the supernatural.

Known as the "Blue Book" he printed up his paranormal primer and issued a copy to his investigators. Troy Taylor author and founder of the American Ghost Society suggests, that though the language of the *Blue Book* is dated to the time it was written, and electronic equipment less advanced, many of the tenets and methods discussed in the manuscript remain relevant to this day.

Price's volunteers quickly started to arrive to witness and record their time in the now empty rectory. Price set up one room as a center of command where he erected his instruments. His volunteers came from all walks of life and many different professions. Some strong individuals performed their vigils alone in the rectory, while others came with groups. Believers, disbelievers and skeptics; all had their own outlook on the paranormal. Some of Price's observers experienced nothing at all during their stay at the rectory. Others experienced odd sounds, unexplained lights, objects moving and full-bodied apparitions. Much of the activity was experienced by multiple reporters, giving credence to the events. Remarkably the nun was witnessed crossing the lawn by a majority of the participants. The messages scrawled on the wall continued to appear. Price's crew were told to mark and date each new message so new messages could be discerned from old. The messages continued to be indecipherable and may were still addressed to the now absent Marianne. A mound of evidence was starting to accumulate.

As Price was often away from the rectory, he found a stalwart individual to appoint as his second in command. Mr. Glanville, his family and several friends were often at the rectory and from 1937-1938 held a series of séances using a planchette (think pointing device such as an Ouija board uses) was able to spell out several interesting conversations that became part of the eventual evidentiary evidence. One alleged spirit claimed to be Marie Lairre who claimed to have been a French nun who had fled her convent in order to

Seance at Borley Rectory

marry Henry Waldesgrave, a member of the family who had held the property for 300 years. The spirit claimed that her "husband" had strangled her and buried her body in the cellar. Price theorized that the former nun had been buried in unconsecrated grounds, and thus felt destined to wander the grounds of the rectory without rest. The story did appear to support the frequent sightings of a phantom nun.

In March of 1938 another alleged spirit made contact with the group. Naming itself "Sunex Amures" the spirit foretold that the rectory would burn down that very night, and that the nun's remains would be found in the rubble. The building did not in fact catch fire that night, although it must have been a very stressful evening's repose for all those involved. Sunex's predictions did come true 11 months to the day of the séance. A Captain W.H. Gregson had just purchased the rectory, the year's vigil complete, and was unpacking boxes of books in his library when he accidently overturned an oil lamp. Books and old wood were no match to oil and fire, and the fire spread quickly. The old brick building was gutted in the blaze, leaving behind brick walls protecting floorless rooms open to the roofless heavens. It was said that the fire started where Sunex had predicted, and that figures could be seen cavorting in the flames.

BORLEY AFTER THE FIRE

Borley Rectory post fire

The walls would remain for another six years until they were finally demolished. With the fire destroying the house, and the investigators gone, one would think that the story of Borley Manor was finished, but that was far from the truth. In some ways the best evidence was yet to be discovered. Many would-be amateur investigators continued to frequent the grounds of the rectory, holding vigils or séances and adding to the mounds of documentary evidence. And the nun's tale was concluded finally, not by Price, but by a fan of Price's who had never set foot on the grounds or participated in the actual investigation. The Canon of Carlisle, the Rev. W.J. Phythian-Adams read Price's first book on the rectory, studied old plans of the structure and photographs of the wall writings. He conducted also a detailed analysis of Borley's history, especially of the history surrounding the Waldesgrave family.

Price had written an account of a psychometric medium he had contacted regarding an apport (an object that had appeared unaccountably) in the sewing room. Phythian-Adams analyzed the medium's account as well. He compiled all of these disparate elements into a detailed report, piecing the different elements together in order to create a storyline of the haunting, a consecutive and plausible storyline. Others had already attempted to interpret the wall writings, in particular, but all had failed to adequately connect the dots. It might have gone down as a clever fabrication, but then Phythian-Adams told Price exactly where to dig.

In August of 1943 Price in the company of a small crowd of notables, including a pathologist from the local hospital, began excavations of the Borley Cellar. At the exact spot Phythian-Adams had indicated, Price hit pay dirt. At the spot the group dug up an antique brass preserving pan, a silver creamer pitcher, a jaw bone with five teeth, and a skull bone fragment. Dr. Eric H. Bailey, Senior Assistant Pathologist of the Ashford County Hospital confirmed that the skull fragment and jaw bone were of human origin, and further noted that the jaw bone was actually a left mandible bone, probably that of a woman. The following day the crew also uncovered two religious medals, one of poor quality gold.

As with everything connected to Borley rectory, the weirdness didn't end there. Price took the artifacts to a well-known art photography studio, A.C. Cooper Ltd., to have the artifacts documented. Two people were holding the skull, moving it into position to be photographed when it inexplicably fell to the floor and broke into four pieces. At the same time an expensive oil painting fell off its easel and also crashed to the floor for no reason. A clock that hadn't worked in over a decade suddenly came to life, ticking merrily away for twenty minutes before never running again. Five months later the Cooper studio was destroyed in an air raid.

The bones of the nun were buried in the Liston graveyard near the Borley property by Reverend Henning in May of 1945, after which the apparition of the nun was never witnessed again on the grounds. But that wasn't the end of the odd occurrences in and around the Borley grounds. With the house demolished much of the paranormal activity appeared to migrate to the nearby church, where organ music was often heard playing in the empty church. Rev. Henning, then rector of the church, made accounts to Price. Price, gathering materials for a third book, recruited fifty new volunteers including Reverend Henning, members of the B.B.C., local residents and strangers.

PRICE'S LEGACY TO MODERN PARANORMAL RESEARCH

Price died suddenly at his home in Pulbourough at the age of 67, in the midst of writing his third book on the rectory. He came under fire by many, especially after his death, as appears to be the usual case. He was labelled a fraud by some, a notoriety seeker by others. His methodology was called into question, his findings dismissed. Some bold detractors even went so far as to label the entire Borley Rectory haunting a hoax, which considering the sheer volume of witnesses and participants clearly seems impossible. Be that as it may, Borley retained its status as the most notorious haunted house in England, and the era of the modern paranormal field investigator was created.

Ghost hunters of our day, from the plumbers that made it big on SyFy show *Ghosthunters* to the little group of weekend warriors that seems to pop up in every small town, owe our beginnings to Harry Price for inventing the protocols we follow today, whether we know it or not. Price also brought the paranormal back to the normal folk. While the SPR with its scientists and aristocrats lent paranormal research an air of respectability, Price brought ghost hunting to the everyman. After all, it was Mr. Glanville's séances that predicted where the nun's remains would be found, and the fire that would gut the rectory for good. And it was Reverend Phythian-Adam's careful studying of the literature that took Price right to the spot. This is a book about ghosts written by just one of those everyman paranormal investigators.

CHAPTER 4: HAUNTED HOUSES

BIG BANG THEORY

The old fort at Pea Patch Island, Delaware provided me with my most memorable night of investigating. The sheer volume of activity I encountered is unequaled by any investigation I've done since. The old fort became a rebel prisoner-of-war (POW) camp during the Civil War. Grossly over-populated, many of the POW's arrived injured from the war, or contracted diseases during their stay at the fort. The old stone walls are surrounded by a mote of non-potable water, and the whole place is damp and dank, being built on a swamp.

Below is the written dialogue of one episode I simply dubbed "The Big Bang" for the enormous bang sound that still makes me jump a foot me every time I watch the segment of video. Of course the bang like everything else that happened in the episode was unexplainable. There were three of us in the kitchen that night, again names have been changed (except for my own) to protect anonymity. The kitchen door leads out to the courtyard area and is close to a battlement still rigged with canons. There were several investigators at the fort that night, but to preserve the integrity of the evidence we were collecting we were all assigned to different areas of the fort, with rotating shifts. At the end of a shift we moved to another section, told to stay in our new positions until another shift change.

The kitchen area was purportedly a hotspot at the old fort. There had even been several eye witnesses that reported seeing a full body apparition of a woman, presumably the cook, who just wandered in one day during a tour to cook her meal. We didn't see the Cook that night, but what we did experience was equally fascinating.

The three of us were in the kitchen with the door open to the courtyard. We were conducting a question and answer session using dousing rods. We had electromagnetic field detectors (EMF) detectors and voice recorders going as well. And I recorded the whole session on a video recorder for posterity. We used the rods to answer yes/no questions, crossed for yes, uncrossed for no, and between questions as neutral. I don't present dousing rod sessions as evidence to clients, but they do provide interesting entertainment on long nights. And I feel they point a direction for questioning. For example, if I ask a question and they begin to swing wildly I continue with that line of questioning, hoping to capture an EVP (electronic voice phenomena – or audio recording otherwise unaccountable). If they appear to point decidedly in a direction

I might take an EMF detector over to the area and see if I get a spike   (*Names changed to protect anonymity*).

Tammy: *(holding the rods)" Ok does anyone want to ask any questions?"*

Robin: *"Can we talk to the person who used to be the cook here? No? Is she not present?"*

On the audio bed you distinctly hear the sound of a footstep or shuffling out in the courtyard. Meanwhile Tammy stops and turns her head, looking toward the door.

Robin: *(asking about the female cook who is seen) "Is she not present? We want to talk to the cook."*

Tammy hears the shuffling sound again, and looks confused. She holds up a hand to pause Robin.

Tammy: *"Wait. Wait a minute."* Listens again.

Mary: *I think I just heard footsteps out there."*

Tammy: *"That's what I [thought]. And I can't tell if it's raining, but I heard, I heard two perfect, two different, very distinct..."*

Mary: *"I heard footsteps."*

Tammy: *"It's not the rain it's footsteps out there. I mean it's raining too but..."*

Mary and Tammy stand at kitchen door looking out into the courtyard. There is a small sound on the audio that might have been an owl. There was at least one owl the park rangers confirmed, that called the fort home.

Robin: *"Is someone out there?"*

Mary: *"Now I don't hear it."*

Tammy replies, *"No I heard footsteps, I heard two."*

Robin: *Retrieves EMF detector and heads out into courtyard." Is someone out here? Someone out here?" Mary and Robin depart the kitchen and words are heard, but not distinguishable. Robin replies to someone. "No we just heard walking. "If you're out here can you walk up to the green light? It will flash and tell us that you're here."*

Long pause. "Can you make something move? Can you move something? Can you give us a sign of your presence?"

Tammy: *still in kitchen putting batteries in a piece of equipment asks in astonishment, "Did somebody just say NO?"*

Robin: *No – meaning it hadn't been her or Mary.*

Mary confirms: *"Neither of us."*

Tammy: *"I just literally heard someone say"* –she mimics in a loud whisper – *"Nooo. And it sounded like it was coming from right outside the door."*

Note: *There is no audible whispered "NO" on the record, except for Tammy's.*

Robin: *comes back into kitchen. Says to Tammy, 'Ok" Turns around and goes back to door. "Are you still here? Is someone trying to communicate with us?"*

Robin and Mary return to kitchen. Tammy says, "I really thought it was you."

Robin: *"I almost thought I heard whispering – points out the door. But this rain, it's hard to... I mean I wouldn't swear to it in a court of law, but I almost thought I heard whispering over at the canon. And then..."*

Tammy: *"Well that walk (meaning the footsteps earlier) was very distinct. Hopefully one of the recorders picked it up."*

Robin: *Says for the record: "Ok, we're back in the kitchen."*

Tammy: *"All right, I'm going to put my voice recorder out in the hallway, because I'm hearing stuff today."*

Robin: *"All right, well we don't need three (voice recorders) in here so..."*

Sounds such as whispering very low on audio in three spots that weren't detected nor reported during evidence analysis.

Section of Video Edited Out

Tammy with rods again: *"Did you work in the kitchen so you didn't have to fight? Could you not fight and that's why you had to work in the kitchen? Aha, uncross please."*

Mary: *"Are you hearing voices out there?"*

Robin: *"Someone is out there."*

Tammy confirms: *Yes there's someone out there. There's flashlights, I just saw flashes of light."*

Robin: *confirming, "mmhmm."*

After the episode, the bang was heard all over the fort and brought everyone running to the kitchen. All of the investigators present would be questioned as to where they were before the bang was heard and asked whether they had been moving around in the courtyard or fort. No one admitted to having wandered around with a flashlight in the courtyard.

Tammy: *"Were you injured? Uncross please" – directing the rods. "Were you injured in battle? Uncross please. Were you injured in Gettysburg? Ok," as rods cross. "Uncross please. I'm going to try that one again. Uncross please."*

Low sound of voices out in the courtyard is heard.

Tammy confirms: *"There's somebody out there."*

Robin: *That one was unmistakable." laughs.*

Tammy: *"Ok, were you injured at Gettysburg? Now we're going to get a no. Rods uncross. Ok, let's go back. You were injured? Were you injured? I feel like I'm playing Jeopardy. Uncross please."*

Mary: *"Was it an accident?"*

Tammy: *"All right uncross. Calm down (rods moving)."*

Robin: *"Did you fight for the south? Small high pitched sound - unidentifiable. Did you fight for the north?"*

Tammy: *"All right, uncross please. Your injury was an accident? Was your injury due to an accident (rods cross)?" Chuckles to herself. "I had to make sure because they [the rods] went all kinds of wacky. Was it an accident that happened here, at Fort Delaware? Did your accident happen on the battlefield? Uncross please. Uncross. Thank you. Are you...calm down, calm down calm," as*

rods start swinging. "Were you injured in a battle in the north? Were you injured in a battle in the south?"

Big bang and yelling as all three women run across the room and huddle together at the far corner.

Gasps. Shushing sound.

Tammy: *"Ok. Ok."*

Mary: *"Why am I holding the rods?" Eruption of laughter.*

It is important to point out that *The Atlantic Paranormal Society* (TAPS) filmed two episodes at the same fort, and in one of the episodes Jason Haws and Grant Wilson were filming in the same kitchen and experienced much the same bang as the three of us experienced that night. Jason actually dropped the rolling pin he was holding at the time, the sound being so astonishingly loud.

CATEGORIZATION OF PARANORMAL PHENOMENON

It's human nature when studying any subject to try to categorize and group like items together. It's how we make sense of a world of otherwise disparate phenomena. Paranormal researchers obviously do the same thing, although different researchers use different terms, essentially the categories below are based on the prevailing theories of the day which we use when conducting investigations. It should be noted that sometimes a location may have more than one type of activity occurring. Sadly for every case in which the evidence fits neatly into a category, I'll have another that defies any such categorization. Paranormal activity has a tendency to defy nice neat boxes, succinct answers and easy to apply solutions. Those whose existence depends on consistency and clear right or wrong answers should probably take up accounting instead. In fact, accounting is an altogether more respectable pursuit.

RESIDUAL HAUNTS

Residual haunts may seem very sinister, but are without doubt the most benign of any paranormal activity. A residual haunting is the result of psychic energies being imprinted on the surrounding environment. The theory is that an event of emotional magnitude can leave an imprint in the surrounding area. This emotionally charged "recording" is replayed when the proper environmental play button is pushed. Think of a residual haunt as being like a music CD. The disk in its case doesn't play by itself. But put it in the machine, and hit the play button and the recording plays out just as it was recorded. Tomorrow if you hit the play button the exact same recording would play. The recording doesn't interact with you, and it doesn't change.

A residual haunt is like that. It's a pre-recorded episode that is waiting for the environmental "play" button to be hit. What causes something in the environment to record an episode? No one really knows, though theories abound. If a building or a location can record such things then it may be that a simple household object can as well, given the right circumstances. Then if the object moves to a new location, and when, or if, the environmental factors trigger the "play back" response the residual episode plays out, though the location has changed.

What causes the recording to be replayed remains a mystery. It may be replayed on an anniversary date or the precise time when the event occurred. The replay may also be dependent on environmental factors such as humidity or barometric pressure. Certain substances in the environment are often present at locations of residual haunts as well. Limestone, granite and water seem to be agents gifted at storing and replaying "past recordings." It has been suggested by some paranormal researchers that such a mix are the ingredients in a battery, a natural battery capable of storing recordings of past events and playing them back when all the right factors are in play. Water in particular appears to have the ability to record a likeness to substances with which it came in contact. In layman's terms, water seems to have a memory. Do recall all the water around Pea Patch Island, in the unpotable mote, and dripping from the walls and ceiling of the fort's surrounding walls. If water truly has the ability to store information then the fort in question was an absolute fortress of residual energy.

Water of course resides in building materials such as wood. Therefore, if the psychic information is recorded in the water molecules of your doorway, that doorway may hold the memory of that event which is replayed whenever the environmental factors are correct. Thus if you strip the old paint off a doorframe, or strip the lath and plaster off an old wall revealing wood that has been covered for decades you inadvertently release activity that has been covered over for a long period of time. Thus the uptick in paranormal phenomena during renovations may be explained.

THUNDERSTORMS AND PARANORMAL ACTIVITY

I also have a theory that thunder storms can cause an uptick in paranormal activity. From my own case files, it appears that often when we have conducted investigations during a thunderstorm, a positive uptick in activity appears to coincide. The night we conducted the investigation at the fort there was a very strong thunderstorm in the area, so strong that the park rangers made us stay in our locations until the lightning had subsided. We went to the kitchen immediately after the worst of the storm had passed, and that was when we started experiencing the activity.

A thunderstorm, where lightning is present, releases a large number of ions into the atmosphere. Ions are electrically charged molecules that dissipate very quickly into the environment. Any electrically charged molecules whether positively or negatively charged, quickly combine with other molecules in the environment, seeking to form a neutrally charged molecule. Any molecule with an uneven charge seeks to even the charge out, thus ions immediately bond with other molecules, disappearing within seconds of release. This is the natural state for molecules, and in this natural state they're very stable.

Lightning, rushing water and sunshine release ions into the environment. And all that extra electromagnetic energy in the air seems to fuel paranormal activity. Perhaps a residual haunt acts like a rechargeable battery, with Mother Nature providing the needed juice to get it playing again. Unfortunately, experiments with man-made ion generators hasn't had the same effect, and use of generators also has the deleterious effect of increasing the number of particulates in the air. It may be that ion generators

BY ROBIN M. STROM-MACKEY

simply don't pack the same punch as a thunderstorm, or perhaps it's the moisture from the storm combined with the ions that makes the difference.

TYPE OF ACTIVITY

To recap, a residual haunting is nothing but a recording of an event. They are very often sounds, such as footfalls on the stairs. They can occur indoors, such as the sounds of a basketball game in an old gymnasium, or outdoors, such as the recurrent sounds of fighting on an old battlefield. Indeed, old battlefields are resplendent in residual sounds. The sound of horses or foot soldiers moving across an old battlefield, voices of wounded soldiers begging for mercy, and even the sound of gun or canon fire. Residual activity may also include smells too, such as the perfume worn by a former occupant, the smell of pipe smoke or the smell of liniment. And obviously residual activity can also be visual, and as such can be very easy to detect. As we know, residual haunts are immutable recordings. Thus, the image may appear to be walking a foot above the ground or walk through a wall. Research of the building will often reveal structural changes to the building such as the moving of a door or staircase, or lowering or raising of floor height. Thus, when an apparition is witnessed walking through a wall, it is probably because originally there was a door there. The residual specter has no intelligence, and thus continues to do what it has always done.

What we were experiencing in the kitchen of the fort was probably residual, stored in the buildings themselves and energized by the thunderstorm, the recordings started to play. The footfalls, whispers, shadows moving and the big bang, all of it seemed to be residual. For one thing, it didn't appear to be trying to make contact with us in any way. Except for the whispered answer, "no," it didn't appear to have an intelligence or consciousness. And one "no" after we had asked a question could be entirely coincidental. Interestingly, while Tammy reports hearing the answer "no" in response to a question, the voice is not recorded on the audio. And the fact that T.A.P.S. also encountered the bang sound during their investigation of the fort makes an even stronger case for it being a residual sound.

Our encounter at the old fort could possibly be categorized as residual, as could many at Gettysburg – possibly the most haunted battlefield in America. All the misery and suffering, recorded in the old stone, rock and water of the location. There at the height of paranormal activity, the night of a major thunderstorm – it's not difficult to believe that what we experienced weren't old troops moving across the fields, and possibly the bang of a now defunct canon sounding.

HAUNTED HOUSES – THE INTELLIGENT HAUNT

Most paranormal researchers agree that the actual haunted house is a relatively rare occurrence. What is meant by a haunted house is an actual intelligent being who has left the corporeal plane but whose spirit remains at a building or residence. It may be that the building was significant to the spirit. In other situations spirits may take up residence in a building that was close in proximity. For example, the home of the spirit may be been torn down, but another house is close, so the spirit changes locations. They may take up residence in a building where they have privacy, such as an abandoned structure.

Spirits do not appear to be irrevocably tied to one location unless they either believe themselves bound or choose to stay. If all that remains of us is our spirit in raw, willful energy, then the sky is the limit when it comes to what we could do or where we might go after death. Thus the spirit of Ann Boleyn has been witnessed in her childhood home of Hever Castle, the Tower of London, where she was held awaiting her trial and subsequent execution, and Pickling Hall in Norfolk where she always appears on the anniversary of her death. If a spirit remains in only one location, it probably does so with a purpose. Perhaps they have unfinished business to finish, perhaps they simply care for a certain location, maybe they're waiting to be reunited with a loved one. They may remain to right what they felt was an injustice done to them. Some theories suggest that spirits that have died a tragic and/or abrupt death may remain in a location because they do not know that they have passed, and thus remain because they are confused.

TYPES OF ACTIVITY

Obviously, the main difference between an intelligent haunt and a residual haunt is that an intelligent haunt can and probably will choose to interact with the human inhabitants of the building. Another obvious difference is that an intelligent spirit will mix it up. They won't cause activity in the same way every time, but will move the china one day, and ring the doorbell the next. Interaction with humans can take on many forms. Auditory activity is probably the most prevalent. You may hear banging sounds, footsteps, doors opening and closing. One may hear music such as a piano playing, or voices may be heard.

Odd smells are fairly common, especially if the spirit had a smell that was distinctive to them. A strong perfume smell may waft through a room and disappear moments later. If the spirit was a cigar smoker, smoke may be smelled when no one in the building is smoking.

Sensations are another way for spirits to make themselves known. You may feel a stroking on your hair or down your arm. In more sinister cases people have reported being shoved in the back as they walked downstairs. In the same vein, many report being held back from falling down the stairs.

Apports and Asports: Depending upon how advanced the spirit may be, objects may appear, disappear or move from one room to another with no explanation. The disappearances may be comical, like your keys disappearing off the hallway table only to be found in the refrigerator. Or they may be more serious in nature, such as a religious amulet disappearing from your jewelry box.

Objects may also be manipulated. We lived in an old home, a home I believe we shared with a small child spirit. Often I would hear my son's electronic toys going off in his closet when he wasn't in his room. Being skeptical as usual, I speculated that the batteries in the toys were wearing down, thus misfiring. However, I never heard the toys go off by themselves after we moved from that location.

Visual: And of course, the spirit can manifest visually. This may occur as a full-bodied apparition, but this is the rarest form of activity – the Holy Grail for paranormal investigators. In the rarest accounts an apparition can look so real that the witness doesn't realize at the time that they're seeing a spirit, but think it's a real human being in period costume. Other manifestations may not appear as solid. You may witness an apparition, but then realize you can see through them. Still other manifestations may only be partially complete, such as seeing a set of legs walking down the steps, but no torso or head over the top! And still other visual manifestations are amorphous, and may appear as a wispy, moving cloud of white smoke, or a dark shadow.

A TRIP TO GETTYSBURG YIELDS A MIX OF BOTH TYPE OF ACTIVITY

My group members knew I was getting ready to write a book about hauntings. Renne was planning a trip to haunted Gettysburg. If paranormal activity is what you're seeking I've never heard of anyone that returned from Gettysburg without at least something to report. Here is what Renne wrote about her trip. Notice that there seems to be a mix of activity from residual to intelligent. Renne appears to be very sensitive to paranormal activity. I often refer to her as my human Geiger counter. On one very active investigation she announced she was feeling chills or being watched, and then just moments later we captured EVP's on our recorders. It happened at least three times during that investigation, demonstrating to me that I should take her sensations seriously, at least to the point of getting gear recording when she reported having one of her feelings.

My husband and I took a trip to Gettysburg PA on 11/23 and 11/24. We decided to stay at The Farnsworth Inn in the Sara Black room. This little room is down at the end of a hall, in the alcove. We almost walked past it, it is so hidden. Charming little room with a canopy bed, fireplace near the bed (non-functional) claw foot tub in the bathroom, and an old wedding dress on a dress form in the corner. I set my little audio recorder up on the fireplace mantle, and turned up the heat, and we left. We did some shopping in town, and decided to eat at the Dobbin House tavern. Before we ate, we asked where the little slave exhibit was located. After going up and down a few stairways, we found the narrow little set of steps and an arrow pointing up. As I took the first 2 steps, I felt a very heavy pressure on my chest, as if someone was trying to push me back down the steps. I kept going and ended up in a little room full of artifacts that were found when they dug out the basement and raised the house. Thought that this had nothing to do with slaves. As I descended the stairs, on the right, was a secret room where the slaves hid out waiting for the Underground Railroad to take them to safety. I learned later that Harriet Tubman was one of the slaves that hid there. It was only about 3 ft. tall, and they would have had to crawl or sit. The heavy feeling on my chest did not go away until we actually sat down in the tavern.

When we returned to the room, we decided to stay in and relax, then get an early start the next morning and go to the battlefield. We had purchased a bottle of wine to enjoy in the room. I sat the wine bottle on a paper bag to avoid the drips staining the dresser. While sitting on the bed, the paper bag rattled, very loudly, as if someone were crumpling it up into a ball. We were both sitting on the bed. As we watched TV, we also heard the deadbolt jiggle. It did this not once, but 3 times. No one was outside of the door, no drafts, and no footsteps. Not being alarmed, we settled in. Then I heard the water running in the bathroom. It ran for about 10 seconds, then stopped. By then, it had been a few hours since either of us had used the bathroom. Just as I was dozing off, I got a very icy chill that made me wake up my husband.

I kept saying "Oh, my God!" The room was nice and warm, and we had plenty of blankets. I made a comment that I knew there was an entity in the room. Then I dozed off again. Later that night, right before the football game ended, I woke up to the feeling of "walking through cobwebs", or something going through me. My arms started to try and push this away, and I screamed "Oh! Oh! Oh!" as I turned over, I saw a black mist move from the foot of the bed, catty corner to the closet. Then it disappeared.

My husband told me the next morning that right after I yelled, OH! He also felt a very icy chill. Morning came, and we got dressed. As I was getting my clothes on in the bathroom, the water in the sink again came on, 3 times for 4-5 seconds each time. I checked the knobs, and they were closed tight. No one had used the sink.

Next stop was the battlefield. I took my EMF meter, just to see what might register. We went to several important sites, one being the high water mark, and found where General Armistead was wounded, and later died.

There was a little spike of 1.3 on the meter.

Then we proceeded to Little Round Top, and Devil's Den. There were no readings on the EMF meter there at all. I took off down the path where Joshua Chamberlain held off the Confederates. About 5 steps down, my meter *registered 2.4. About 10 more feet in and my meter jumped up to a 5.7. And at the end of the line where they mounted the bayonet charge I got a reading of 6.5. I think the 20th Maine division is still fighting there! What a thrill.*

We headed back to our room and then off to dinner at the Dobbin House dining room. What a treat! The second night was very calm, although I did not sleep well, even after walking all day. I will note that my iPhone 6 did not work very well, despite having a full cellular and Wii -Fi signal. My alert tones did not work, I could not open my e-mails, and calls and text messages were difficult. This only happened in our room. I guess this was my fault, as I told the entities that they were welcome to play with any of my devices. I have not listened to all of the audio, but have picked up some whistles, rattles and the sound of an old toy squeaking as it was run across the floor. I also heard a cat meow that wasn't in the room. This was an awesome trip, and I can't wait to do it again.

HAUNTED OBJECTS

The call came in late one Saturday evening. The young woman on the phone, we'll call her Ann, was upset and needing advice. The house in which she resided with her parents had transformed from a peaceful retreat to a house of fear. Strange and unaccountable sounds were heard and lights  turned on and off. Then one night Ann went down to the basement to flip a breaker that had shut off. As she stepped to the basement floor she witnessed a tarp tied around a box of old books come unaccountably untied and fly across the room. It was this event that made Ann decide to call me. She was mainly concerned for her parents; being very religious, they were talking about calling in the family pastor to rid the property of evil spirits. Ann on the other hand wasn't as frightened as she was stymied. What had caused this sudden onslaught of activity in a home that until recently wasn't haunted? She wanted some answers, and she wanted to know how to make the activity cease in order to restore her parents' peace of mind.

I made the usual enquiries. The house was recently built. There was no known history of misfortune surrounding the land upon which it sat. The activity was a new occurrence. I was trying to think of some reasonable explanation and then I remembered the tarp which suddenly seemed to point directly at the solution. I asked her to tell me more about the books.

She explained that she had just recently purchased the box of old books which included some very personal papers [her emphasis] and possibly a journal. Wanting to protect the box she had put it in the basement with the tarp tied over it to protect it from the damp. Bingo! I surmised that Ann and her family had unwittingly exposed their home to a haunted object.

Just as houses, land or people can be the center of a haunting, so too can objects. Given the premise then, a haunted object moved into a building can cause the start of activity, and moving the object out can make the activity stop. Often haunted objects are items that were of personal significance, such as a personal diary or a painted portrait. Then again the items themselves may be mundane and unremarkable such as a wooden bunk bed that started a nightmarish journey for a family in Wisconsin (81).

THEORIES BEHIND HAUNTED OBJECTS

There are three theories as to why an object may be "haunted." First is the theory of the psi projection such as in a residual haunt. This theory contends that certain emotionally charged events can leave an imprint on the environment, such as a location, building or object. Activity may either be auditory or visual (See Residual Haunting). Certainly psi-projection theory may explain haunted objects. If a person's consciousness or part of a person's consciousness could imbed in a building, it should also be able to imprint in an object. Thus when the object moves locations so does the haunting phenomena.

Taking psi projection a step further, perhaps an object of great sentimental value, for example, became imbedded with the consciousness of the deceased. The old journals are just such type of object, extremely personal and emotionally charged. Thus if someone were attached to an object in life they might return to it after death. It might be that the spirit desires to see the object given to the proper person. Or perhaps they might not wish to see their beloved object fall into the wrong hands.

I can offer a third theory as well, Retrocognition. In Latin retro meaning backward or behind and cognition meaning knowing, was a term coined by F.W.H. Myers which he used to signify having a knowledge of the past which one could not have learned or inferred by normal means. Retrocognition is the ability to perceive experiences from the past clairvoyantly, usually as a spontaneous replaying of past events such as in a vision or a dream. Thus when the object is brought into the building a person suitably gifted clairvoyantly would be able to read the object, perhaps reliving the events of the past. To the clairvoyant the activity might feel like a haunting, but what they would be experiencing is the past events that happened to the previous owner. Thus if you were walking down stairs and felt as if you had been shoved, it might not be you being shoved, but the person who owned the object in the past.

Returning to Ann and her dilemma, when she asked again what she should do, I had a *definite* answer for her. And the beauty was that the answer didn't require hours of investigation, nor daunting research into the history of the property. Simply remove that box of books out of her basement and get them out of the house I told her; and then see if the problems ceased. "Why?" She asked. Ann was understandably fond of her little treasure trove of Americana. But I explained to her that she wasn't the only one. I told her to move the box out and see if the problems ceased. If not, I opened the door to her to call me back and we could schedule an investigation. That late Saturday call was the only time I ever heard from Ann. I can only speculate, therefore, that moving the box out of the house restored peace and order to their home, making any further intervention unnecessary. Whatever happened to the box of books I can only guess? It's probably buried at the back of some shed or garage where it will remain until someone else falls prey to its charms.

PSI PROJECTION HYPOTHESIS

I've often been stymied by the two classifications of the residual and intelligent haunting. If the intelligent haunting is very rare and the residual haunting more common, then why on investigations do I seem to get intelligent responses to questions or requests? If I ask for a sign that something is present and I get a bang on the wall. If I ask a question and get an EVP response is that not sign of intelligence? If we're out on an investigation, and as happens fairly often, one of my investigators reports the feeling of being touched, is that not a sign of a spirit attempting to interact with us? If this were the case then intelligent hauntings would be as prevalent as residual. It had become increasingly clear that the delineation between residual and intelligent haunt had far too much bleed over, and that a new hypothesis was needed.

Parapsychologists, it turns out, have been working on this new hypothesis for some time now. Dr. Andrew Nichols, professor, parapsychologist and paranormal researcher posits a theory he calls the "Psi Projection Hypothesis," a theory he feels might explains all the types of phenomena experienced at a haunting (1). The hypothesis suggests that strong emotions may cause an imprint in the environment and that an aspect or aspects of a personality may be able to imbed themselves as a form of replication at a location. If enough of a person's personality is able to imprint on a location after the person dies or perhaps remains after the person leaves, it may have enough personality to actually behave in a seemingly intelligent manner. Incidentally, death may not even be a contributing factor to the copying that occurs. My computer has this pesky idiosyncrasy when I try to delete photos. I'll highlight the photos to delete them and it will make copies of them instead, and where I had one bad photo to delete, now I have two – the original and the replica. This theory is also reminiscent of the Egyptian belief described in Chapter One of the ka. The ka wasn't actually the soul of the person (the soul going onto Auru, the Egyptian heaven), but a replica of the person – the ghost – that stayed with the body. Recall also the Norse philosophy that the body died, but lived on in a sort of half-life. In these philosophies I see distinct similarities.

In the "psi projection theory" the personality replica would be able, on a limited basis to interact with people. It might be able to answer simple questions such as what is your name, or did you live here? Quite possibly it would be able to make auditory sounds or even manifest visually upon request. And in some limited capacity it might even be able to effect matter, move an object etc. But not being the actual soul of a living person, it would not be able to change, or understand the changes going on around it. It would probably not have a memory and not be able to learn new things such as the year it is now. It might be able to interact, but never to remember new experiences. For the ka or replica ghost the year would always be 1868, and she or he would be living in their old farmhouse – and you would be the ghost!

So how might such an imprint or copy be made? Quantum physics as a specialized area of science really began with the discovery that light acts both as a particle and a wave. As such sometimes it flows as a wave does, but its flow can be staunched until light dribbles out through a blockage one particle at a time. Within the brain human thought appears to move as waves as well, with electrical impulses flowing across neurons at lightning speed and varying frequencies. We know this to be true because we can test brainwaves with an electroencephalograph or EEG machine. We might speculate, Dr. Nichols suggests, that thought like light might move as both a particle and a wave. And if this were true we could theorize that our bodies would be constantly surrounded by a sea of thought particles, think the multi-colored auras reported by mediums who may not have been too far off. This idea of a psi field has been accepted for decades by parapsychologists, and is further suggested by consciousness studies. Think Carl Jung and our old friend William James for theories on a collective and ever present stream of consciousness.

The psi field extends beyond the organism and saturates the environment around it. It is capable of interacting with the psi fields of other organisms and perhaps even objects. Nichols likens the effect to that of a strong magnet, which when introduced into an energy field alters the pattern of that field. Think about the childhood experiment with the metal shavings and the magnet. Remember how the magnetic shavings would immediately line up in the direction of the magnet. The molecules of a magnet are aligned or distributed in one organized direction. Therefore, if a magnet is introduced into an electromagnetic field the field will realign to this new magnet. Accordingly, if a strong emotion or emotions is interjected into the environment it will act as a magnet, and reorganize or realign the thought particles.

Parapsychologists use the analogy of tapes, although this metaphor is somewhat dated with the new technologies emerging. Audio or video tape depended on a coating of easily magnetized particles to make recordings. The tape itself moved through a device which produced magnetic impulses. These magnetic impulses caused the particles on the tape to realign into a pattern that matched the magnetic impulses, which resulted in a recorded image or sound – or both.

Supposedly a very strong emotion, or many strong emotions, sent out into the environment over time could cause the thought particles in the environment to realign in patterns that matched the original thoughts, and that could be perceived by someone with a suitably developed psychic ability. Psychic ability seems to be easily equated with the strength of an individual's antenna. Some may only be equipped with the stupid rabbit ear antennas that sat atop televisions until recently, and needed constant readjustment. Other people may be equipped with the large, roof top antennas that brought in far more channels, while still others were receiving images from satellites in space and could receive all the channels – all for free. Lucky dogs.

But what does the antenna actually detect? It may be that individuals with heightened psi abilities may be sensitive or hyper sensitive to electromagnetic fields. Thus if the enter an area with unusual amount of electromagnetic fields they will feel uneasy, or watched. They may even have physiological reactions such as becoming nauseous or ill. This hypersensitivity may allow them to pick up on electromagnetic resonance or anomalies in the area more readily than a person without this sensitivity. Anomalous electromagnetic fields can be natural, as in areas with seismic activity, or manmade such as buildings located near power lines. They may also pick up on electromagnetic resonance which is one theory as to how a spirit may communicate with us.

Traumatic events would cause stronger imprinting upon the environment, thus sites where murders, suicides or battle occurred would have stronger impacting projections. Think of the most haunted sites you remember, mental hospitals, prisons and battlefields always surface at the top of the list. Nichols also explains that sites with unusual electromagnetic or geomagnetic properties are more likely to be regarded as haunted.

Such sites with seismic faults or underground water sources may further create a "containment zone" for activity that holds paranormal activity for longer periods of time. Although haunting phenomena does tend to decrease in both regularity and intensity over time, something that Nichols likens to entropy when the particles are eventually scattered.

These hypothetical thought-particle imprints might carry either a telepathic or psychokinetic charge – meaning they might be perceived more subjectively or objectively as thoughts or impressions or as physical disturbances. Telepathic imprints would result in more subjective phenomena, such as seeing an apparition, feeling cold spots, hearing sounds of footsteps or voices or merely sensing a feeling of being watched. The psychokinetic impulses would result in more objective phenomena such as recordable sounds like footsteps or knocking, objects actually being moved or manipulated such as in poltergeist cases. Residual haunts could be explained by a type of "psychic residue," phenomena that is repetitive and non-interactive, left over from a former resident. Poltergeist activity could be explained by the dynamic changeability of a human agent who is present and constantly changing the psychic thought patterns. And grudgingly, Nichols also admits that these random thought-energy particles may hold the essence of consciousness – or as I have suggested – a copy of the personality of an agent. Remember my computer making a copy of my photo as I try to delete it, this would be more like copying the entire hard drive of the computer.

MEMORIES OF THE DEAD GUY

The medical field has known for some time that organs taken from one person and transplanted into another is not necessarily as simple as changing parts out on a car. Despite being a blood type match, the donor organ cells contain DNA that is specific to the deceased, and cause the recipient's body to reject the new organ, sensing that the organ is foreign to the body. This rejection response requires suppression through heavy medication for the rest of the recipient's life. In some cases, though the DNA of the transplanted organ will continue to resonate or interface with the recipient's consciousness, and to the point that the recipient may undergo marked personality changes. They may develop likes or dislikes for certain foods they had not had in the past. They may become moody. In some cases they even acquire some of the memories of the deceased.

The DNA of our body, a copy of which is in every cell, has been studied extensively for some time now, and scientists have only been able to ascertain the function of a small portion of it. A whopping 95% of the DNA appears to have no function, and scientists have labeled it junk DNA. But there is increasing evidence that this junk DNA does serve a purpose, that it is our interface or receptor between non-local communication and the body, thus every cell produced by our body could be acting as an interface or receptor to information. Thus each organ, organ system and cell could interface with each other to facilitate the exchange of hereditary information. Consider how many of our cells die and grow every day, this storage and dissemination of hereditary material is probably vital to the continuation of the organism.

Do recall your high school chemistry class (hopefully you didn't sleep through it) and the study of atoms. As you may recall at the center of the atom was this tiny nucleus which contained the atom's positively charged proton(s) and neutron(s), and then circling this were the atom's electrons, which really orbited a long distance away from the nucleus. One example compared the distance between a nucleus and its orbiting electron to a football field. Place the nucleus in the center of the football field and the electron(s) could be orbiting as far away as the goal line at any given time. And the distance between the goal line and the nucleus? It's a vacuum of non-local space. The illusion of matter is that it's solid, when it really isn't. 99.99% of matter is space, thus our bodies are 99.99%

open space. And what is in all this empty void? It's believed that in this incredible storehouse resides information and energy. This is the nonlocal space where our cells and organs interact and exchange hereditary information, and it's the nonlocal space where our living organism interacts with the environment around us both sending and receiving information constantly (43).

Thus an organ removed and transplanted could still be resonating (acting as an antenna) with the non-local consciousness of the deceased. Though still in the theory stage, it's not an altogether new idea, as quantum physicist Erwin Schrodinger suggested as early as 1944 that DNA could function as a "quantum antenna" for "nonlocal communication (43)." How do the cells and eventually the organism collect information outside itself? One theory is that information is sent via electromagnetic resonance in regard to systemic cellular memory. Resonance occurs when one vibrating system or external force causes another system to oscillate, it is vibration of cells at the same frequency.

DNA doesn't contain all of the cell's information, but acts more as a computer processor, receiving encoded information via electromagnetic waves, and translating and disseminating information via proteins to the cell. Apparently all cells are equipped with countless oscillating structures that move and groove via the stimulus they receive from nonlocal space. Every cell in the body oscillates at its own frequency of between 100 and 1000 Gigahertz. The oscillating of cells, creating waves in and between cells is nonlinear, quantum processes. And it is believed this oscillating, wave behavior can be simple or complex. This oscillating action causes resonance between molecules that have identical frequencies, i.e. those cells that have the same frequency will be dancing to the same beat. And all the molecules that vibrate on this frequency, when resonating will not only act like a whole, but be a whole. In other words they will act in the same manner at exactly the same instant, whether they are near one another or not – distance not being a factor.

EMF, EMR AND THE SPACE IN BETWEEN

Electromagnetic fields are everywhere, in the core of the Earth, in outer space, within our brains, traveling through our bodies. It powers our electronic devices and communicates with our very cells. Are ghosts electromagnetic energy, and do they give off electromagnetic fields? Possibly. But then any time a ghost was around we should be able to detect it with our EMF gauges, and while this is sometimes true, it is not *always* true, which is part of the frustrating quirkiness of paranormal investigation. Vince Wilson, author of the *Ultimate Ghost Tech: The Science History & Technology of Ghost Hunting* suggests instead that they may be electromagnetic waves which imbed in an environment as an electromagnetic resonance (EMR) that react when conditions are correct and frequencies and wavelengths are in tune with the human brain This resonance might cause our brains to feel it's experiencing a sensation or memory not our own, such as happens to the organ transplant patients (1).

People often report walking into a room and feeling a hostile environment, or sensing a feeling of dread. This may be because they are sensing the EMR in an area. Suppose too, being at a purportedly haunted location and feeling a touch on your arm or a push on the stair. It might not actually be a spirit you were interacting with but the EMR. You would be experiencing the shove down the stairs as it happened to someone in the past and recorded as an EMR in the present. This might also explain the idea of possession as well. Sometimes at locations investigators will start to take on a different personality, they may begin to cry uncontrollably or start acting uncharacteristically aggressive. It may be that they're not being possessed by an actual spirit, but falling under the influence of the EMR in the area to which they are particularly in tune. Some report having flashbacks to the past. Under extreme situations people have actually witnessed an event as if they were there, such as standing on a battlefield and seeing the soldiers actually battling it out. But again, regardless of how strong the impressions, if the events are immutable, they remain just that, a recording that does not change. Thus the residual haunting takes on a whole new dimension. You might not only be able to see, hear or smell a former occupant, but also experience their sensations as well.

This might also be true of seemingly intelligent Hauntings as well. Perhaps more of a personality or an entire copy of a person's consciousness became imbedded as EMR in the environment. This could explain how the spirit could appear to answer questions or interact with someone within the environment. It can appear to have a personality either kind or angry, as the person may have been while alive. It may even be able to convert the electromagnetic waves into psychokinetic energy needed to slam a door, move an object or play the piano. It may be able to manifest a reproduction of itself by manipulating the electromagnetic field that all matter uses in order to appear solid.

As such they may be able to be photographed or recorded on an audio recorder. The spirits would still only be a copy, however, and in as such would never grow or change. They wouldn't for example know what year it was, wouldn't become rabid followers of the presidential candidates, and remember from one day to the next what happened. They would be more like my son's iPad friend Siri, able to interact and communicate but only to a point. Don't get me wrong, at times Siri can be quite glib and has a wonderful sense of humor. My son's favorite game is to ask Siri how to divide 0 by 0. She always gives him the same answer to this question, the one that she is programmed to make. And while it's a quirky answer, it always the same. Siri appears intelligent, but in the end she's just a clever copy of a human personality.

How residual or intelligent a haunting may be would depend on factors in the environment, the physical factors of the location, possibly the climatic factors present at the time the imprint was made. All of these might affect how complete a copy was actually made.

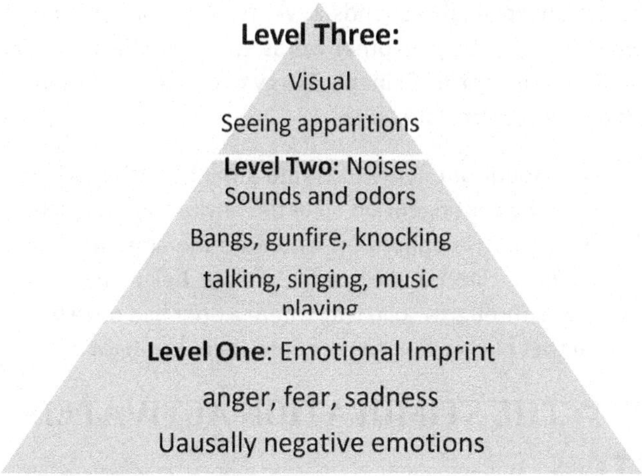

Level Three:

Visual

Seeing apparitions

Level Two: Noises
Sounds and odors

Bangs, gunfire, knocking

talking, singing, music
playing

Level One: Emotional Imprint

anger, fear, sadness

Uausally negative emotions

Wilson suggests that the theory again could explain both residual and intelligent hauntings and suggests a categorization of both by level of activity. For a residual haunting he suggests you use a metaphor of a computer file with an interrupted download in mind. It's an imperfect file, and while you have some information you don't have it all. Therefore, you would have only some aspect of the personality recorded, but not all of it.

RESIDUAL HAUNT

Level One: In keeping with the hypothesis, a residual haunting may be only a partial imprint of a personality. Therefore the first level is just an imprinting of a strong emotion. You might notice you feel a certain emotion while in one room that is not explainable nor wholly rational. And while you might never experience any paranormal activity in the room it might still creep you out. Consider the example from Chapter One where I describe the weird feeling I got from spending the night in the back bedroom, and also the example of the uncomfortable man cave that Aaron suggested.

Level Two: Include Odd smells and unexplainable sounds. Level Two is a combination of an emotion combined with some form of energy. In other words, there may be a residual emotion such as sadness but it takes some form of kinetic energy to create the desultory sounding footsteps pacing in the bedroom upstairs.

Level Three: Wilson feels that the amount of energy to create a full-bodied apparition would be greater still, and would also be contingent on all of the environmental factors being correct at the time. The residual style apparition would be the apparition that appeared to float above the floor in an old building because floor height had been changed, or who would appear to walk through a solid wall where a door had once been. They're more a recorded hologram that plays when the conditions are just right.

INTELLIGENT HAUNT: THE STIMULATION ACTIVATED RESIDUAL IMPRINT

Level Three:

Apparition Communication

Level Two:
Voices, Talking
Whispering
Singing
Humming

Level One: Sounds
Knocking, scratching , dragging
footsteps

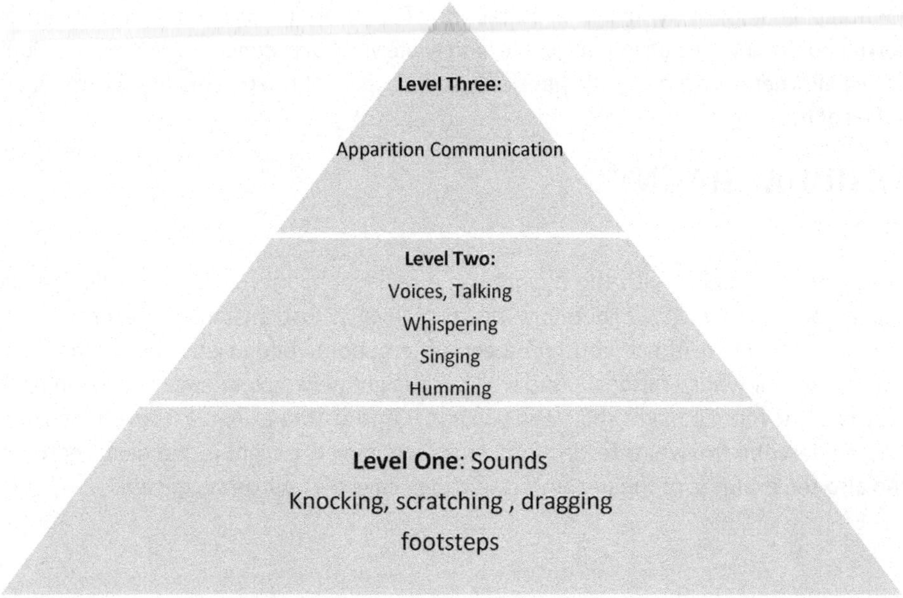

If an intelligent haunting is a more complete copy of a personality it would make sense that at least on some level the energy present would be capable of some type of limited communication. He labels it a *Stimulation Activated Residual Imprint*, meaning that upon being *stimulated* by someone in its environment the "spirit" could be triggered to respond, but that the responses are limited in scope.

Level One: would be a low energy response, such as knocking sounds or the sounds of footsteps that would suggest the spirit knows someone is present and is trying to tell you it is there.

Level Two: Includes an aural response such as talking, singing, humming. While an entity may respond to a question with an answer, true intelligence needs to be carefully weighed. Case in point, we recently recorded an EVP that was incredible in clarity though weak on message. We three females were talking with our male client Aaron in a closed building by ourselves. Aaron remarks, "That place creeps me out, and I don't know why." And then directly after you hear a completely different, but incredibly distinct male voice says, "I don't know why." The two voices, both obviously male, were also most obviously different in tone and pitch. One would conclude upon listening that there were two men in the building at the time, but we investigators knew that there was only one.

We were stunned by the clarity of the voice. It sounded like another male was in the room with us, even though we knew beyond a doubt that there wasn't. The tone and pitch of the second voice was distinctly different from the first voice. One of my investigators assumed because of the clarity of the voice that it must be an intelligent haunt. But looking at what the voice says isn't terribly enlightening. It is merely parroting back the exact phrase Aaron had already said and doesn't contribute any additional information.

For something to truly show intelligence it would have to be able to view and acknowledge changes in its environment. For example, if I were at a possibly intelligent haunt during an investigation wearing my group sweatshirt, a truly intelligent entity would first acknowledge me by name, after I introduced myself, and then ask what the Greek letters on my shirt represented.

Wilson cautions against assigning intelligence to trigger responses, like the EVP I just mentioned. If I ask is anyone here, and I receive a "yes" EVP is that really a sign of intelligence or an energy simply responding with a stored response. Remember the artificial intelligence personality Siri from earlier. Could not an intelligent haunt be compared to a type of environmentally stored artificial intelligence that once stimulated would be programmed to respond. I will admit that the vast majority of EVP's my group captures could be easily categorized as just such trigger responses.

THE JURY MAY STILL BE OUT

After writing about the two theories, I must admit I felt pretty disappointed. After all, I've dedicated the last ten years of my life to researching and investigating ghosts. If all activity can be summarized as a type of imprint or imperfect recording on an environment than all my time, money and effort has been for nothing. But then I remembered my ongoing investigation at Aaron and Lindsey's house in Hartly, Delaware and Wilson's caveat that a *true intelligence would have view and acknowledge changes in its environment.* During my second investigation two of our investigators were doing a session in the master bedroom. In the white noise of a rainstorm faint female whispering can be heard as if she was having a conversation with someone else. During this small snippet of conversation one can distinctly hear the phrase, "Yes, I see him." One of the investigators in the room at the time was a man. It was one of the more stunning EVP's I caught, not because it was the clearest, but because it appeared to be an entity demonstrating that it saw us and that it knew one of us was a man, in other words viewing and acknowledging changes in its environment – in this case a strange team of people in its house.

Clearly this one small EVP isn't enough to make a case for an intelligent haunting. Lindsey has clearly admitted activity in the house that at least on two occasions appear to meet the criteria of viewing and acknowledging something in its environment. On at least two occasions Lindsay recalls that a presence in the home has seemingly alerted her of danger. One evening Lindsey had gone out to greet husband Aaron who was coming home from work. While standing to converse with Aaron she happened to glance into the side mirror of Aaron's work truck. Reflected in the mirror was a sight that left Lindsey in a panic. Lindsey clearly saw flames. The flames were so shockingly real in fact, that she spun around to look at the front of the house, specifically at the chimney to see if her house was ablaze. She saw nothing. However, now somewhat in a panic, she ran into and through the house to the attached porch on the other side. On the porch, she found the ashtray ablaze. In her own words, "There was no way his truck could have [shown a] reflection of the porch but "something" made me run out there to "check on it" and if that didn't happen we would've had a fire."

The team returns repeatedly to this property because of the stunning amount of evidence it never fails to produce. Not only does every investigation yield some type of activity, but the activity does seem to show some level of actual intelligence – which is the truly exciting part of paranormal investigation.

IS MY HOUSE HAUNTED OR IS IT MY IMAGINATION; THE PSYCHOLOGICAL EFFECT

It should be noted that there is a final possibility that haunted houses are a product of our imagination. University of Kentucky Professor Emeritus, Robert Baker (now deceased) was an avowed 'ghost buster' who believed, "there are no haunted places, just haunted people (81)." He argued that in his 50 years studying ghostly phenomena, he came across nothing that deterred him from that stance. I hear his voice, thick with a southern accent in the back of my mind as I write this book. In the 1997 documentary *Hauntings*, "the only place ghosts exist are in the human mind." He concluded that they were a product of our imaginations or perhaps hallucinations, and that creating them led to our psychological satisfaction. He concluded that ghosts filled a gap or a void in our lives (*81*).'"

There are a few psychological possibilities for hauntings as well. Dave Schumacher of the Paranormal Research Group suggests magical thinking, sheer human imagination, and the desire to experience a paranormal event, subjective validation and confirmation bias.

In other words, if a person is inclined toward believing in the paranormal they're more likely to attribute unexplained phenomenon to being paranormal. For example, I was speaking with a colleague who was house-sitting for a person who collected antiques. One of the beloved antiques was an old church pew. My colleague said that the object made her uncomfortable, and noted that if anything would be haunted it would be an old church pew. Given her bias, had she noted strange sounds or movements in the house while she was staying in it, which is likely as she's already in an unfamiliar environment, it's quite likely that she would have attributed these things to being paranormal and likely blamed the church pew as the culprit.

In other words, she was already suspicious of the object because it seemed "spooky" and needed only the confirmation of a strange event to leap to that conclusion. Certainly, some objects do elicit emotional responses from people. A creepy painting which seems to follow you with its eyes or the leering face of my brother's Bozo the Clown doll come to mind. If a person is half the way there, perceiving something as "spooky," may be all that's needed to push them toward belief.

CHAPTER 5: OTHER THINGS THAT DEFY CATEGORIZATION

POLTERGEIST

Poltergeist activity is normally associated with haunted houses, and thus is usually lumped in with residual and intelligent haunts. But if the prevalent theory of poltergeists is correct they actually have very little in common with the average haunted house. True poltergeist cases are fairly rare, and the stronger the activity the more sensational they become. I did, however receive an inquiry about one case that I believe was honestly a poltergeist situation. Being a minor and living in an awkward situation she never agreed to our conducting an investigation, so I was never able to test my theory. I've changed the names and locations for anonymity's sake. We'll call my young correspondent Allison. Allison wrote me about a dire situation that was occurring in her home. In her email, she wrote:

"Hi my name is Allison. I'm 17 years old and I and my family have recently moved into a new house. On the third day [after] moving in, it was about 2 am, my uncle heard someone walking downstairs with high heels on and he went to check and no one was there. So he told us about it but we thought he was crazy. Then the next night me and my father were woken up by loud footsteps and kitchen chairs moving and cabinets being slammed. It's been going on for about three weeks now and every night it's getting worse and worse and me and my family are so scared , do you have any advice ???"

I wrote back immediately and asked her some additional questions pertaining to the activity, the property and the move itself. I was also careful to ask about any other teenagers living in the house. It turned out the townhouses were brand new, but had replaced an older house. She also indicated that an old cemetery dating back to the 1800's had also been in the near vicinity. She admitted that she was the only teenager in the house. However, there were also four other smaller children living in the home as well as a male adult family member. Essentially the mother had brought her two children to live with a family member and his three children, seven people trying to live in one townhouse. Add to the fact that the young lady had to change schools and leave friends behind. A theory was quickly forming in mind that the explosiveness of the activity – loud, tumultuous and angry – had very little to do with the old cemetery or house that had been removed, and very much to do with a teenager in an uncomfortable situation venting off steam. She admitted it continued most nights starting at 2 or 3 am with stomping sounds in the family room and kitchen area.

She went on to tell me that her mother and she had done a ritual one evening where they burned a white candle. For two days the house was quiet, and then it started up again. She went on to grudgingly admit that the male family member was not someone that she liked, and that his small children were not well behaved and didn't listen to authority figures.

I asked her if the activity only happened when she was in the house. She replied that she had asked her family members whether anything happened when she'd spent a couple of nights with a friend. They told they thought that the activity still took place.

The word poltergeist is German word literally meaning noisy ghost. But this may be a misnomer. The Spiritualists of the 1900's speculated that a spirit was responsible for the activity, using a human agent as a power source. With modern studies in PSI, the theory of a spirit channeling through a human has fallen somewhat out of disfavor. Many modern paranormal investigators now believe that the activity is created solely by the human agent. Whether the activity is created by a human, or by a spirit through a human, nearly all researchers agree that the chaos created is manifested by psychokinesis (PK).

Psychokinesis (PK) is the ability to control or manipulate objects via the mind. In the case of poltergeists more specifically recurrent, *spontaneous* psycho-kinesis (or RSPK) is to blame. Poltergeist activity is usually created by sub-conscious bursts of psychokinesis, usually emanating from an adolescent as they grapple with an inner conflict. They are most often female, but some very famous cases have involved males as well. (Epileptics and hysterical subjects are also cited as possible candidates.) RSPK is an ability that appears to be strongest in young people, but fades as a person ages.

Usually the young person has no idea that they are the agent of the activity. The whirling tempest in their head is primarily in their subconscious. Of course, the activity sparks fear, which raises the stress level, which causes more activity, and often an escalation in the virulence of the activity occurs, and you've got the perfect storm as they say. The youngsters in question are often resistant to believing that they are the agents creating the havoc and often have to be convinced. One strong indicator that the teenager is the one creating the mess is to remove the adolescent from the premises. If the activity only happens when they are in the building, it's a strong sign that they are ones around which the activity revolves. Likewise finding a way to resolve the adolescent crises is a good way to end the deluge.

Poltergeist activity usually manifests itself as strange noises such as knocking or scratching sounds. The sound of music being played, doors slamming and pounding on walls can happen. Electrical malfunctions can occur with lights being turned on and off, or electronic equipment malfunctioning. It can also encompass items being lifted, flying (usually slowly) through the air and breakable items being smashed into walls or falling onto floors. The items are usually lifted without anyone witnessing it, and there are even accounts of items not belonging to the domicile suddenly appearing (apports). Possessions can disappear entirely, or be found in other places. Sometimes only the sound of an item being broken is heard, the object being found intact.

There have been historically infamous accounts of poltergeist activity, excruciating situations in which people have been brutally and continually attacked. But as emotionally harrowing as a poltergeist attack may be, such activity doesn't usually result in physical injury, although the nastier of poltergeists have been known to bite, kick or pull hair. And others have thrown rocks or dirt.

In some of the more extraordinary cases the adolescent may even be able to manifest a subconscious separate entity, perhaps a manifestation of the Id of the adolescent. Being a creation of the darker regions of the mind, the embodiment of a person's primal fears, these creatures are interpreted as being malevolent. Think of the glowing eyes that Allison reported seeing in her closet. Were the eyes a separate entity, or more likely the embodiment of Allison's fears brought to life?

Thus, I saw Allison as being a strong candidate for RSPK. Here was a young female adolescent who had just moved. Moving is traumatic enough, with changing schools and leaving friends. Now she's also living with another family. Consider the scenario of seven people attempting to live harmoniously in one small townhouse. Stir into the mix teenage hormones and angst, and it certainly it seems a recipe for disaster.

Notice the type of activity described. I thought in particular the sounds of high heel shoes walking downstairs was a telling detail. High heel shoes are the footwear of teenage girls, not ghosts. And Allison goes on to describe the activity as "kitchen chairs moving and cabinets being slammed." This activity sounds more like a child having a temper tantrum, which is what I would do if forced to live with three naughty children and an inconsiderate adult.

Note the episode that Allison describes. She and her mother had lit a white candle in a type of ritualistic cleansing, and the activity stopped for a couple of days. The act of lighting the candle probably helped soothe Allison's fears. She and her mother were doing something about the situation, which probably made her feel more in control of the situation. Sadly, the comfort provided only lasted a couple of days.

I did ask her if the activity only happened when she was around, and she said no it happened whether she was in the town house or not. But she was asking her family members after the fact, and people have notoriously poor memories. I suggest to my clients that keep a log of activity, in this case noting who was in the townhouse, what time of the day or night things happened and what types of activity occurred would prove a more reliable way to collect information.

In an interview, Jennifer Lauer, Co-Director of the Paranormal Research Group describes a very similar situation. She said:

> *"There was one [client] in particular. They called us late at night and we had to drop everything and get a team and go out there. It was a case of RSPK. The popular theory behind poltergeist activity being that there is a human agent that is affecting the environment with their minds. It had to do with a young female. After we did an investigation and told her that's what we felt that the case was, we explained that the activity was probably coming from her. We explained how the brain works, and how the brain functions and how that can happen, and that it's a natural cause. We explained that it's been studied under lab conditions and how it has been reproduced and that it's not a "crazy-person" thing, but that it happens more frequently than people understand or recognize.*
>
> *She didn't want to believe it. She wanted to believe something else. However, after we brought that from her sub-conscious into her consciousness by making her aware of it, it [the activity] stopped....Then everything is ok, because the issue is resolved in their mind. Especially if it's PK, because PK is done in their mind. By making them aware of it, it solves a lot [of cases] of them (45)."*

SHADOW MEN

My son and I had an unsettling few days one spring; unsettling even for a ghost hunter with some experience. My son and I were alone in the house as my husband was away on business. Any single mother can tell you that staying by yourself with a small child, or children, is an unsettling experience. There are enough explainable but frightening things with which to contend. Burglars, rapists, thieves who knows who might break in to hurt you or your family as you lie groggily asleep.

THE DARK MAN

Mythology speaks to archetypes. Archetypes are personalities that show up again and again in legends and verbal histories of a culture. They encompass the most basic fears, hopes and desires of a people. The enthralling aspect about the theory of archetypes - whether the legends are from Russia, Africa, Asia, Europe or North America – is the similarity of experience across the human spectrum. Symbolized by a fox in one culture or a mongoose in another, the basic characters represent the same human desires or fears. And living alone, what I feared most was the dark man, that nameless danger, that dark shape in the night.

WHAT WE EXPERIENCED

Therefore, it's not surprising that the dark man is exactly who appeared to us. My son awoke three mornings and reported a strange man standing in the hallway. He felt the form he saw was more than merely the shadow thrown against the wall as he sat up in bed. On the first sighting, he described the form as wearing a striped shirt, but upon further questioning he couldn't be sure. He could never identify any distinguishable features. On two occasions, he described the being as standing in the hallway and looking around the corner and into my bedroom. On the third occasion, he described the dark form as bobbing up and down in a strange way, and then dissipating as my son called to me.

With the plasticity of youth, my son first interpreted the dark man as being his grandfather who had recently passed away. On subsequent viewings he wasn't so sure, however. And, after sensing my own uneasiness, he became increasingly disconcerted. It goes without saying that children feed off their parent's reactions. My son became increasingly uncomfortable being alone in his room, and if I came into his room unannounced he reacted violently, often with a, "why didn't you say you were coming in!" I must admit, that I have never caught sight of the dark man. But I did find myself looking over my shoulder while dressing, and waking up several times a night to look out in the hall. I wasn't getting much sleep. I was edgy. During the day I was tired, distracted and cranky. Worst of all, I didn't know to whom I should turn. Now I admit all this rather sheepishly. I've been researching the paranormal field for a number of years, and I've willingly walked into situations just to experience paranormal phenomenon. It is vastly different, however, to seek out the paranormal in someone else's domicile or building, than to have an unknown quantity in your own home. And to make matters worse, we were living in a home that did not have a prior history of paranormal activity. This was a completely new phenomenon and so I had no idea what to expect.

SEEKING ANSWERS

I finally sought some advice from friends with whom I discussed several possibilities. We considered natural as well as supernatural causes, how light and shadows might be flitting across the walls as cars drove by. It was late in the winter and was getting light late in the morning. When my son and I arose it was still very dark, and thus my friends and I speculated that headlights thrown against the wall of the stairwell might cause the illusion of movement. We further hypothesized that someone standing on the street corner waiting for a ride and illuminated by headlights might be causing the illusion of a form.

One early morning I set up my equipment and recorded video and audio. I used my EMF detector to check for any odd electrical anomalies. After which I went through all the evidence diligently. And I got...absolutely nothing. Not only did I not capture a moving form in my hallway, I recorded no electromagnetic spikes or any odd audio recordings. I also did not see any strange lights moving across the walls casting shadows that might be interpreted by a small boy as a moving form.

My son saw the figure only the three times, and never after I conducted my mini-investigation. All three times my son witnessed the thing he called out to me, upon which the creature would seemingly disappear. I never saw the figure. Still it makes one wonder if what my son saw was real, and if so what it wanted? Years later I learned about shadow men, and decided that perhaps that is it what we had unwittingly attracted. In some ways it fit the description of shadow men, the fact that it seemed genuinely interested – especially in me. Also the fact that it didn't hang around like a traditional haunting would. Or maybe it was car lights on the wall. Either way, I was relieved when the phenomena stopped for good.

SHADOW PEOPLE

Shadow Men are unlike other types of hauntings, and thus some paranormal investigators categorize them independently. These beings look like shadowy figures, dark masses with no distinguishable facial features. Some are described as having red glowing eyes. They are almost always described as being male, although some accounts detail them as bald, sexless and with a large, broad silhouette. The shadows appear to move of their own volition. They often move quickly through a room and are witnessed disappearing through a wall or door (42). If they move across you you're most likely to feel extreme cold. And yes, they have been known to touch, grab and pull on victims. Unlike other types of hauntings, shadow men appear to be intelligent.

Being intelligent they also appear to be acutely aware of the presence of witnesses. It seems they either act secretly as if trying to avoid detection or act brazenly with behaviors demanding attention or fear. For example, many witnesses report that they see shadow people out of the corner of the eye, noting that they appear to lurk in the darkest corners of the room, or peer around doorways as if spying on inhabitants. Other accounts are more sinister, speaking of shadow people that stroll out in full view, sometimes sitting on the edge of a bed or standing in a doorway menacingly. From the accounts I've read, they seem to appear most often to children or adolescents, and many witnesses have suggested that they felt the creatures gained strength by feeding off their victim's fear.

They seem to prefer nighttime for their activities, although there are accounts of shadow people showing up in the broad daylight. They may make an appearance once never to be seen again, or they may make appearances at odd times over a series of years. One witness noted that one fedora clad shadow figure harassed him over a decade, usually appearing when the witness was the most distressed or anxious, seemingly to relish the misery.

Paranormal writer and blogger Jason Offutt of MysteriousUniverse.org categorizes shadow figures into five distinct categories based on appearance and behavior (**40**).

> 1. **Benign**: *These creatures may be seen only once or a few times, such as the one my son witnessed. Their behavior appears more like a residual haunt in that they may always display the same behavior every time they appear, for example always appearing at the same time, walking the same path across the room. They may or may not acknowledge witnesses. Aside from being spooky, these beings don't appear to have a desire to terrorize or unduly frighten witnesses. Other accounts describe benign shadow figures who are playful, or that appear to act in a clownish fashion.*

> 2. **Negative Shadows**: *These creatures appear to lurk in dark shadows and can cause feelings of terror from their witnesses. For these creatures intimidation appears to be the goal.*

> 3. **Red Eyed Shadows**: *These creatures are always negative. They are described at staring openly at observers with blazing, red eyes and are described as feeding off people's fear.*

> 4. **Hooded Shadows**: *These creatures are sometimes described as looking like a medieval monk in hood and robes. They emanate feelings of deep rage.*

> 5. **Hat Men or The Men in Black**: *Offutt notes these creatures are "the most curious." They appear to be wearing a fedora style hat and are sometimes described as wearing a suit. If this suggests a "men in black" style appearance it may be on purpose. Offutt notes that these fedora-clad, shadow men have been reported in numerous cultures across the globe, and it has been suggested that these may actually be inter-dimensional beings traveling not across the galaxy, but from a different dimension to make contact and/or study our world.*

THEORIES BEHIND SHADOW PEOPLE

There are several theories as to what shadow people might be. The first is that shadow people are the spirits trying unsuccessfully to materialize, and thus are seen only as amorphous shadowy forms instead. This is the usual explanation, especially for the more benign or silly of the creatures. Another theory is that they are beings from another dimension witnessed when our own dimension partially overlaps their own, which may explain why they are only partially visible. Some paranormal investigators suggest that shadow people are evil or non-human creatures or perhaps even demonic spirits which evoke terror purposely.

Offutt suggests they may be categorized as djinn (jinn). In the Islamic tradition djinn play an important role as entities that are non-human. These spirits may be gay, human companions or dark predators depending on their dispositions. They are said to lurk in cemeteries or the ruins of human habitations. They can be great deceivers, sometimes disguising themselves as a departed loved one.

Sleep theory may help to explain some sightings. In the in-between state of wakefulness and sleep is known as the hypnogogic state. It is a period when the brain is extremely receptive to "ideas, images, sounds, feelings, impressions and intuition," a period when a vaguely imagined dream may take on the feeling of reality (38). Patients experiencing a hypnogogic hallucination report flickering lights, visual hallucinations, a feeling of being paralyzed and report feeling like they are being held down on the bed or a feeling of pressure on the chest. This might be explained as old hag theory or sleep paralysis, except that at times people who experience shadow people in broad daylight have reported the same phenomena.

An overactive imagination or neurological disorders such as schizophrenia can cause hallucinations and visual disturbances. High levels of electromagnetic fields have also been known to cause visual disturbances and hallucinations, and should not be discounted as a possible explanation. Seeing a shadow figure in an already dark hall? It could of course be a trick of the light.

CRITTERS THAT FOLLOW YOU HOME

I was getting ready for an investigation. I'd done the phone interview with the client, and then did an initial walk through. It's a fairly mundane procedure, done during daylight hours when I determine whether there is enough reported activity to actually warrant a full investigation. It also allows me to figure out where the activity is occurring and where I will need to have my team set up equipment. I was comfortable with the client, Lindsey, who honestly seemed more curious than frightened.

The Thursday night after the walkthrough was serene, I did the walkthrough after work. There were no problems that night. Friday was a normal workday with no untoward stress. Friday night, however, was one of the most bizarre of my career. When I woke the next morning, while memories were still sharp I recorded what had happened. Here is what I wrote:

October 10, 2014: Around nine pm we were putting my son to sleep. He has a small sugar bear [glider] named Hiccup. We had Hiccup out and were playing with him. Sugar gliders are like tiny flying squirrels. He'll run up your arm or leg and then leap to another person and land on their head or back, run around, jump to someone else... My husband, son and I were all in on the little adventure. Eventually we put Hiccup back in his cage, tucked my son into bed, and went to bed ourselves.

It was around 1130 – midnight. I had been sleeping, but then I noticed that my husband had come up to the foot of the bed. We were talking about something, but as soon as we stopped talking about it I seemed to forget what the conversation had been. I thought this odd at the time. I wondered to myself, "Why can't I remember what we were just talking about?" I didn't have time for further reflection because I realized that my husband, had brought Hiccup in with him. The little creature leaped off Gene and was running around on the bed. I followed his movements, because I didn't want him to get loose and lost. Hiccup ran up the furrow in the covers close to me and I cupped my hands around him in preparation of gently lifting him up and containing him. As I was cupping him my husband put his headlamp on [he keeps a small flashlight, head-lamp by the bed at all times]. As the light beamed down on my hands Hiccup seemed to disappear. I thought he had burrowed deeper into the sheets so I was ruffling the covers trying desperately to find him when my husband asked me in a very bewildered voice, "What are you doing?"

Slightly exasperated I replied, "What do you mean what am I doing? I'm trying to find Hiccup."

"Hiccup isn't in here. He's in his cage," Gene said.

"No he's not, he's right here. I just had him in my hands," I explained starting to get confused and still talking to my husband at the foot of the bed. "You were the one that let him loose. Help me find him."

"What are you talking about? I've been here asleep the whole time, I haven't been playing with Hiccup."

At this point I may have been struggling to wake up fully, because it slowly dawned on me that Gene was in fact beside me in bed, and that I was playing with an imaginary Hiccup, and sitting up in bed conversing with...no one. "If you've been asleep the whole time, then who was I talking to?" I asked. "

That was your son, he got up to go to the bathroom," my husband explained. "I just saw the bathroom light turn on."

"It was not our son. He's not been out of his bed." How I knew this fact so adamantly I cannot explain.

I simply knew our son was tucked up in his bed fast asleep.

My husband didn't agree. "I'm pretty sure it was your son. I saw a dark figure at the foot of the bed when I woke up, and saw him turn around and head down the hall to the bathroom."

We discuss this possibility a little further, until my husband finally gets out of bed and goes to my son's room. He is sound asleep in his bed, but Gene does note that the light is on in the bathroom. Not an alarmist, he comes back to bed wryly pointing out, "I think you brought something home from your walk-through." He then turns over and goes back to sleep.

It's hot in the room, however, and I realize that I'm too warm to sleep without opening the window. In order to open the window, I need to get up and turn my back to the bed and doorway. There are two reasons I don't want to do this. The first I just mentioned; the idea of turning my back to whatever is in the house is unnerving. The second is because we have a large four-poster bed that stands about 2 feet off the ground. It's easily high enough for an adult to crawl under. Eventually I realize that I'm being paranoid, and I did get up and open the window.

The cool air helped, and I fell back asleep. But this time I have a distinct dream that the blanket I am sleeping under is slowly being pulled off me by a force from underneath the bed! I jerked awake. I'm now realizing quite vividly that whatever is playing with me is reading my thoughts. Somehow, I'd conveyed my worries about what could be under the bed, and it had used that information.

I managed to go to back to sleep. Once again, I had a very vivid dream that felt like it was being manipulated from outside myself. This time I get the cliché' haunting experience, the feeling of being held down in bed. I know it to be a dream and I also recognize my own sleep paralysis as something separate from the sensation. Groggily I finally wake up enough and tell it verbally twice, "Get off, get off me." I'm no longer panicked at this point, I'm more annoyed, because I realize that there is something that is playing with me, perhaps trying to scare me, but that the creature is a bit of a buffoon.

Of course, this is the third time I've been awoken this night by crazily vivid dreams. I'm annoyed, I'm worried and I'm awake. As I'm lying in bed I hear the creaky step outside in the hall creak as if someone was on the step. Then I hear another small noise I can't identify. I nudge my husband awake again, and ask him he has his handgun with him [lest we have a human invader]. He assures me he does. But this is the final experience I have that evening. Each successive incident seemed like it was losing energy.

We did ask my son in the morning if he had heard or seen anything, or been out of bed last night. He said no to all three. He did remind me of the time he himself had a dream that Hiccup was loose on his bed. His calls had awoken me and I had gone into his room and woke him up. He, like I, had been adamant that Hiccup was loose. I had forgotten that incident.

*** End of Account ***

Being a paranormal investigator, I find this story extraordinary on so many levels. And I can say that I can pick it apart now, only because of the amount of time that has gone by, without any further reoccurrences. It's much easier to be critical when you're not actually emotionally involved. But let me start with the easier answers.

The third occurrence, when I felt like an entity was holding me down on my chest and arms is probably the most easily answered. Indeed, I answered it at the time I wrote it, chalking it down to sleep paralysis. Sleep paralysis is something that occurs naturally in mammals. It's a type of protective tendency that sets in when an organism is in its deepest sleep, causing a temporary paralysis of the limbs. In this way if I dream I'm fleeing from an assailant, I don't actually start flailing in bed. In the same vein if my poodle, Uther, is dreaming that he is chasing a squirrel he doesn't actually take off running and throw himself inadvertently off the balcony. Its nature's way of keeping our bodies safe when we're in our deepest, most vulnerable stages of sleep.

Sleep paralysis (SP) is a physiological response, quite natural. Coupled with this I apparently had the "Old Hag" syndrome going on – old hag meaning a witch. The old hag was known for visiting victims at night and sitting on their chest. What actually happens is that because my chest and arms were paralyzed it felt as if something was holding me down. Because I was only partially awake, my body was still not responding, instead feeling like it was under spectral attack. SP is a fairly common phenomenon. I might also have experienced a hypnogogic or hypnopompic hallucination which are also common with SP. Such acute episodes can be caused by stress, fear, being overtired. They also occur more regularly if someone is sleeping on their back or on their stomach.

The second dream as well is easily dismissed as a nightmare. I was already emotionally distressed, and probably had a bad dream because of it. I didn't for instance actually see the sheets being pulled down.

That leaves the first incident. Obviously, the night left me bewildered and I sought the advice of two experts I knew in the field. Greg Pocha, Director of Parapsychology, Afterlife and Paranormal Studies for the Eidolon Project Canada (eidolonproject.org) theorized that I had experienced a somewhat rare sleep anomaly called a False Awakening (FA). An FA is the polar opposite of an SP in that the person is not paralyzed but moving about freely, acting out their dream. They feel like they're awake, but they're sound asleep. In my FA I was sitting up in bed, conversing with my husband and chasing an imaginary critter. I didn't actually wake up until my husband turned on his headlamp and started asking me questions. Pocha speculates that I had a Type 2 FA which is accompanied by sensations of confusion, tension, stress, apprehension, feelings of foreboding, feelings of heightened expectancy and feelings of ominous oppression. Apparently Type 2 FA's can also produce hallucinations, such as seeing people that are not there; husbands standing at the foot of the bed, for example, or imaginary sugar gliders running around on the covers. FA's are more common in lucid dreamers as are SP's. Until that night I'd never experienced either an SP or an FA.

Pocha pointed out that I likely have a telepathic connection with my son, which he speculated is common among mothers and their children. Note that my son had had a similar dream about his sugar glider getting out. This is one of his first pets, and required specialized care. Hence, especially when the animal was new to the house, my son would often suffer bouts of anxiety. I've always considered myself about as sensitive as a rock, so this suggestion surprised me. And then he spent a night away at a friend's house. He left me to take care of his pet, which I did. However, I awoke in the middle of the night in a panic over whether I had fed Hiccup his nightly apple slice. I was so concerned that I went down stairs and got him another, just in case. Hiccup ate well that night. When my son came home the next day I asked him how his night away had been. He said it had been fine, except in the middle of the night he had awoke in a panic, thinking he'd forgotten to get Hiccup his apple. Had his panic over his pet radiated to me?

Pocha's answer seemed to tie up the experiences I had in a nice, neat scientific bundle. I might have been subconsciously anxious about the upcoming investigation and that anxiety created not one, not two, but three lucid dreams resulting in an SP and an FA experience – all in one wild ride of a night. I didn't know I was feeling terribly worried about the investigation, but that's why we call it a subconscious or below consciousness.

For skeptics this appears explanation enough, except for two minor details.... First my husband saw a similar dark figure at the foot of the bed, which in a stretch we might say was a shared telepathic hallucination. Second, the dark figure we saw at the foot of the bed turned around, walked out of the room, down the hall and tripped the motion sensor night light in the bathroom! Pocha's response, "I will have to agree with your husband's first, and most logical conclusion. That it was indeed your son that was seen at the foot of the bed. Why? It must be fairly obvious that you were suffering from episodes of sleepwalking. Thanks to chromosome 20 (the exact gene is still unknown) there is a genetic link passed down, so the likelihood of your son suffering the same noctambulistic fate is better than average. I can safely surmise that the chances are excellent that your son was indeed sleepwalking, being silhouetted from the light of the motion detector that he had just set off. In your words the figure turned around and headed back down the hall. Apparitions tend to take the easy route and just fade out. As well you state that you were struggling to wake up, apparently your husband was in the same state, as apparently you woke him up. This gave plenty of time for a sleepwalking boy to return to his bed and be asleep - because he was never awake."

This is not to say that Pocha dismissed the idea that a spirit could follow someone home. In fact he vehemently warned me to take some precautions against such a fate. He just felt it unlikely that on an initial walkthrough I would have caught the attention of something that would be so interested in me as to follow me home. I wasn't doing anything provocative enough to garner attention. Incidentally, I also asked another parapsychologist acquaintance of mine about the incident. His explanation was more to the point. Heck, he could have tweeted it to me. "Yup," he said, "it sounds like something followed you home. "

Remember that lost kitten you found as a kid that followed you home? It seems possible that spirits are capable of doing the same. I've read or listened to accounts of paranormal investigators that came away from an investigation with more than they bargained on. It can also happen to laymen as well. I got an email one day from a young married man. His comely, young wife worked at a hospital. They lived in an apartment where nothing had ever happened, until just recently. They felt as if they were being spied on in their bedroom and once the young woman had woken up to find a man leaning over the bed looking at her? Was it possible that his lovely wife had managed to attract the attentions of a ghost? Hmmm, so the choices are hang out at a hospital with all that sickness and death or spy on a pretty young lady in her bedroom at night? Possible something followed her home? I'd say!

The prevailing theory of spirits is that they are intelligent, willful energy. If that is the case why would they not be able to move about as they chose, changings locations at will? These restless souls appear to be more curious than anything. They may come for a night or two, or stay for a week, but then they appear to get bored and move on. Pocha candidly agrees, noting, "Ghosts have total and complete freedom and free will on their side. Although many are "stuck" by their own accord or ignorance, all have freedom to go where they please unless boundaries and a safety net is set up." And he noted that hospitals and the like are rife with ghosts who are likely to follow someone home. A house is haunted because a spirit feels the space familiar or attractive, but hospitals, asylums, prisons are unpleasant places, places of misery and disharmony, and spirits that find themselves there are more likely to want to leave.

SPIRITUAL BOUNDARY SETTING

Pocha noted that spirits, "all have freedom to go where they please unless boundaries and a safety net is set up." So how does one set up a spiritual baby gate to keep critters at bay? Various experts suggest smudging with white sage cleanses a house or apartment of an undesirable interloper. Any new-age store worth its salt [pun intended] will carry either dried white sage or white sage incense. You merely light the sage or incense stick. The dried leaves will slowly smolder producing a very pleasant smoke. (You'll want to hold a bowl underneath the smoldering stick to catch ashes.) You then walk the perimeter of the room, making sure to get into every corner. It is also suggested you work from the top of the house down, and from the top of the walls down to the floor. Move from the back of the house forward, ending at the front door. Smudging is said to cleanse an area of unhappy emotions and restore harmony. If this is a bit too oogey-boogey to your way of thinking, consider that it can't hurt anything, and it smells really good. I actually have one investigator on my team that carries around white sage with her everywhere she goes. She also swears that when she smudges her own house her husband becomes much more sanguine, a side effect she quite enjoys.

Another technique is to reason with the entity, establish parameters or even suggest they go on their way. If one believes that a spirit is of human derivation, then one ought to be able to reason and negotiate with it as they would with a human being.   For example, I told the husband of the nurse to discuss with his wife the distinct possibility that they had become the unwitting recipients of a stray. I suggested at night when they got ready for bed that they communicate with their interloper, reminding him that it was their home and that it was not appropriate for him to invade the private space of their bedroom or spy on them at night. The point is that as a family you have to set the rules, and present a solid front. It's also helps you to feel that you are taking back the control of the situation, which is extremely powerful psychologically speaking.

If you are going to try to consciously make contact with spirits, such as attending a paranormal investigation, séance or ghost tour you should come equipped with some type of protection. Whether you believe in spirits or not, the very act of your exploring the possibility means that you give the idea some credence. And if you believe even nominally in the existence of something beyond the ordinary, and you open up an avenue of communication, then you should at the very least take some precautions. Not all energy is good energy, just as not all people are nice people. If you open yourself up to communicating with anything, you run the risk of having something aggressive or negative taking you up on the invitation.

Before and after every investigation my team now performs some type of quick blessing. Keeping it fairly generic so as not to offend those of varying religions, we now invoke our guardians or astral gatekeeper or higher being to keep us safe and not allow anything to attach itself to us. I also require my members to wear protective talismans depending on their belief backgrounds, such as a crucifix, Star of David, or pentagram (which FYI is an ancient of protection, *not* a symbol of Satan worship).   The ancients believed iron was a ward against demons and evil spirits. I actually had a blacksmith whose specialty was Celtic designs make a pair of iron bracelets, which I wear now on every investigation. They rust, however, so I don't shower with them! Again iron and talismans and blessings may seem very oogey boogey to the skeptical person, but again I ask what does it hurt? There are books written about spiritual and psychic protections as well, if you are interested in learning more on this subject.

THE NIGHT THAT HICCUP DID ESCAPE HIS CAGE

Now, I should state that the house I live in is not haunted, not in the traditional sense. That is not to say that really bizarre episodes have not occurred here. Weird things have usually happened at or around the time I was conducting paranormal investigations. Thus we have long periods of peace and quiet when absolutely nothing odd happens, followed by short periods of time when weird things happen unnervingly often. Considering the amount of psychic anxiety that seemed to follow Hiccup's coming to live with us, it isn't surprising that this didn't became one of those odd, unexplainable things that happen to us periodically. Per my earlier story, my son had dreamed that Hiccup had escaped his cage. And I had already suffered my false awakening dream regarding Hiccup's decampment. And then one night we heard our son yelling from his room, "Hiccup is out! He's out of his cage!"

I dutifully dragged myself from my bed into my son's room only to find that Hiccup was loose and running around on my son's bed. How he got loose is what has puzzled me the most. An examination of the cage latch indicates that the cage is either latched or it is not. The cage has a wire hook on it. When the door is closed and the wire hook is latched, it has to be unlatched by hand. When the hook isn't latched the door stands slightly ajar on its own. You can't mistake the open position for the latched position, and there is no in-between position possible. When the door is left standing ajar Hiccup is out in a moment, especially at night as he's nocturnal. Therefore, if my son hadn't latched the door it wouldn't have taken Hiccup as long to get out as it did.

Not long after this episode we had another strange incident with the family dog. My husband asked me in the morning, "Did you bring Uther (our standard poodle) upstairs last night?"

Being kind of groggy, I replied nonchalantly, "no, I don't think so."

"No, really, did you bring Uther up last night?"

Really not getting what all the fuss was about, I again answered in the negative, and then asked, "Why do you keep asking me that?"

"Because, I left Uther tied downstairs last night on purpose. You came upstairs at the same time as I did to go to bed. So how did Uther get up here?"

I then recalled having awoke briefly in the night, and distinctly hearing the dog come up the stairs. I told my husband this and added a plausible, "Maybe he slipped his collar and came up on his own."

"If that's the case, how did he get tied to the bedpost?"

An examination of the dog proved to me that he was in fact tied to the bed by his leash. But whoever, or whatever had tied Uther in the middle of the night had looped the leash high up on the bedpost leaving the dog very little room to move. We never satisfactorily answered either conundrum. Both odd phenomena only happened once.

So, long story long, the answer is yes, if you seek out the paranormal you are likely to find it probably sooner than later. Mediums often talk about attracting beings to them naturally, but personally, I think that *anyone* that shows an interest in the paranormal, that opens themselves to communicating with the spirit world becomes a type of beacon to spirits. And once they know they've been noticed, like an attention starved toddler, they hate to lose the spotlight.

CHAPTER 6: MAN-MADE GHOSTS

"There is only one place ghosts exist, "the human mind. It is an

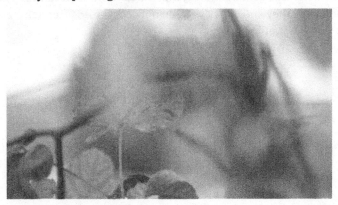

invention of the human mind."

Robert Baker, Professor Emeritus University of Kentucky, Discovery Channel Documentary, "Hauntings" 1997

"I think therefore I am." (written originally in French it read "je pense, donc je suis" – added simply because French is cool)

René Descartes, Discourse on the Method

Whenever I think of the late Dr. Robert Baker I hear his thick southern Kentucky drawl as he makes this bold statement. As I began to write this chapter I kept hearing his prophetic words, and decided I couldn't agree more. But not for the reasons that Dr. Baker suggested. I don't think Dr. Baker was incorrect about the power of the human mind for invention, certainly we are wildly creative beings. I do, however, disagree that ghosts are simply created in the human mind, and therein lies their environs. Where I feel Baker was naïve was in his under-estimation of the power of the human mind to shape its reality.

In Chapter Four I described two rather similar theories about how ghosts are imprinted on an environment, a partial or more complete copy of a human personality left in the area. This suggests that a ghost is created, exactly as Baker speculated, in the human mind. I suggested briefly, that death wasn't even a necessary factor in this imprint. It's possible that we through our will, create and give life to the very creatures of the night of which we are most frightened of finding. Take the witch hysteria of Salem, when townsfolk swore they saw witches riding brooms. Did they make their testimony up or did they really believe they saw the spectacle they described? Did the very belief that witches were real and could fly through the air on broomsticks drive what they witnessed? And what about the fact that ghosts in Japan are described sans feet? Is it possible that the Japanese culture believes that ghosts have no feet, and thus when someone sees a ghost it invariably has no feet? The most obvious example of manmade ghosts would be poltergeists, the product of recurrent, spontaneous, psychokinetic outbursts of the tormented adolescent mind. Is it possible to create an entity from pure raw emotion, or invent one out of thin air? The case studies in this chapter suggest that such may be the case.

THE THING IN THE CRAWLSPACE

Michelle Belanger, occult author of *Haunting Experiences; Encounter with the Otherworldly* describes just such a conundrum in her book (46). "It's a universal childhood fear," she says. "The thing in the closet. The monster under the bed. All the hungry, malevolent things that lurk just beyond our sight in the dark and forgotten places of our homes...." Belanger was in college, when she met a young man she names Evan. She met Evan on the first day in fact of college, when he invited her to the university's gaming club. Evan apparently was from a rather well-to-do family, and this allowed him to live off campus in the lower half of a rented duplex. He apparently was somewhat of a geek with an active imagination. He was into anime, and gaming, and decided somewhere along the line that he was new-age pagan.

He was also convinced the rented duplex he lived in was haunted, and apparently would discuss his "feelings" with anyone he could get to listen. To share expenses, Evan asked a couple to move with him, an older guy named Karl, and his girlfriend Amy. In his late twenties, Karl worked full-time and Amy stayed home and did the housework and the laundry, an arrangement Belanger found quaint in this more modern era. But Belanger approved of Amy, as being a pragmatic young lady. Raised Jewish, she nominally adhered to her upbringing and didn't go in for all of Evan's supernatural mumbo jumbo. That's why when Amy told Belanger about, "The thing in the basement," Belanger took it more seriously.

It seems that Amy did the laundry for herself and Karl, and thus spent a lot of time in the basement which housed the shared washer and dryer. It was apparently a most, distinctly unpleasant basement to begin with, as basements in older homes tend to be. Dusty, dirty, dank and filled with cobwebs and the carcasses of generations of dead bugs, it had cinderblock walls with flaking white paint, with moldy, water spots in some areas. There were a couple of small windows in the basement, but they were so dusty and filled with cobwebs that even on a bright day the light they let in was gray and washed out. This lowly cave below ground was lit by the tepid light of one hanging light bulb whose dim illumination kept the darker recesses in constant shadowy gloom. Under the stairs were old boxes filled with junk, perhaps someone's forgotten Christmas decorations, or they could have contained desiccated body parts. Underneath the thick layers of dust, it was impossible to tell." Whatever the junk under the stairs, it was of no one's concern except for the fact that the area was the center of Amy's uneasiness. Whenever Amy was in the basement doing laundry, with her back to the stairs, she consistently felt that something was watching her.

Not being of a hysterical nature, she rationalized it as just being uneasy in a dim, creepy basement. But the feeling of being observed continued. "It was a pervasive impression, something that made the hairs on the back of her neck stand up, especially when she had her back to the crawlspace." That was bad enough, but over time, she started to feel that the presences was taking an active and malevolent interest in her. "The shadows appeared to grow deeper.

During her final encounter with the peeper under the stairs, Amy was again at the washer and dryer with her back to the crawlspace. She had just emptied the dryer of a load of whites, and was moving a load of darks from the washer to the dryer. She was trying to ignore the feeling of a presence behind her as she worked, as there really wasn't anything she could do about. "And then she got the distinct impression that whatever was back there was starting, very slowly, to creep forward. She could not shake the impression that the thing – whatever it was – was exploring the space beyond its dank little realm of duty boxes and moving closer to her. Doggedly trying to finish her work and ignore the chills running up and down her back, Amy kept thinking to herself, "It's just my imagination. It's just my imagination. And then the lone bulb that lit the cellar popped and went out leaving her in darkness (46)."

Amy dropped her laundry, abandoning it where it lay, and hightailed it up the stairs refusing to go back down. "There was a moment of panic when she realized that her route of escape would actually take her closer to the unseen creeping thing, but her urge to flee overrode any other concerns."

Belanger notes that Amy was understandably reluctant to tell anyone about her encounter in the basement, fearing that her sanity might come into question. However, she staunchly refused to return to the basement, and she therefore had to explain to her boyfriend that she had abandoned his laundry for all time.

Meanwhile the atmosphere in the apartment was changing in ways that were hard to describe definitively. In the weeks since Karl and Amy had moved in the atmosphere in the apartment had seemed to turn darker, more oppressive. "It wasn't something anyone noticed all at once, but gradually the place seemed darker. A sense of threat hung in the air like something was lurking." Evan became over-anxious and started missing classes. Karl and Amy's relationship became strained, and they fought often, usually over silly things. Belanger finally had to admit that something appeared to be affecting the occupants of the apartment, and finally decided to check out the basement, although she was reluctant to believe that there was something nasty living under the stairs.

Belanger a paranormal investigator and medium reports that what she found living under the stairs wasn't a spirit per se, but a wad of negative emotions left behind, just as the boxes had been abandoned. Only over time this castoff emotional energy had begun to coalesce into a clot of negativity that was starting to take on a will of its own. Belanger admits that at this stage she herself was new to the paranormal research and still labored under the false illusion that, "all ghosts are dead people." Says Belanger,

> "I'd learned that hauntings were caused by death, almost universally. Spirits got tied to a house or other residence because that was where they died and they had failed to move on. I had a basic notion that some ghosts were more like echoes or psychic video recordings [residual hauntings] imprinted on the energy of a place, but I did not grasp the notion that spirits could have inhuman origins...."

She was surprised when she poked around under the basement stairs and found nothing but an oppressive yuck in the air. She admits it had no sentience, no sense of self, but just a, thick, heavy, twisting cloud of ick that felt for all the world like a "big otherworldly slug slowly creeping up the stairs."

> "As I peeled back the conceptual layers of my impressions, I started to realize that it wasn't just a bug clump of generalized ick. There were strata of emotions, mostly negative ones. People arguing. The upstairs neighbor worrying about money. Evan's fears about flunking out of college. Amy, secretly holding back a need for independence out of a desperate love for Karl. Images and feelings that seemed connected to other people, all of them worried or frightened or generally frustrated about life. I didn't have a word for it at the time, but I had come face to face with my first psychic residue. "

It was following Amy, or probably more to the point, attracted to Amy, because Amy was a source of pent up negativity. Belanger assessed that Amy's desire for freedom was outweighed by her love of her boyfriend. Thus Amy's negative energy became a source of attraction to the residue.

If we consider a Level One residual haunting described in Chapter Four, Belanger's psychic residue would be the raw emotions imprinted in an environment. Sadly, many human emotions are negative, thus feelings of anxiety, rage, depression, sadness and loneliness might all be left generally stamped into a space, left to unwittingly affect the emotional state of those that inhabited said space. It's much the same as when you walk into a room where two people have been fighting and the tension in the air is palatable. You may quickly feel your own mood change for the worse, affected by those emotions around you.

According to Belanger these psychic residues (Level 1 residual hauntings) can either build up slowly over time adding layer upon layer like an onion, or collect all at once due to a traumatic event such as a murder. These residues tend to collect in low-traffic areas of a dwelling such as attics or basements, as the energy in high-traffic areas is constantly moving, keeping the area uncluttered, in much the same way that dust bunnies collect under the furniture and not in the walkways. Allowed to collect for too long in the forgotten recesses of a structure, the residue can start to take on a life of its own, although it never acquires intelligence. They can be mistaken for a traditional haunting as they tend to exude the same negative emotions with which they were created. And sometimes they can trap the echoes of the events with which they were formed, which can seem like the events are replaying themselves – think Level 2 or even Level 3 residual haunting.

Belanger reports that she had been reading about Pagan grounding and energy transformation, and she was able to break down the residue and move it outdoors where it would be absorbed by the Earth, which may seem far-fetched to skeptics. However, if we concede that we can imprint an environment with a certain amount of our energy, then we should consider the idea that there should be some way to also change or cleanse the energy in an environment.

THE PHILIP EXPERIMENT

We've discussed theories and looked at a case study about how residual energy can be recorded into an environment unconsciously, resulting in phenomena that resemble a classic haunting, i.e. a dead guy haunting a space. If we have the ability to create a ghost unconsciously with a bit of emotional junk, could we create one consciously through concentration and motivation? Do we have the ability to create one *through human will alone?* Can we make up a spirit and have it come to life? One such famous experiment seemed to suggest the answer to this question is to some extent, yes.

The Philip Experiment was conducted by the Toronto Society for Psychical Research (TSPR) beginning in 1972 and ending around 1978 (**52**). The focus of the experiment was to see if a group of individuals could actively create a poltergeist, or tulpas (a thought created spirit) as some have called it. It was to be created out of concentration and imagination, a completely fictitious creature, and then given a kind of existence via the willpower of the group. It was also to demonstrate the theory that a poltergeist was a force created out of human projection or spontaneous and often unconscious psychokinesis. The success of the experiment went a long way toward explaining the theatrical séances of the spiritualist movement. It appeared to demonstrate that, parlor tricks aside, human psychokinesis might be to blame when trumpets trumpeted and tables danced.

The experiment was conceived and directed by Dr. A.R.G. (George to his friends) Owen and his wife Iris Owen. Born in Bristol, England in July 1919, Dr. Owen had a Bachelor's in mathematics and physics and a Master's and PhD in mathematical genetics from Cambridge University. During World War II he invented an aerial radar system for the British War Office that is still in use today. After the war he was both a research fellow and a lecturer in genetics and mathematics at both Trinity College and Cambridge University. During his career he wrote some 40 scientific papers in the fields of mathematics, statistics, genetics and population theory.

Iris (May, Pepper) Owen, born in Meldreth, Cambridgeshire, England in 1916 was an emancipated woman herself. During the war she worked as an Armed Forces radio intercept officer for the Enigma Team. Later she worked as a nurse in a cancer radiotherapy clinic. After moving to Canada, she became a lecturer for the Toronto Ryerson Polytechnical Institute, speaking on parapsychology.

The couple immigrated to Canada in 1970, when Dr. Owen accepted the offer of the Toronto New Horizons Research Foundation's offer to do research in parapsychological studies. Aside from their various other pursuits, it seems that Dr. and Iris Owen had an avid interest in the study of poltergeist activity. During his time in Canada he was able to study and document several high profile poltergeist cases aside from conducting the Philip experiment. For the remainder of their lives, the Owen's would conduct experiments and research into the existence of psychokinesis (52).

To set the record straight, for certainly there is a lot of misinformation on the internet regarding the Owen's research; both Dr. and Iris Owen were Christians, being members of the United Church of Canada. Both already had a belief in the survival of the soul after death. Their parapsychological research was not intentioned to prove the existence of the survival of the soul after death, but to study the existence of psychokinesis (PK), and to test the theory that PK or recurrent, spontaneous psychokinesis (RSPK) was actually the agent involved in poltergeist cases. The evidence was good that PK also went a long way toward explaining the physical happenings at many of the séances during the spiritualist movement.

The point of the Philip experiment was to determine whether several individuals could pool their small, untrained natural PK abilities collectively to produce demonstrable physical results. Could humans collectively and *willfully* create physical phenomena through psychokinesis under controlled conditions?

A relatively random group of eight individuals was selected. Aside from the Owen's, none of the group had experience in paranormal research, nor was considered to have any extraordinary psychical abilities. They consisted, in fact, of extremely ordinary individuals: a housewife, an accountant, a sociology student, a bookkeeper, an industrial designer, a psychologist and a former Mensa chairperson were selected. Certainly an odder combination couldn't be found if one tried! They became known as the Owen Group.

The idea was fairly simple, if not time consuming. The group's first task was to create a fictitious character and make up a biography about him. They named their character Philip Aylesford and then made up a sufficiently tragic history around his life and untimely death.   They were also tasked with creating a history of Philip that was somewhat rooted in history but was also rife with historical inaccuracies. According to Owen, "It was essential to their purpose that Philip be a totally fictitious character. Not merely a figment of the imagination but clearly and obviously so, with a biography which included intentional historical errors.

Philip they decided had been an English lord born in 1624. There were intentional contradictions in the bio, including that Philip had been reincarnated several times. Didington Hall, Philip's home of residence is an actual residence, but the description of the hall did not match the actual building, and Philip never resided there.

Philip lived in the time of Oliver Cromwell. He was a staunch supporter of the King, and was Catholic. Married to a woman older than himself, Dorothea, his wife, was the daughter of a neighboring nobleman and was described as cold and frigid in bed. The couple had no children either because Dorothea would not or could not bear them. Theirs was a loveless match.

Out riding the boundaries of the estate one day, Philip encountered a gypsy encampment. Among the gypsies was a haunting dark eyed, raven-haired beauty named Margo. Philip fell instantly in love. Knowing he could not lose her, he arranged to have Margo live in the gatehouse, near the stables of the estate, where he could frequently and clandestinely visit his amore frequently.

Sadly, this arrangement did not sit well with Dorothea, who undoubtedly had strong objections to her husband's mistress residing on her very property. She devised to have Margo brought up on charges of being a witch. In fear of his reputation and standing within the community, Philip stood by mutely at Margo's trial. Margo was convicted of witchcraft and condemned to burn at the stake.

Stricken with remorse, the beleaguered Philip wandered the battlements of Didington Hall in despair. One sad morning, his lifeless body was found at the foot of the battlements. He had thrown himself to his death, his guilt and anguish too much to bear.

Secondly, the group was tasked with gaining knowledge about the time period in which Philip lived. This would help with visualization and also help determine fact from fiction.

The group conducted research on the politics, religion history and customs of the period. A member of the group visited England, and provided the team with photographs of the region in which Philip had lived. One member sketched a picture of Philip so they would have a face to meditate upon.

In September 1972 the group began meeting once a week in the "Philip room" where they would discuss Philip and his life, meditate together, and try to produce a collective hallucination. Owen believed that extended, collective concentration in an atmosphere of trust and good will could produce the type of poltergeist type thought form that existed, not in the material world, but in the mental or astral plane. First the group had to be comfortable with each other and the spirit they were trying to create. Another component of the experiment was simply to produce a feeling of good spirit, and fun. They were to create an atmosphere of childlike enthusiasm and creativity. From the serious adult perspective, what the team was trying to do went against the laws of physics, but children created more in the imaginary realm, and never considered the laws of reality. Thus the group told jokes, sang songs, created rhymes and simply tried for an air of fun.

In the early sessions the group attempted to create a single mental image of Philip. They tried to envision his daily activities, and think about his feelings for Margo and Dorothea. Some of the members reported feeling a presence in the room, and some claimed that they had encountered very sharp images of Philip in their minds. Yet, over the course of nearly a year the group had produced no substantial phenomenon. The group needed a change.

It was British Psychologist, Kenneth J. Barcheldor that suggested the group should steal a thing or two from the Spiritualist séances of the 1800's. Create an atmosphere of mystique he suggested. Turn off the lights, light a candle, gather around a table and surround themselves with objects from Philip's fictional life and era. The group would sit in a circle and place their hands lightly on the surface of the table and invite Philip to appear.

Soon after the group made the changes things started to get interesting. At an early session, suddenly a loud and distinct rap was heard, the members recalling later that it was so loud it made the table vibrate. The group later confided that they "felt" the rap more than heard it. Following closely on the initial rap were knocking sounds. Very soon after the group began trying to converse with Philip, using an agreed upon system of yes and no answers. One knock would signify yes, two meant no. Through this system the group began to query Philip for details about his life. At the start the group noted that the only questions Philip appeared to answer were questions about his life and historical data – apparently drawing from the collective unconscious knowledge of the group surrounding the historical era from which they had drawn.

Once Philip made his initial contact, the phenomena began to escalate quickly. Auditory knocks, raps and bangs produced a unique sound experience that could not be reproduced by researchers, and hence could not be explained. Philip himself seemed to form a very distinct personality, as noted by the vehemence or lassitude of his responses. On some topics he displayed strong opinions noted in the loud responses. On other subjects the sounds were quieter and more hesitant. He demonstrated strong likes and dislikes. However, when the group queried Philip on his wife Dorathea they heard in response scratching noises that seemed to come from the table or chairs.

The table became the main focus of the activities surrounding the experiment. The group members noted that there was a sense that the table itself was alive when Philip came to visit. After the knocks and scratching noise oral phenomenon began as well. Group members reported that they could hear whispering in their ears, although none were ever caught on tape. And then the table around which they all sat started to move. Suddenly and then violently the table would jump off the floor and start sliding around, despite having thick carpeting underneath. On one account the table actually began to "dance" according to the group, tilting up to rest on one leg at a time, and then spinning around.

Obviously, with the physical phenomena beginning to occur violently at times, the research team started to have doubts as to validity. Was one of the members knowingly hoaxing the experiment? They placed paper doilies on the table where the teams' hands would rest, trying to foil anyone's attempt to try to move the table by hand. Cameras were brought in to film proceedings, placed strategically in order to capture any tampering of team members' knees moving the table. And yet, the table danced and moved, shaking seemingly of its own accord.

Philip seemed to gain in strength, despite the team's growing uneasiness. He also seemed to be taking on a personality of his own, doing things unexpectedly. The lights would dim, and would only brighten when team members asked Philip to turn them back up. And if one of the team members arrived late for a session the table would often dance across the room at them, pinning them in a corner against the wall. The group would sometimes feel a cold breeze blowing across the table top. Members asking if Philip himself could command the wind found he was able to send a whirlwind of air across the table, landing in the participants' faces. At one session it was reported that a fine mist-like cloud formed over the center of the table, reminiscent of séances of old.

As activity accelerated the public and the media became more curious. In 1974 a movie was reportedly produced by the group under the title "Philip, the Imaginary Ghost" which chronicled the experiment's conception. The media quickly responded. CBS Television sent a crew out to film a documentary, "Man Alive." In front of a studio audience of 50 people, Philip turned the lights on and off, levitated the table and produced booming raps.

In a later session one of the group members reminded Philip playfully that he was just an imaginary ghost. While they meant it light-heartedly, the offhand comment seemed to break the illusion, the manifestations diminished and then ceased not long after. Apparently fake manifestations don't take kindly to being reminded of such.

However, the experiment and its results spawned immediate imitators. Not five weeks after the end of the original experiment a new group began the Lilith project. Lilith was supposedly a French-Canadian spy during World War II. Other groups, in conjunction with the Owen project also conducted similar experiments. Thus Sebastian (a medieval alchemist) and Axel (a man from the future) came into being. Every group that followed the original protocol was able to create –after a certain amount of time – the same type of results.

Did the group produce a ghost per se, in the classic sense? No. Not only did Philip not manifest in a traditional style haunting. The raps, bangs, scratching sounds, the moving, levitating, dancing table; all of this type of physical phenomena was reminiscent of a poltergeist type haunting. Also note that Philip never materialized in an ethereal form, and no audio was ever captured of his speaking. At times whispers were heard in the ears of the group, but again none were ever captured on tape. The sessions were not interactive, as would be a human conversation. Philip answered questions from the biography that had been created for him or answered historical questions that could arguably have been drawn from the minds of the sitters. Philip appeared to have an intelligence, but again it was more of an artificial intelligence.

MAN-MADE GHOSTS OF OLD – TULPA

From the magical ideation of the giant pyramids of Egypt, to the unfathomable creation of the Great Wall of China (incidentally the only man-made structure visible from space) to the erection and total destruction of the New York Twin Towers; from the unbelievable advances in science and medicine; to the harnessing of electricity, the creation of the light bulb, the computer, the internet, heart transplants, prosthetic limbs, moon landings, space stations, genetic engineering, race annihilation...for good or for evil the human spirit is capable of unbelievable feats of imagination. All of these wonders began as an idea and then was made a reality. If the human race can fathom such wonders and then give them substance, why should we question their ability to create a spirit?

The idea that a "spirit" can be created and given substance merely through emotional residue or from pure concentration is not a wholly new idea. The Tibetan Occult tradition speaks of the tulpa (the word literally means to build or construct) which is a thought-form created and given life through intense concentration and the repetition of the proper mystical rites. They believed that all conscious beings in the universe from the

Supreme Being, to the deities, to humans were capable of giving concrete existence to an idea, in much the same way as a building is imagined and then built.

The tulpa is a creature of pure imagination created consciously and pointedly in the deeper regions of a person's imagination. Like a child's imaginary friend, a person wanting to create a tulpa visualizes what their thought-friend looks like, sounds like, imagines their personality and then concentrates on creating that creature within their mind. There are apparently ten different types of tulpas that can be created from humans, to talking animals to supernatural figures. Supposedly with enough will-power, time and attention, a thought-creation can seem to develop and mature into its own being, residing in the creator's mind. Once mature enough, however, the Tibetans believed a tulpa could eventually leave the mind of the creator and move into the physical world, though they cautioned that only creatures created for the good of mankind should ever be brought into the physical realm purposely.

It was also believed that a tulpa could sometimes be created by accidently. A lonely traveler crossing the steppes might unwittingly create a tulpa through fear, boredom and imagination. Or a group of individuals, such as isolated villagers, superstitious and afraid, might unwittingly create a collective thought-form, a creature created by and embodying their fears.

Do consider that modern Psychological Science is still debating what is now labeled as Dissociative Identity Disorder (formerly Multiple Personality Disorder) in which a human mind can be caused to fragment into different and distinct personalities due to trauma of a physical or sexual nature at an early age. Proponents of DID suggest that a person can create wholly separate personalities as a coping mechanism, a way of distancing themselves from sustained and wholly intolerable assault. Considering the study of confirmed cases of multiple personalities makes the idea of a tulpa not seem that preposterous. Certainly the human mind appears capable of fragmenting accidentally or purposely into separate and rather unique personalities; and perhaps we can consciously create a whole separate personality with the desired, projected traits we wish we ourselves possessed.

Tulpas were sometimes created in order to perform a task for their creator. But when in the physical realm they often had a pesky predilection of taking on their own will, morphing into something completely dangerously unpredictable.

ALEXANDRA DAVID-NEEL

The French opera singer turned writer and explorer, Alexandra David-Neel (born Eugenie Alexandrine Marie David in 1868) was the first westerner to earn the title of a Tibetan lama, and the first westerner to write on the tulpa tradition. David-Neel, a steely explorer who lived to the ripe age of 101 years, despite many explorations into the wilds of the Tibetan Himalayas, decided she wished to create a tulpa of her own. She began by imagining the most benign character she could imagine, a type of Friar Tuck, short, fat and jolly. She imbued him with a personality, history and background. She shut herself away and performed the necessary meditation and magical rites. The monk started to form and take on a personality in her mind. After many months of envisioning the friar into being she allowed the chains of her mind to be broken, and her creation the freedom to move out of her mind and into the real world.

At first, she would catch glimpses of the monk as a shadowy figure in her peripheral vision. Eventually, however, the monk left the shadows behind and could be spotted moving about her apartment. In Neel's own words, "He became a kind of guest, living in my apartment. I then broke my seclusion and started for a tour, with my servants and tents. The monk included himself in the party. Though I lived in the open riding on horseback for miles each day, the illusion persisted. It was not necessary for me to think of him to make him appear. The phantom performed various actions of the kind that are natural to travelers and that I had not commanded. For instance, he walked, stopped, looked around him. The illusion was mostly visual, but sometimes I felt as if a robe was lightly rubbing against me, and once a hand seemed to touch my shoulder (**49**)."

What was even more startling, other traveling companions were sometimes able to see him, and would ask David-Neel about the stranger traveling with her. "Once, a herdsman who brought me a present of butter saw the Tulpa in my tent and took it for a live lama"(**49**).

David-Neel had envisioned him as a friendly, open personality, but over time her monk started to develop his own ideas. According to David-Neel, "The fat, chubby-cheeked fellow grew leaner, his face assumed a vaguely mocking, sly, malignant look. He became more troublesome and bold. In brief, he escaped my control." Fearing that things might start to go badly now that the sly friar had jumped his bonds, David-Neel decided he must be destroyed, in the same way he had been created. It wasn't as easy as that, however, but took six months of concentrated, sometimes emotionally tortured meditation before she was finally able to reabsorb her thought-form back to the subconscious depths from whence he'd come.

IN THE JEWISH TRADITION – THE GOLEM

Jewish Occult writings have a similar belief. Their thought-being brought to life is known as the golem. The word means shapeless man, a creature molded of the earth and created through imagination and magical ideation. Golems were created to serve their masters as servant or protector. In the Talmud (the Jewish book of civil and ceremonial law and legend) the golem means "shapeless" or "imperfect man." Adam is referred to as a golem in the Talmud, meaning a man created from earth without being imbued with a soul, at least for the first twelve hours of his existence. The Bible mentions the golem only once, in Psalm 139:16:

> Thine eyes did see my substance - גלמי golmi, my embryo state - my yet indistinct mass, when all was wrapped up together, before it was gradually unfolded into the lineaments of man.

An interesting cross reference is from Job 10:8

> "Your hands shaped me and made me. Will you now turn and destroy me?"

One legend of the prophet Jeremiah speaks of him creating such a creature. Stories in the Talmud of the Third and fourth centuries suggest that certain rabbis might have possessed the knowledge to create such creatures, using magical rituals that followed God's divine process of creation. Medieval Kabbalistic legends revolved around the Sefer Yezirah, the Book of Creation, often cited by Jewish rabbis during the middle ages as a book of magical spells. It gave instructions on the making of a golem, although rabbis often disagree on the finer points of the instructions. Most versions suggest that one must first create a figure resembling a human being, and then invoke God's name in order to bring it to life, as God is the ultimate creative force of the universe.

Another version suggests a shape must be molded from earth (clay). The diviner must then walk or dance around the figure while saying a combination of letters from the alphabet and chanting the secret name of God. In order to dissolve the creature, the diviner would walk around it in the opposite direction while saying the words and letters backwards. According to the Sefer Yezirah certain letters of the alphabet and numbers signified parts of the body and accompanying astrological correspondences. Much of the western occult tradition still draws on such practices.

Jacob Grimm (co-author with brother Wilhelm of the Grimm's Fairy Tales) wrote in his 1808 *Journal for Hermits (Zeitung für Einsiedler)* of the golem tradition. A great collector of folklore, Grimm recounted legends of the Polish Jews who, "After having spoken certain prayers and observed certain Feast days, make the figure of a man out of clay or lime which, after they have pronounced the wonderworking Shem-ham-phorasch over it, comes to life. It is true this figure cannot speak, but it can understand what one says and commands it to do to a certain extent. They call it Golem and use it as a servant to

BY ROBIN M. STROM-MACKEY

do all sorts of housework; he may never go out alone. On his forehead, the word Aemaeth (Truth; *God*) is written, but he increases from day to day and can easily become larger and stronger than his house-comrades, however small he might have been in the beginning. Being then afraid of him, they rub out the first letters so that nothing remains but Maeth (he is dead), whereupon he sinks together and becomes clay again (39). Perhaps the most well-known legends surrounding golems centered on the Rabbi Judah Loew ben Bazalel the Maharal of Prague (1513-1609), although some accounts name Rabbi Elijah of Chelm instead. Rabbi Loew, Jewish scholar and author of several books on law, philosophy and morality would have been staunchly against creating a golem, no matter what the reason – or so his proponents believe. However, as the legend is told, Rabbi Loew created a golem from clay to protect the Jewish quarter from Blood Libel (an accusation that the Jews used the blood of Christians in certain rituals, and especially in the making of their Passover bread – an ugly accusation that began in the Middle Ages and survived until the early 20th century), and as a servant to do chores requiring physical strength.

Despite their diminutive beginnings, golems were said to grow to outstanding proportions and thought to possess great strength. One version of the legend says it occurred in the spring of 1580, near the time of Easter, when a certain Jew-hating priest was trying to incite his Christian flock against the Jews. So Loew created the golem to protect the community through the season of Lent, however at some point or another the golem began to go off the tracks, eventually threatening the lives of innocent people. Rabbi Loew was forced to do something quickly. In one version of the legend, Loew removed the Divine Name from the golem rendering him lifeless. Another account suggests the golem went mad, and escaping his bonds ran away.

During the Seventeenth Century the legends of Rabbi Loew and the golem were recorded in the manuscript Nifloet Mlhrl translated as the Miracles of the Rabbi Loew which became the basis for Chayim Bloch's *The Golem: Legends of the Ghetto of Prague* (translated into English by Harry Schneiderman). Legend has it that it became the inspiration for Goethe's ballad *The Sorcerer's Apprentice*. And it seems likely that the golem myth might have inspired the British novelist, Mary Shelley, to create the creature Frankenstein. J.R.R. Tolkien, probably not incidentally, included a character named Golem in his *Lord of the Ring* series. There remains a Golem museum in the Jewish Sector of Prague.

THE MONSTERS FROM WITHIN

Notice in the accounting of the Philip experiment, David-Neel's tulpa monk, the Rabbi Loew's golem and Belanger's physic residue under the stairs, all appear extremely similar. All are constructs of the human mind, and except for the psychic residue, all consciously and pointedly created. None of the creatures appeared to be particularly sentient, but all possessed a will. All of them gained in strength over time, becoming something more and different from their inception; and possibly dangerous to their creators. Philip would chase latecomers into corners with the table, and the golem threatened innocent people, David-Neel's tulpa gained a sly, malevolent countenance and the psychic residue followed Amy up the stairs. Both in the tulpa and golem traditions the creatures were known to eventually go mad and run away, slipping the bonds of their creators entirely. If they didn't escape, they imminently faced destruction. Could the monsters of folklore be much the same? Bigfoot, vampires, werewolves and broom riding witches, might they have begun in the human mind, brought to life via the collective, willful fears of people, in the same way that tulpas were said to be accidentally formed by superstitious, fearful villagers? If what we perceive in our minds we can make real, then perhaps we have ourselves to blame for our nightmares.

CHAPTER 7: COMMUNICATIONS FROM BEYOND DEATH

WHEN DALE CAME TO VISIT

I worked for a year as an Occupational Therapist's Assistant in the rehabilitation department of a nursing home. It was a truly unique experience working with the geriatric population.

Many of them loved to talk, and their lives were often fascinating. I met a woman who had hand-sewn the space gloves for the likes of Buzz Aldrin and Neil Armstrong, and a congenial gentleman who still bore shrapnel in his leg from fighting in World War II. And then there was Dale....

Dale was charismatic and gregarious. He was a wonderful story teller and had a sense humor that often had me roaring with laughter. Then again, he also had a stubborn streak that defied understanding, and even at the age of 81 he expected to be the man in charge. Most of all he had that gift that so few people possess, of making you feel like there was no one in the world with whom he would rather be. He was also solidly and unapologetically a devoted old lecher who flirted with every female of the species he ever came across. He was good with women, he liked and understood them.

Dale's other great passion was cars. His entire life had revolved around these wonderful machines, and many of his stories were about the vehicles he loved. Dale had been a highly respected mechanic, and for decades he'd built and serviced his own race cars. He and his son had both driven them, but when he realized he didn't have the aptitude as a race car driver, he'd hired one and financed the racing team.

He'd had two very eventful marriages. His second wife had been twenty years his junior and only a few months older than his eldest son, a fact that caused some consternation in the family.

I worked with Dale for a number of weeks, during which time we became very close. When the day came that he was discharged from therapy, I found that I missed our conversations. When lunch time came I began taking my peanut butter sandwich down the hall to Dale's room. Our friendship survived until his death. I'd moved on to a different job by that time, but I still visited him when I could, dropping by on a Friday afternoon. Then one sad Friday I went to his room to find someone else in his bed and his belongings gone. I asked at the desk, though I feared the answer. He'd passed away earlier in the week.

I had been a paranormal investigator when I knew him, and I often invited him to visit me after he passed, to let me know he was still around. When strange things started occurring around the house, therefore, it wasn't a complete surprise.

It was late one night, with my husband asleep beside me when I heard a distinctly loud, breathy voice from the bathroom exclaim, "Yes!" I remember it was so distinct that I lifted my head off the pillow and asked if there was anyone there. I got no reply.

One Saturday morning, shortly after I heard a large bang coming again from the master bathroom. I thought something had fallen, but I never found the source of the bang.

My father had adopted a hobby of repairing old clocks, the wind up kind, after he retired. His collection of old clocks grew so large that he gave a few of them to me. Two of his mantel clocks I carefully keep wound and running all the time. One afternoon I decided to wind the clocks only to find both of them were set *an hour ahead*. If you've dealt with old clocks you know that they have a way of running behind, sometimes profoundly behind. The evidence that something odd was going on was starting to mount. Then one evening my husband and I were lying in bed together. I was reading a book and he was on his laptop. We were both very much awake. My husband suddenly asked me, "did you just move your feet?"

"No," I replied wondering why he asked. "I've just been lying here quietly." I went back to reading.

A couple of minutes later he again asked, "Did you just move your feet?"

"No," I again replied. "Why do you ask?"

"Because it felt like someone just sat down on the edge of the bed right by my feet."

"That's weird," I said. "But no, I haven't moved." I went back to reading.

Suddenly my husband jumped out of bed and walked very quickly into the master bathroom. The leap out of bed was so abrupt and out of character I immediately asked, "What are you doing? What's wrong?"

With a look of utter confusion on his face he replied, "It just felt like something pinched my leg!" My husband is not the kind to be easily rattled, and he doesn't count every odd occurrence as being something supernatural, so when he reports being pinched by an unknown quantity I tend to believe him.

Odd things had started to occur so regularly that I started keeping a log of the events, as I suggest my clients do. Then one Saturday I held a meeting for the paranormal group at my house. We had a couple of new members and a lot of new equipment to learn and I wanted us to do a trial run before our first official investigation. A couple of the ladies were trialing their new Mel meters which is an instrument for measuring electromagnetic fields and ambient temperature. Another member and I were setting up and trialing the new surveillance camera system. Trying to figure out the system's interface was taking all of my concentration. So I wasn't paying close attention to the ladies as they wandered about with the meters. At one point they asked if they could go out in my overstuffed garage. They'd gotten a strange EMF spike in my kitchen that appeared to have disappeared out the wall. Reluctantly I told them they could go out in the garage, wondering what could possibly be of interest in my garage. They came back in a few minutes later, very excited. They'd gotten a 7 point spike in the garage. I really didn't think much of it, concentrating still on the computer interface of the DVR. We finally got the cameras up and operating and we all sat down with our meters and voice recorders and did a short dress rehearsal of an EVP session – a type of question and answer session. We were packing up when one of the team members came up to me with a question. She asked me what I thought of mastiffs.

"Mastiffs? They're a big dog. That's about all I know. Why?" I asked rather stymied.

"That's the picture I get in my head. He looks kind of like a mastiff."

"Who?" I asked, now thoroughly bewildered.

"The man who I see. Remember I said we'd gotten those EMF spikes. I think it's the man that looks kind of like a mastiff." And then it dawned on me. Dale had been of Germanic background and build, with a thick head of blond hair. Having been six feet plus, he might have given the impression of a large beast. I went to my office desk and fished out a picture I had of him. I showed Maya the photo. She looked at it for a while, and then said, "Yes, I think that's him, but he's younger now. He's more like fifty years old. Oh, and he's happy we're talking about him now. He's happy you know he's here."

A few nights later I told Dale that he didn't have to stick around on my account. It was then that I thought I felt a brush on my hand. After "our talk" the activity became less frequent and less intense, eventually ceasing altogether. Dale had moved on.

AFTER DEATH COMMUNICATIONS; A TEA PARTY FOR TWO

Most paranormal researchers begin their studies because they're looking for some type of assurance of the soul's survival after bodily death. And thus far in looking at haunted houses – an imprint of a person's personality, or poltergeists – psychokinetic outbursts by a human agent - there hasn't been much to indicate the survivalist theory. It was this that bewildered the psychical researchers during the spiritualist movement as well. Medium controls appeared to be a creation of the mind of the medium, and physical phenomenon that occurred at séances, when it wasn't trickery, could be postulated as being psychokinesis again.

It was at my father's funeral, he of the antique clocks, that a long-time friend gave me what turned out to be a truly touching present, a used, somewhat dog-eared book about After Death Communication (ADC) experiences. Having been in the paranormal field for a couple of years, I've greedily read and spoken to anyone I could that might feed me information about the paranormal. But this book about After Death Communications - or ADC's - was truly different from the paranormal researcher's point of view, because it wasn't written from a paranormal investigator's point of view.

I can admit that I had never heard the term ADC used before in the paranormal field. I was rather astounded therefore to find that this is a field of study being undertaken, not by parapsychologists but a rogue few in the medical and grief counseling fields.

The Society for Psychical Research, in the 1880's, dedicated quite a bit of time to studying what are often labeled Crisis Apparitions. Edward Gurney wrote the majority of the classic two-volume set entitled *Phantasms of the Living* on the topic (**35**). F.W.H. Myers author of another classic, *Human Personality and its Survival of Bodily Death*, felt that Crisis Apparitions, apparitions of the deceased that occurred twelve hours before or after bodily death, were the release of the human consciousness and did not necessarily indicate the survival of the soul after death (**79**).

Other of his associates thought that telepathy was involved, the living being messaged telepathically by the dying with the crisis providing the energy. But what about an experience among the living and the dead that occur weeks, months or sometimes years after death? These are much harder to explain as a telepathic message floating around in the ether. Skeptics would quite obviously explain them as constructs of over-active imaginations or a hallucination brought about by grief. There are reported occurrences, however, where ADC's have been witnessed or experienced by more than one person at the same time, making fabrication or imagination harder to explain.

While still a relatively new field of study, there is a growing amount of research in the area, albeit anecdotal, which encompasses Crisis Apparitions, but also experiences that occur quite some time after death - sometimes several years after death.

The official definition of after death communications is quite specific. ADC's are communications we have with a loved one, be they friend or family member. The messages originate *without the use of a psychic medium, rituals, therapists or other devices.* The communications are spontaneous and unique. The experiences range from strong evidence such as the sighting of a full body apparition to rather weaker evidence of interpreting a "sign."

What makes this subject significant is the great number of people who claim to have had an experience. A survey conducted by Tilburg University (Netherlands) asked respondents to anonymously answer the question as to whether they felt they had ever had contact with someone deceased. The survey reported that 25% of Europeans answered yes (125 million) as did 30% of American respondents (100 million). Spouses of deceased partners came in roughly at 50% yes responses, and parents who had lost a child reported a 75% yes response (74). It would seem to suggest that the likelihood of having an ADC increased the stronger the bond with the deceased (my assessment). Another study suggests that 42% of Americans had reported having an ADC, while 67% of widows responded positively to the question (56).

Bill and Judy Guggenheim conducted the first in-depth research on ADC's reporting their findings in the 1988 book *Hello from Heaven*! (59) The book documented 353 firsthand accounts of ADC's; selected from some two-thousand interviews and 3,300 first-hand accounts the couple had collected. Respondents ranged in age from children to the elderly (ages 8-92) and represented a wide cross section of social, educational, socioeconomic and religious backgrounds. According to the Guggenheim's, "after-death communications appear to be the most common form of spiritual experiences that people have (58)." I can contest to this. Of all the accounts I have received in my paranormal researches, ADC experiences are by far the most frequent.

CATEGORIES OF ADC'S

After Death Communications are usually arranged in distinct categories. I have attempted to arrange them from what I consider to be weakest to strongest (**58, 56, 59, 88, 89, 90**).

Symbolic ADC's: Certainly the most frustrating of all ADC's as they have the least validation. They often appear coincidental. One might find a medal or coin that was significant to the deceased, or hear a song on the radio that was of significance in some way. The grieving party may have asked for a sign, which appears to come – belatedly. Experiences involving symbols are a common occurrence and they often involve things occurring in nature, although they may not seem to fit with the normal. For example, my father was in love with blue birds. He did research on blue bird houses and had them erected on his property as well as mine. Only blue birds never came to roost. Usually he was trying to shoo out the wrens that inevitably took up roost in the houses. The year after he died we had a blue bird family move in and raise a nest of blue birds. It was the one and only time blue birds ever nested in our birdhouse successfully.

On another occasion, I brought home a clock from my parent's home. I had bought my father the clock, therefore it had significance to both of us. It had the most beautiful chime, which was the reason I had bought it for him, as a gift. Sadly, when I brought it home it no longer worked. One night my husband wound it up, and it worked without hiccup for a couple of hours, and then never worked again.

Lucid Dreams: These dreams occur when you are asleep. The SPR discounted any evidence reported when a respondent was asleep, despite the fact that in sleep we may in the best state to collect telepathic communications. We are at that time in the least likely state to collect and analyze data effectively. Lucid dreams are, however far more intense, colorful and more vivid than an ordinary dream, which tends to set them apart. They may involve one or two-way communication.

Upon waking these dreams are still fresh in the person's mind. The dreamer can usually remember what the deceased was wearing, where they were at, and what was said. The dream state makes a natural environment for the ADC experience, speculating that in sleep a dreamer is more conducive to psi phenomenon (ESP) as the mind is being directed by the unconscious.

I had my own lucid dream a couple of months after my father died. We were a close family and the separation for all of us was excruciating. It had been a particularly grim day, but no grimmer than others I had had in the recent past. I dreamt that night of my father, but it was vivid. If I'd dreamt of my father since his death I have no recollection. But this dream was clear as if we were two people sitting in a room together. My father was showing me his new stereo system in the dream. My father had custom built stereos and television systems as a career, so it was just like him to be showing off a new system. And the fact that I got the receiver stuck on the Cubs game fit as well. Dad had been an avid baseball fan, though I personally have no interest in the sport. I woke up feeling better than I had in many months...euphoric even...as if Dad had actually come for a visit.

Visits during the Alpha State: These might also be called hypnogogic or hippocampi hallucinations, they occur in a relaxed state, but not while the person is sleeping. Meditating and prayer can also put a person in an alpha state, when arguably a person is far more open to having a telepathic experience. Suddenly you open your eyes, and your loved is standing there. However, you have a tough time believing what you're seeing because you may or may not be awake.

Out-Of-Body experience (OBE) these experiences can happen while a person is asleep or in a deep meditative state. As always anything that happens while asleep or in a near sleep state becomes suspect. These experiences are often highly dramatic, as the person seems to leave their physical body and travel to visit a loved on. One can seem to go to a nearby locale, or somewhere on the earthly plane or even seem to ascend to a place outside the physical universe – like heaven. Heavenly visitations often are reported as beautiful, serene locales filled with beautiful flowers, birds, butterflies, sparkling waterways and stately trees; places filled with radiant light, vibrant colors and exuding emotions of joy and love. OBE travel happens at the speed of thought, and are similar to the experiences of those having a Near-Death experience (NDE). It should be noted that people in perfectly good health have also reported having an NDE type of experience.

Sensing a Presence: the most often reported phenomenon is often the most discounted. It is the feeling that your loved one is near, a feeling that they are watching over your shoulder, though she/he can't be seen or heard. You just feel them there. My husband, the stoic one reported having just such an experience. He was going through a very tough episode in his life. His father was deathly ill and my husband was trying to work and go to college all at once. When day when he was feeling particularly low he reports that he suddenly felt the presence of his deceased sister in the room with him.

Olfactory Stimuli: Olfactory experiences, where people report smelling an odor distinct to the deceased are also reported. Our sense of smell is actually based in our reptilian brain stems, the most ancient and primitive portion of our brains. The sense of smell evokes instant and deep-seated emotions, often under the radar of our conscious minds. Take the painter I met in Beaufort, South Carolina who told me the story about her ADC that occurred to her when she was alone. Sitting in a chair in her living room suddenly she began to smell her Grandmother's perfume. Her grandmother had of course been dead for quite a few years at the time, but she was distinctly smelling her Grandmother's scent in the room. The ordeal unnerved the artist so much that she literally fled the house, though she admitted that Grandmother had probably only been paying a visit. The woman also told me that her sister had reported a similar experience where she too had smelled the deceased's perfume. Sometimes more than one person will smell the distinct odor at the same time, which of course lends credence to the episode.

The Oogey Boogey Effect: Often reported are a wide variety of physical phenomenon. Lights may blink on and off. Televisions, radios, stereos and electronic toys may malfunction unaccountably. Objects of significance such as photographs or portraits may be moved, turned over or fall off the wall. Messages may be left on computers, answering machines or other electronic devices. Basically, the phenomenon will take on the characteristics of a normal, intelligent haunt. My hearing the large thump in the bathroom or having my antique clocks suddenly jump ahead one hour unaccountably might be examples.

Hearing a Voice: People often hear a clear, audible voice, while others report a message received telepathically. The messages are often short and direct. Still others report the ability to have an entire conversation with their departed loved ones telepathically. My mother told me rather dramatically one day on the phone of a frightening experience she had had. She was in her bed one night when she distinctly heard my father call her name from the living room. Being not fully awake she patted the bed and told him to come lay down. Then she realized… he was dead. I would further add that sometimes what is experienced is more of a strange buzzing in the ear as if the person speaking is not sharing the same frequency. I've had this phenomenon occur to me once, and have also had this phenomenon reported to me by others. The story of Leonora Piper also suggests this phenomenon, when as a child Leonora first hears the long, sibilant S sound in her ear, which eventually becomes a message from her departed aunt, which incidentally happened at the moment of the aunt's death.

Feeling a Touch: Those who have a very physical bond with a departed person may experience a touch of some type that is distinctly recognizable to the deceased. One might feel simply a slight touch on the hand, such as I described earlier. Other forms of tactile messages might include stroking of the hair, a pat, a tap on the shoulder, a kiss or even a hug.

Partial Appearances. The Guggenheim's divided the category of visual stimuli into partial and full apparitions. An ADC may involve a wide range even within the partial visual category, from a semi-opaque mist, to simply an outline of a form, or a colored light. They may simply appear as body parts, i.e. just the head and shoulders appearing, or just legs running down the stairs. Some may be transparent, others translucent, while others are completely solid. Many visual ADC's occur in the bedroom, with the loved one being seen at the foot of the bed.

Full Appearances: While it may be mystifying some people have reported seeing and touching their loved ones. They see their entire body, and they feel solid when touched. In one account I read the deceased, upon request, actually picked up a pen and wrote out a message, before disappearing. The message remained behind. Usually the deceased are expressing love, happiness, gratitude or well-being. If they'd been injured in life, they appear whole and healthy. And it's not uncommon for those who died very old to appear younger. They usually choose that period of their lives when they were at their prime – such as Dale appearing to be much younger than he had been in the photograph. They may or may not try to communicate with you verbally. Mostly they appear to demonstrate to you that they are fine, and you needn't be concerned for them.

A former student recalled the morning after her father's funeral, waking up on the couch in the family room and seeing her dad making up the fire - just as he had always done. She didn't think much of it, until she recalled that her father was dead.

Odd Visions: Some people report seeing a two-dimensional picture of your loved one, or a picture that appears like a hologram right out of Star Wars. They liken the experience to seeing a 35mm slide suspended in the air. The colors of the image are usually vibrant.

The voice may sound clear but far away. Suddenly, if you are awake, the line will seem to go dead unaccountably, without the sound of a hang up or dial tone after.

SOME FACTORS THAT INCREASE THE VALIDITY OF AN ADC

Crisis Apparition: Timing is important in verifying the validity of an ADC, especially if an experiencer has the ADC before they've heard of the deceased's sudden and unforeseen death – i.e. Gurney's crisis apparition scenario.   The contention that a person's experiences an ADC because of a grief-induced hallucination would not be an arguable in this case, as the experiencer would not be grieving.

ADC's Occurring Years after Death: Some people experience an ADC years or even decades after death. It is unlikely that an ADC of this distance would be caused by active grieving or a telepathic message sent by the dying at the moment of crisis... The research suggests that ADC's long after death usually carry a much more important message.

Evidential ADC's: Often the message of an ADC is something the experiencer had not already known, or could not have known, before the occurrence. They may be told where an heirloom is hidden, or where money has been deposited. Sometimes important items are revealed to them that they hadn't known existed. This type of ADC helps raise the validity of the event.

Important Message ADC: Sometimes the life or property of an experiencer is saved during an ADC. One woman reported hearing her deceased husband's voice one night calling her over and over from the family room. Upon going to the family room she found smoke, and realized that she had a chimney fire. She contends she got out of the house safely only with her husband's help.

Messages have included otherwise undiagnosed medical issues, emergencies, potential automobile, aircraft, industrial, fire and leisure accidents, fires, warnings about children and adults who may be in trouble. Obviously these messages, when proven correct prior to the event are provide compelling evidentiary proof that something paranormal is afoot.

This category includes people who received protection from potential automobile and aircraft accidents, medical emergencies, criminal activities, industrial accidents, a building fire, and undiagnosed health problems of children and adults. These accounts provide very compelling evidence that our deceased loved ones are indeed watching over us and can and do intervene when they are able to do so.

Preventing suicide: These are accounts by people whose suicide was averted by a message from a loved one. Research further indicates that messages received during suicide attempts are often from family members who had also committed suicide, warning the person not to make the same mistake.

Bill a troubled youth was doing poorly at school and strung out on drugs. At one point he decided to commit suicide. At the time he was living with his mother and grandfather. Bill's grandmother had died a couple of years earlier. On the day Bill decided to end his own life he reports that he went down in his grandparent's basement where he intended to hang himself from a rafter. He started to string up the rope, when he looked at the basement steps where he saw his grandmother motioning to him. Using hand gestures, Bill didn't report actually hearing her say anything to him, she indicated that he shouldn't do this. He took the rope down.

The story of Bill, a long-time friend of mine, is just one example. Incidentally, sixty percent of messages from beyond are from those who had committed suicide themselves (58).

Multiple Witness ADC's: Regarding validation having two or more people witness and confirm their experiences of a communication is certainly more powerful than testimony by one person alone. Sometimes witnesses are not in the same locale but have the same experience, which they confirm during a later conversation. Remember the painter from South Carolina who smelled her grandmother's perfume, and then found out later her sister had experienced the same phenomenon.

THE WHY OF ADC'S

Many people feel a profound happiness from having an ADC, and it helps to shorten the grieving period. It is both an affirmation that the soul survives death, and that their loved one is ok. People who are terminally ill often find peace in the process of dying, where before there was fear. Many use the ADC to continue on a sort a relationship with the departed, albeit a mostly one-sided relationship.

Yet others are startled and or scared after having an ADC. For my mother it made the grieving process worse, in some ways. Hearing her husband's voice made her miss him all the more. She didn't really believe she'd had a communication from beyond, just imagined it. Years after experiencing her ADC, while helping me edit this book she still said she was uncomfortable even speaking of the event. Many with a deeply religious background will resist believing in ADC's, as it's not part of their religion's doctrine. Some conservative church leaders even contend that ADC's are demonic or evil in nature. Critics and skeptics will contend that ADC's are self-induced delusions or hallucinations, brought on by grief.

Whether you believe you've had an ADC or just imagined it, the power of the ADC is that it can be comforting. Did I really think my father had returned from the grave to visit me in my dreams? I don't know, although the dream was unlike anything I've had before or since. After having the dream I did feel happier than I had in a long time. Did it make our separation easier to bear? Unequivocally, yes. Whether it was a construct of my unconscious or an actual visit from my father, the pain was lessened by the experience, and therein lies the power of the ADC.

THE WHEN OF ADC'S

The why of ADC is variable. Some seem to occur to help with the grieving process, and occur fairly soon after death. According to other accounts, sometimes they seem to happen a year, five years, ten years or more after death. Sometimes they seem designed to appease the desires of the departed, like Grandma stopping by to see the new baby, born after she passed. Still others happen during a crisis moment in the life of the living, where the departed makes an appearance in order to be of assistance - as in the story below. In other words the experiences, their time table and the messages behind them are extremely unpredictable and individual. These experiences are different from the traditional haunting in the fact that they occur once or perhaps a couple of times, but then stop.

Recalling the stories I had collected over the years from family, friends and acquaintances I started to realize that, actually the vast majority of "ghost stories" I had gathered were actually ADC's. They're simple and rather homespun in the telling, and I'm guessing most families have their own share of strange stories. It's the time my Dad knew the phone call was to tell us that Grandmother had died. Or the time my husband reports feeling very down and just knowing suddenly that his departed sister was with him. They are what they are, stories, unverifiable for the most part., intriguing but not reliable. Indeed, many, if not most, are based merely on gut feelings.

PARANORMAL RESEARCH PERSPECTIVE

From a researcher's perspective ADC's don't get much shrift. There's enough difficulty for us investigating a property with a recorded history of paranormal activity. Activity doesn't happen on cue, making a ghost hunter's job difficult to begin with. And as I've said in the past, we can't grow a ghost in a test tube, and then grow another thousand just like it. That's what the scientific community demands of scientific research and what paranormal researchers just can't deliver. If we want to be taken even somewhat seriously no self-respecting investigator is going to take your word that you saw a butterfly and just knew your mother had sent it. That's not to say that you saw a butterfly and that your mother sent it. It's just to say that no paranormal researcher is going to accept that as valid survival evidence.

If you're seeking some type of validation for an ADC I have a few suggestions. First, after you experience something unusual write it down as quickly as possible. We think our memories are sharp but they're not, and details will get blurred almost immediately in your mind. If you're experiencing repeated phenomena, as in the story of Dale, then again keep some type of log system, where all such phenomena is recorded in one place. If multiple people are experiencing it, write those experiences down as well. Recall the initial experience Leonora Piper had as a child. Her mother had the amazing foresight to write the experience down with the date and time of the experience, only to find out later that the aunt in question had actually died at that particular instance.

Experiences that happen when you're sleeping, such as my lucid dream, will be taken less seriously than an event that happens while awake. Thus our experience with the dark figure at the foot of the bed would hold less credence than my husband's experience of getting pinched. It is true that psi researchers believe that while asleep we are more open to communicating telepathically than say in the middle of a hectic work day. However, from a credence standpoint something that happened at noon while one was fully awake will hold far more validation than something that happened at midnight when you were roused from sleep.

If you receive a message during your ADC again record the message as quickly as possible and accurately as you can. If it eventually proves true you will have the written proof that you got word of the event before it happened.

Multiple witnesses will always make for better evidence. If you find that another witness has had the same experience as you, quickly pause. Have both parties write down or somehow record their impressions, and then compare the impressions. The more alike the impressions are, independently recorded, will raise the credibility of the experience.

Beyond that you need to decide personally if you'll accept that your loved one returned with a message, or whether you had some type of hallucination brought on by grief or something that occurred that day that started you thinking about the deceased. They're personal experiences. If you do wish to discuss your ADC, instead of contacting the local paranormal group in your area it may make sense to contact AD researchers instead. The Guggenheim's maintain a website with a forum where ADC's can be reported and discussed.
Check out http://www.after-death.com/Pages/MessageBoard/ to join the discussion.

NEAR DEATH EXPERIENCES

Across thousands of years and every culture ancient or modern, these strange experiences have been reported. The ancient cultures described such an event as a vision, an enlightenment quest, a mystical experience or a visit to the underworld. The vocabulary they used would fit their cultural views, but the experiences would contain similar criteria. Near-death experiences have been described by Buddhists, Christians, agnostics, men, women and children, and again the words with which they describe it and the interpretation they took away from it are seen through their cultural and religious lenses, while the experiences they describe are eerily similar.

Many of the modern advancements in cardiac care began in the 1960's when defibrillation, heart massage and the administering of oxygen were found to be effective methods of revival for those who had suffered a heart attack. The result was that a far greater number of people were being successfully resuscitated, even after heart and brain function had ceased. Medical professionals began hearing stories from patients (slowly at first) about having experiences during cardiac arrest that indicated a consciousness that defied rational explanation. The number of reports was minimal at first, as most people who had such an experience kept it to themselves. Many who had an NDE staunchly refused to share their experiences with their doctor or other medical personnel for fear of being thought irrational?

When a medical student, George Ritchie had suffered double pneumonia in 1943. He suffered a bout of extreme fever and a tightness in the chest, and at one point ceased breathing. His heart stopped, and the attending doctor pronounced him dead. A male nurse in attendance became distraught and convinced the doctor to administer a shot of adrenaline into the heart, it wasn't a normal procedure at the time. It worked, and after nine minutes when Ritchie had been clinically dead he was revived. During that nine minutes Ritchie had experienced an NDE. After graduating as a psychiatrist Ritchie wrote a book entitled *Return from Tomorrow* about his experiences and began lecturing to medical students. Raymond Moody was one such student. Inspired by Ritchie's experiences, Moody began studying the phenomenon, and in 1975 wrote his global best-seller *Life After Life* in which he coined the phrase near-death experience.

In the way of things, Moody's book inspired a courageous few in the medical profession to begin questioning the phenomenon. That is not to say that the initial number of cases was large. Researchers quickly found that people were often reluctant to speak of their experiences. Not only were they highly personal, but those who were bold enough to speak of NDE's were usually ignored, their stories dismissed as the words of someone incapacitated and probably hallucinating. And at the time very few people had ever heard of a near-death experience. Eventually a few fairly comprehensive NDE studies were conducted, and the field began to gain some traction, When researchers began systematically soliciting responses from people who had been successfully resuscitated they found that NDE's were both more prevalent than they believed and shared strikingly similar characteristics. In the United States 4.2% of the population reports having had an NDE.

A near-death experience is a profound, usually life-changing, psychological or mystical event that occurs to someone who is near death, or feels themselves in life threatening danger, or extreme emotional crises. Not everyone in these situations experiences such a vision, or altered consciousness experience. And not everyone that experiences an NDE immediately recalls it or recognizes what they experienced. There are a number of similar elements which will be described below. The more of these elements a person reports experiencing the deeper and more profound the NDE is thought to be. While most NDE's are reported as profoundly peaceful and loving, some few are described as terrifying or dark in nature. Nearly all report an altered life view and changes made in their lives after an NDE. Not all changes will be immediate, some take years to accomplish. There is some indication that even when an NDE is positive, it takes time to come to grips with it emotionally and psychologically. A life-changing experience exerts a burden on the individual to find a way to mesh it with ordinary life. Thus many who experience NDE's are reluctant to speak about it, first for fear of being ridiculed, but second because they feel overwhelmed with the import of the message and what it means for their lives. Some even experience bouts of depression afterwards.

COMMON FACTORS OF THE NDE

Psychiatrist Raymond Moody described twelve different elements to an NDE experience in his book *Life After Life*, noting that most people did not experience all twelve. A rating system was developed to determine how in-depth a person's experience had been. Those who only reported one or two of the twelve are not classified as having had a true NDE, although even these individuals often report a significant life change after the experience. The greater the number of the twelve elements a person experienced the greater the depth of the NDE is thought to have been. Each NDE is extremely unique to the viewer, yet they to tend to run as a coherent sequence of events, with these twelve elements reported consistently in some order or another 60, 87, 88 44).

MOODY'S TWELVE COMMON ELEMENTS OF AN NDE

The ineffability of the Experience – in other words often expressed is the frustration that words are completely incapable of describing the event. For many the unmeasurable love and joy they felt pale to that of the earthly plane. Still others may feel that what they experienced is sacred and thus unutterable.

A feeling of peace and calm. The extreme pain and terror is gone of a catastrophic accident or medical emergency is passed. They report feeling whole, healthy, pain free and euphoric; peaceful after the intense trauma.

Realizing they are dead: It is very unsettling to hear someone pronounce you dead, just at the moment when you're feeling euphoric and whole again. Sometimes viewers report hearing a noise following this pronouncement, often described as a buzzing, whistling, loud click or murmuring sounds. Again we have the description of a buzzing sound such as Leonora Piper described, and what many people report when having an ADC, what I experienced as well one evening after an investigation when it appeared that something had followed me home. It's as if different planes of existence are on a slightly different audio frequency that takes some tuning in, like the tuning of a radio.

Out-of-Body Experience (OBE) Very often the first visible perception is of floating out of one's body, or floating above and looking down on one's unresponsive body. Often experiencers will report having seen and heard medical personnel trying to resuscitate them, and recount those experiences with unbelievable accuracy. In one case, after

being found unresponsive in a park, and having been in a coma after a week, a patient recognized the nurse who had been attending his resuscitation. He told her what had been happening in the emergency room during the critical moments of his revival and told her where, in the rush of events, she had placed his dentures. She later verified the events. Indeed in a review of 93 OBE cases, 92% of responders were found to have described the events accurately, 10% with some error, and only one patient's account was found completely erroneous, which rules out the probability of hallucination or delusion (74).

Despite leaving the body, viewers are often relieved that they still have a consciousness, a sense of identity, and the functioning use of their senses. Many report a heightened sense such as 360-degree vision. Those who were deaf can often hear, those who were blind report being able to see. They cannot, however, communicate with others in the room, and they may find that they can now move through walls and closed doors, and that the laws of physics no longer appear to apply. Sometimes experiencers report moving somewhere away, simultaneously, from the bodies to other places. Travel is at the speed of thought.

Through the Rabbit Hole: And then suddenly people report that they are literally sucked into a dark space. A few describe getting stuck as if in a very confining black tunnel, of which they need to crawl through. Others report moving rapidly through extreme darkness, or a dark funnel, with an indescribable light at the end. It usually starts as a pinprick of light at the end of the tunnel which grows as the person approaches. Sometimes the tunnel is described as multi-colored, sometimes as spiraling. Sometimes they are alone in the tunnel, other times they report seeing or merely sensing other beings in the tunnel with them. Sometimes there is even an accompaniment of music reported. As they get closer they often describe a sense of acceleration. Sometimes a wind or feeling a wind whistle by is described.

At the end of the tunnel...A brilliant illuminance is often described, to which the person travels or ascends.

Being on a Different Plane of Existence: People report feeling like they are in a different world. A sense of being on a different plane of existence such as a foreign landscape, or a spiritual realm. Through this celestial illumination are often spotted people, animals, plants, a lush outdoor landscape and sometimes whole cities or beautiful buildings. Beautiful exotic flowers and lovely music are often described.

Communing with the Dead: Seeing and sometimes speaking to or communicating with loved ones, or sacred figures such as a saint or Jesus, or meeting unrecognizable beings with whom communication appears to be telepathic are reported. These beings may be loving, consoling or terrifying. Often a conversation can ensue, sometimes messages or information are given. People who had died when they were very old and infirm may appear much younger than they were when passing. Those who died as children may appear grown to adulthood.

Panoramic Story of Me: Some report a life review sometimes from birth forward to death, sometimes in reverse. Life reviews are described as panoramic with the person involved in bright Technicolor representation. They often involve an assessment of a life, what was learned, what accomplished. Other people or beings may take part in the judgement process or offer suggestions. Sometimes the whole life is shared, others see only segments of the whole. Others feel a flood of knowledge both about life, or the nature of the universe. Many start to understand that the smallest gesture or word can have lasting implications. Everyone and everything is seen as interconnected. A heightened sense of cognition and observations are often reported; thoughts and impressions occurring at an extremely rapid rate as if the person's mind is a recipient of information sent.

The Preview: Sometimes those that get this far in an NDE will be given a glimpse of what is ahead. Because time is nonexistent in this plane and certainly nonlinear, they may get to see future events as if happening now. Certainly, this raises issues about the impression of free will and choice. In a dimension where time is not relevant, can a person be held responsible for deeds they have not yet committed? Is the story of us already written, and we but actors on the stage?

The Property Line: Many report getting a sense of a border, one that should not be crossed, lest return not be an option. People have reported such elements as a wall, a river, a valley, a bridge or a gate, in other words either a natural divide or an architectural divide. At the border may be relatives or enlightened beings which either direct or suggest the person not cross the divide. It becomes fairly evident intuitively that the person has to make the choice, and that the choice is irreversible. Death results in the body if the border is crossed.

The Man behind the Curtain: Some people report being drawn to, enveloped by and conversing with the brilliant (but not blinding) light, which knows their deepest thoughts before they've thought them, and communicates with them telepathically, emanating immense joy and unconditional and boundless love. Those of religious backgrounds often conclude they have come in contact with the Supreme Being or an angel. Others report seeing people in the light of religious significance such as speaking with Jesus. Those without religious leanings have described the light as simply being a being made of light. Often the light-being asks them a question. Respondents phrase the question differently but agree that it amounts to the same question, "Was the life you lead worth it, knowing what you know now?" In other words knowing now what lies beyond life would you have lived your life differently? Respondents report that the question is asked in a Socratic manner without reproach, as if the being truly just wants to know.

Return to the Body: Sadly, return to the body is usually quite abrupt and traumatic. Some people speak of being pushed back into their bodies via the head, others describe being sucked back through the tunnel forcibly. After an idyllic interlude being foisted back in an ill or damaged body, experiencing pain and trauma once more is extremely upsetting. There is in many cases a reluctance to return to the body, to the pain and slow recovery process that will be necessary. They may be made to understand that their job on earth is not yet finished, or they must complete a task before returning. Often there is a horrifying feeling of loss once they are revived. They may experience vast depression or anger at being back in their broken bodies. Often medical personnel to whom they try to speak of their experiences will be less than supportive, causing them to feel a sense of isolation.

Many of the same elements are reported in both positive and negative NDE's, but with different emotional tones.

It should be stressed that people have reported NDE's that were at the time of the clinically dead and/or without brain function. (That is not a necessary criterion however, as people who are physically healthy but in extreme crisis or danger have been known to experience NDE's as well.) This is what has astounded the medical researchers the most. How could someone without brain function be revived and recount accurately what was going on in the emergency room? How could someone in that state also recount a fantastical journey so similar to what others have reported?

Certainly, skepticism plays a role in the researcher's analysis, and they have compared the stories to the effects of drugs, to hallucinations and delusions, and none of these states are able to produce any or all of the same effects. People having a hallucination, for instance, rarely recall their experiences with lucidity (**60, 87, 88 44**).

CHANGES DUE TO AN NDE

Even NDE's not categorized as deep often lead to profound changes for those who experience them. Experiencers no longer ask profound questions such as is there life after death, or is there a God? They report that they now know, because they've seen it, that there is a survival of consciousness after death, and that profound love and joy await them beyond the boundary. They become more focused on the big picture versus the mundane. They develop a sense of self that is not dependent on how others perceive them, but how they perceive themselves. Often they become more self-confidant and adventurous. But these changes often take years to develop, as initially they often feel isolated from those who have not had a similar experience. Studies of long term effects of NDE'rs shows that there is usually an increased spiritualism that is reported, and that those who have had these experiences come to value family and friends more, and monetary success and career less. They now know what is of value in their lives. They often develop a desire for knowledge, exploring different world philosophies and quantum physics.

The majority of experiencers (somewhere between 84-92% of study responders) report developing a heightened intuitive ability. They find themselves able to read people, and develop empathy to other people's problems. Many report remarkable psi abilities afterward that range from being able to read people's minds to diagnosing disease, to seeing auras. It is frightening or at the least unsettling to suddenly have these abilities, and many NDE'rs will start to avoid public places to avoid getting deluged with information.

OUT-OF-BODY EXPERIENCES

The Out-of-Body Experience (OBE) or astral projection as sometimes called, has already been discussed briefly along with NDE's, as being the most often first experience reported during an NDE. However, a person can experience an OBE alone, sometimes accidentally, and sometimes consciously. There are even websites that teach people how to initiate an OBE, and what to expect once they have left their bodies. The fact that 5 out of 100 people, or possibly as many as 35 out of 100 people report experiencing an OBE sometime in their life has prompted researchers in psychology and parapsychology to study the phenomenon more closely. OBE's occur most often in people 15 to 35 years of age, although not all researchers agree that age is a criterion. Drug use such as smoking marijuana, or practicing meditation appear to increase the incidence of OBE, which may explain the younger ages reported. For the most part socioeconomic status, age, education, birth order, gender and religious background do not appear to have any correlation to OBE. Anyone can experience an OBE regardless of their background. Most often they occur only once, and not by initiation, although having one OBE may preclude having multiple such experiences.

The experiences themselves are very vivid and often profoundly life changing. People report seeing their bodies from across the room, or merely finding themselves outside their body in another place. A feeling of physical paralysis may preclude the event. Some perceive their astral selves as a cloud or a globe of light. More frequent is not to perceive a second body at all. It's rare to perceive yourself in body, though some do, clothes and all. Less than 5% of viewers report seeing their body connected to their soul by some type of tethering, silvery thread despite the occult literature on OBE's.

Experiencers often report odd phenomenon during OBE's. They may experience heightened sensations and energy, again as if being in a body was somehow muting our sensations. They often report hearing odd loud noises or feeling vibrations. As they leave the body they may also sense the presence of shadowy figures nearby, who appear threatening, but rarely approach. The odd sensations are almost unanimously involved with vision and hearing, rarely are the other senses involved.

Projectors may feel themselves flying very quickly through the air, moving through walls or ceilings, and finding themselves in remote places. Often these places are not a location the experiencer has ever been to before, and may only appear to parallel our world. Very often the places are more fantastical, like dreamscapes - resembling those of an NDE. Then again a person experiencing an OBE can report visiting someone very much alive. They merely have to think of the person and they are there. Sometimes the people that are visited will report having seen their visitor, conversing with them, or even touching them in some manner. The visitor may be described as translucent but still visible, much like the classic apparition. Some researchers have been able to confirm with the visited, which certainly adds credence to the report. Still others have reported a doppelganger type of experience with the astral projector appearing to be physically solid as if they're actually there in body. Physical contact can be made, conversations had. The visited person may never suspect that the visitor is there in anything but physical form.

The burning question for researchers is of course whether a person's consciousness actually leaves their body, or whether the consciousness splits and half of the consciousness leaves the body, or whether leaving the body is merely an illusion. From a researcher's perspective the prevailing theory appears to be that leaving the body is an illusion, made possible because the person is in a sensory deplete meditative state, or in an event of sensory overload. Some people are able to retain consciousness in their body while perceiving an OBE, which argues against the soul or consciousness leaving the body entirely. OBE's very often occur as someone is falling asleep as in a hypnogogic state. They can also occur spontaneously as when the person finds themselves in a stressful or life-threatening situation, which is probably why they are often lumped in with NDE's. It has been suggested that while the perception of leaving the body may be false, being in a relaxed and open state may open the person to experiencing psychic phenomenon. Perhaps what a person is experiencing is clairvoyance, and the illusion that they are leaving their body enhances the perception of seeing something from a distance.

According to one survey:

- o *44% of OBE's occur during sleep, known also as lucid dreaming though not in deep sleep. The lucid dreamer reports that the experience is very different from a typical dream in vibrancy and detail*
- o *32% occur when awake, though usually in a relaxed state*
- o *28% report being somewhere in between asleep and awake, or the hypnogogic state (80).*

o *25% of respondents reported having an OBE during some type of crisis or period of high stress, overwork, or physical emergency (61)*

What makes OBE's different from an NDE is that they can be initiated and studied under controlled circumstances in a laboratory. A subject with known psi abilities may also find themselves capable of initiating an OBE and then his/her body can be studied for physiological changes. Remote viewing experiments can be conducted with the subject being instructed to project themselves to a certain location and then report back. Remote viewing experiments were even studied by our own military for a time, although not all remote viewing experiments were preceded with an OBE.

CHAPTER 8: PHYSICS, QUANTUM PHSYICS & REALITY

Photograph used with permission.
Edward Thompson, *"Storm approaching Pripyat"* (2012).

IMPLICATIONS OF NDE STUDIES AND CONSCIOUSNESS

One of the mysteries of near death experiences remains the fact that if the brain is not functioning a person should not be capable of having lucid memories of an event. If, as mainstream science would have us believe, consciousness is centered in the brain, and is a function of firing neurons, when those same neurons cease firing all consciousness should cease as well. So how could a person have an NDE or any memory of a catastrophic event if their brain is not functioning?

If the brain stops but consciousness continues then the implication is that consciousness is independent of the brain. This of course is a bold assertion, and not one to sit well with the scientific community who are profoundly materialist. However, let's examine some of the science that suggests that a non-local consciousness may actually exist, and may exist in some form or another despite the death of the body, which is after all the entire point of studying all of this "weird stuff."

Recall in Chapter Four when we discussed the rare but documented case studies of transplant patients, where patients who received an organ would sometimes undergo changes in their personality that reflected those of the deceased. In some cases their choices changed. Suddenly they might start listening to different music, or eating different foods. In still other cases they would undergo more marked personality changes. The DNA that exists in every living cell cannot possibly code for every like or dislike, every personality characteristic and every memory a person possesses. The implication is that the DNA is not a receptacle for information, but a type of tuning device that reads information that exists outside the body, from a consciousness that exists in non-local space.

Near-Death experiences also suggest a non-local consciousness. When brain function ceases, people report a heightened sense of consciousness, as if the material body is somehow shielding them from a full awareness of consciousness, which they can only fully experience after they have left their body. A materialistic theory of consciousness, a theory that consciousness is merely an illusion or byproduct of our functioning neurons does not explain how conscious thought can continue even when brain function ceases. After Death Communications and crisis apparitions further suggest a consciousness that exists outside the body, thus the personality survives even when the body ceases.

But what is non-local consciousness, and what scientific studies suggest that such a thing is possible? In order to answer these questions we need to examine (briefly) some fundamental theories in physics, quantum physics and consciousness studies.

Classic Physics

Let us start with electromagnetic fields and their infinitesimal ability to store information. Electromagnetic fields are fields produced by electrically charged particles whose patterns travel in waves.

These fields possess what appears to be an infinite capacity to store and encode information. Think if you will of the seemingly infinite capacity of the internet for comparison. All the information is identifiable by their differences in wavelength. Information is encoded within interference whereby two waves overlapping create their own specific pattern.

When two waves oscillate (moving or swinging back and forth at a regular speed) at the same rate they are said to be coherent, and this coherence enables interference. Information stores within a coherent field is like a hologram (yes, think Star Wars) which is a picture that looks 3 dimensional but is only 2 dimensional. This holographic property is what allows us to retrieve information about an object as a whole from any place in the coherent field.

Definition of interference: Wave interference is the phenomenon that occurs when two waves meet while traveling along the same medium. The interference of waves causes the medium to take on a shape that results from the net effect of the two individual waves upon the particles of the medium (**76**.)

As usual a picture is worth a thousand words. If we envision two waves of water, for example colliding, this is what the net worth would yield us. If we take what we see from waves in water to include other types of waves, sound waves, light waves, we can begin to understand intuitively what happens when the two waves collide.

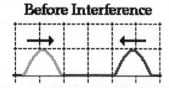

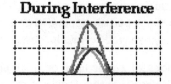

FIELDS AND WAVES

To take a concept from classical physics consider the theory of the field. A field is a difficult concept to comprehend because it cannot be seen, but its effects can be felt. Consider a gravitational field for example. Without it none of the planets would continue to orbit the sun in such neat formation. While we cannot see a field, we can see the results of the field in our physical world. A field requires no outside medium to exert remote influence, it both occupies the nonlocal space and is a type of space.

Fields ensure correlation and rhythmic cohesion throughout the system. The electromagnetic field is one of the four fundamental forces of nature (along with gravity, and strong and weak nuclear forces). Electromagnetic fields are a purely physical phenomenon whereas charged particles and only charged particles are forced to move. Electromagnetic energy is integral to all material systems in our universe from galaxies to the atom. It is the energy that fuels our bodies, brain, heart and muscles as well.

Aside from providing energy, electromagnetic fields can also store an infinite amount of dphase speeds and frequencies store information without causing interference or a disturbance throughout the field. All of our sensory information is provided by waves of one type or another. The colors we perceive, for example, are thanks to light rays, soundwaves bring to our ears the words of our loved ones. Sending and receiving, and converting different frequencies is how our wireless internet, our radio, television and mobile phones work as well.

QUANTUM PHYSICS AND PROBABILITY

In 1802 Thomas Young, physician and physicist, conducted what are now called the Double-Slit experiments, and made a groundbreaking discovery. In his simple but brilliant experiment, Young forced the light from a single source through a narrow slit in a board, and then two more narrow slits within a fraction of an inch of one another, to shine on a screen behind. Without belaboring the outcome, he discovered that light operates as either a particle or a wave. That is, depending on the experiment design, light can travel in waves, unless sufficiently hampered when it seemingly dribbles particle by particle. Light, however, never acts as both at the same time. This attribute has been labeled complementarity. Both particles and waves are thus complementary aspects of light. Einstein would later propose that other things such as atoms also shared the wave particle duality. Therefore matter is also complementary. Whether an atom was acting as a wave or a particle depended on when and how you observed them. And then sometimes they behaved in ways inconsistent with either waves or particles.

Photons are particles of either light or another type of electromagnetic radiation. Experiments with isolated photons indicates that a photon can also sometimes act as a wave, meaning that the photons are entangled with one another as they move in a wavelike pattern. Entanglement is a quantum phenomenon whereby particles that are separated by distance still possess properties that indicate they are still connected beyond time and space. They become linked together in such a way that they now operate as one, and one particle can no longer be described without mentioning its counterpart. Once entangled, two particles though separated by great distance still operate as one, thus whatever happens to one particle happens to the other instantaneously. This is known as nonlocality, and has led to the quantum physics theory of nonlocal space; a multidimensional space with uncertain and unpredictable outcomes – known as probability waves.

At the subatomic level scientists found they could not calculate accurately both the position and the momentum of a particle simultaneously. Thus they could only estimate all the possible outcomes and then observe. This function is known as the superposition of wave function, in which a wave can no longer be described as a real wave, but instead as a probability wave. German physicist, Werner Heisenberg posited the uncertainty principle, saying that observation was impossible without altering or changing an object fundamentally. If one looked for a particle in a certain location and found it there based on chance alone as often happened, did that mean, he suggested, that observation alone created physical reality – albeit at the quantum level, thus ascribing consciousness or conscious will a power over or a means to bend matter and energy to its desire?

Something that is observable is said to be in an eigenstate. In the eigenstate an object exists at a measurable time, location and quantity. Thus the baseball thrown through your front window at two pm is exists in a series of eigenstates. We can know when and where the ball came hurtling through. We can even measure the trajectory and thus nail the little bugger who threw it. But tiny particles that cannot be measured or located with any degree of certainty exist instead in a probability limbo. Until it is observed and the wave function collapsed does it become reality? This is known as the Copenhagen interpretation that holds that nature is fundamentally probabilistic and suggests that the will of the observer has a direct influence on shaping subjective reality. Because we do not know what state an object is in until we observe it, until we observe it, it exists in all states at once. (You gotta love quantum physics!)

Directly negating the positivism of the 19th century, quantum physics suggests that there can be no objective observation at all. The observer determines where and how a particle will be perceived. The very act of observing and measuring effects the results, as everything in the process is interconnected. Therefore all observations of reality are subjective because the observer's mind determines what will be perceived. Take it a step further, perhaps the very act of observation creates physical reality, suggesting that consciousness may be more fundamental to the universe than either matter or energy.

Keeping in mind that 99.9% of matter is empty space (recalling your high school chemistry again). As you probably recall, atoms are comprised of a nucleus, a tiny portion of an atom which houses the proton(s) or positively charged particles, and the neutron(s) the neutrally charged particles, and the electron(s), those tiny negatively charged particles orbit the nucleus in electron clouds. Imagine the nucleus in the center of a football field. The electron(s) could be orbiting anywhere on that football field at any one time, and everything in between is empty space. In this infinite structure less void or absolute (or true) vacuum reside quarks which are fundamental, elementary particles – the building blocks of matter, electrons, gravity and electricity. These different elements have become enmeshed with one another that as such they are now one element and no longer exist. It is a void of infinite possibilities and at absolute zero temperature the true vacuum possesses an infinite amount of, as yet, untapped energy. Physicists and Nobel Prize winners Eugene Wigner and Brian Josephson as well as Mathematician John von Neumann further suggest that within this vacuum is that which is the basis of our consciousness.

In 1920 psychologist, Karl Lashley proved that there was no single area of the brain where memories were stored, but that memories were stored throughout the brain as a whole. His associate, Dr. Karl H. Pribam further suggested that the brain worked more as a holographic receptacle. If one were to take a holographic photograph, what appears to be a three-dimensional image recorded on a two dimensional platform, an image created on a flat surface with a coherent laser light, and smash the photographic plate into a hundred pieces, each piece, in principle, would contain an exact and complete image of the original. All of the information contained in the original image would also exist on the fragments because of interference patterns. Throw a pebble into a pond and you can see first-hand what interference patterns look like. The circular waves move outward and intersect with one another, creating a pattern of weaker and stronger waves, with some waves being neutralized entirely.

Information can be stored in interference patterns in a coherent field. Where the waves are interacting, like our water waves, to form a particular pattern, the interference pattern are distributed across the physical medium of the field. Waves that cohere or form the particular pattern carry and thus store the information of the hologram. The information in a hologram is not stored in the field itself but in the physical medium of the field, thus the entire image can be retrieved from even a small portion of the original. I only hope that is a coherent explanation!

Unlike the field described in classical physics, in quantum physics non-local connections can be made instantaneously. Between particles that are entangled distance and time are of no matter, as they operate as a single unit. In a classic pond the rock goes into the pond at a certain location and the waves emanate out from that location. In the quantum pool the rock goes into the pond, metaphysically speaking, at all locations simultaneously and the waves form patterns at the same time. That also means that the information stored within is available at all places at and at all times and in its entirety. Fundamentally different is the way information is stored and the speed of retrieval. Dutch Nobel laureate, Gerard't Hooft has speculated that the entire universe may be based on the holographic principle, a theory compatible with string theory, which is a multi-dimensional theory.

In string theory the strings which are attached to a brane are single dimensional oscillating lines (wave function) floating in space-time. As yet the medium of holographic storage is unknown, remembering that the information is stored in the medium, but is thought to be stored on the strings or branes, what used to be known as the ether. Scientists have now proven that a vacuum even at absolute zero degrees, -273.15 degrees Celsius is still contains a plenum of energy, and it is still constantly fluctuating and creating new quanta which then disintegrate immediately. These quantum fluctuations are known as the vacuum's zero-point energy. It is still creating and destroying virtual particles from anti-particles. Virtual waves appear and disappear randomly, virtual meaning something either seemingly real or a possibility of being real. There appears to be a constant universal fluctuation of creation and annihilation. The entire universe may be an interconnected holographic field filled with information.

SYSTEMS THEORY AND LIVING ORGANISMS

The concept of coherent fields has been suggested not only in physics but also biology. How does a single egg cell and sperm cell form an entire infant? It doesn't appear possible that two cells could contain all the information necessary to form all the different organs, skin, hair, teeth…. Working with limb regeneration of amphibians in the 1920's Paul Weiss suggested the concept of morphogenetic fields, organizing fields of formative information which guides the development and organization of cells in a living organism. Alexander Gurwitsch further postulated that neither the cell's individual properties nor its relationship with adjacent cells could explain the role of individual cells during embryogenesis. Information is exchanged in cells via resonance, vibration with the same frequency and phase. Resonance exists at the smallest subcellular level as electron spin resonance and nuclear magnetic resonance. Living organisms all have a living system with rhythmic oscillation, vibration, or periodic motion. Each has its specific frequency. Every cell in a living organism has countless vibrating molecular structures within, tuning forks for information transfer perhaps. These vibrating structures have a specific oscillation.

The reciprocal information transfer between the field and the cell structures would take place through resonance at the cell's specific frequencies. Like tuning in a radio station, the information would only be received if the cell's frequency was tuned to the correct resonance or so the concept suggests. A living organism is in constant communication with its constituent parts, and is therefore truly more than merely the sum of those parts. But is an organism a closed system. It makes more sense that such a complex system would have some type of external communication system.

QUANTUM PHYSICS AND NON-LOCAL CONSCIOUSNESS

Quantum physics, as complicated as it is, is still only a study of closed systems and nonliving matter. The idea of integrating the laws of quantum physics with living organisms – chaotic systems in constant change and flux – has still not been accomplished. Some scientists felt it was impossible to compare non-living matter to living matter. Yet Schrodinger and Einstein felt quantum physics *could* be applied to living systems to explain their chemical and physical attributes, and thus the study of Quantum Physics was as yet incomplete.

But what of consciousness, what of that defining part of a human being that makes us who we are? What do philosophers and psychologists think of human consciousness, and wherein do consciousness theories appear to tie into some theories of quantum physics? There are basically three schools of thought regarding human consciousness, materialism, dualism and monism.

MATERIALISM

Certainly, scientists and psychologists have failed to explain consciousness adequately. It is that intangible quality of humans that sets us apart from other animals. Does a cat, for instance, contemplate the mysteries of the universe, or a dog ponder a higher being? Does a worm query global climate change, or a fish stage protests for cleaner water?

Heck, I can't even train the fish in my fish pond to come to the surface for nightly feedings. They're thinking, "The big shadow falls over the pond and then several items drop into the water and then we miraculously find food floating on the surface. It's all very mysterious!" I mean really, you guys are that dense?

Is our consciousness merely the function of firing neurons, physical, electrical and chemical processes? We have already discussed the theory of holographic memory in the brain. But are memories consciousness? Are we merely the sum of our memories? That hardly seems to explain the ability to take those memories and change or adapt, to puzzle through problems, to make sudden leaps of intuition. Consciousness remains one of the great unsolved mysteries of science.

Several prevailing reductionist theories suggest that the brain is merely a bundle of neurons, sending and receiving information, undergoing constant physiological processes, keeping the organs running and allowing for organism survival. Consciousness which would reside in the brain, and be dependent on brain function would therefore be at worst merely an illusion, a human conceit of preeminence, or at best tied to certain brain functions – as yet unexplained. Anything of a paranormal range would be impossible under materialism as everything was contingent on brain tissue and firing neurons. Thus a person could not have an NDE if no brain function was occurring. Psi abilities would undoubtedly be impossible as well. How could we possibly know anything about the outside world except to experience it physically? The survival of the soul after physical death would certainly be ruled out. If our consciousness is an illusion of physiological processes and those processes cease with death, then death is truly the end.

RADICAL DUALISM

Based on the writings of the French philosopher René Descartes the neurophysiologist, John Eccles and philosopher of science Karl Popper all suggested a theory of radical dualism. Consciousness and the brain, while radically different, are still highly interactive. What is meant by radical is the idea that the mind and physical matter are separate natural domains, which despite being separate, nevertheless interact with one another whenever necessary. For example, consciousness is not necessary in order for the brain stem to keep the heart pumping blood or the stomach from digesting that wonderful hamburger you ate for lunch. These are purely materialistic functions of the brain. Consciousness would come into play on Monday morning when you drag your unwilling body from sleep and head off, unhappily, to work. Proponents of this philosophy cite several theories of quantum physics. The collapse of probability waves caused by conscious observation and measurement is one model that seems to support their theory. We consciously decide to go to work, despite our hesitation, and our minds make going to work a reality, thus the wave collapses.

This obviously stands in direct opposition to a materialist paradigm of brain function in which a will is an illusion. The brain, and therefore consciousness is merely a function of, or an attribute of physiological processes. Thus there is no such thing as mind, as it is all reducible to physics and chemical processes, thus there is no choice of whether to stay in bed or go to work. Certainly the brain function of my goldfish is arguably materialistic. "We are hungry and will search for food now." The goldfish would never consider eating a healthy salad over the delicious hamburger simply because they were watching their calories. According to Descartes theory, animals are merely physical automata. But a human, through conscious effort, can make such a decision, demonstrating the dualism between what the pure animal instincts demand and what the mind contemplates and decides. Pure materialism reduces the human down to a merely functioning machine, the sum of neurons firing in a brain, which seems ridiculously simplistic.

WEAK DUALISM

Also called epiphenomenalism suggest that specific areas of brain function trigger certain experiences of consciousness, but that consciousness has no effect on brain or bodily function. Weak Dualism again appears to reduce consciousness down to mere chemical processes, and neglects to explain that we act for specific reasons. If we feel pain we change the way we're holding our body, if we feel cold we find more clothes to wear, thus our minds continually affect our physical reality. It also does not take into account that we can be trained to consciously slow our heart rate or control our breathing, for example. The neuroplasticity of the human brain also argues against weak dualism, as certain sections of the brain can change, adapt and learn new functions as work with individuals with brain damage has demonstrated.

Summing up radical and weak dualism, the late John Beloff, parapsychologist concluded:

> "Pure materialism is, I contend, a philosophical mistake and therefore not a genuine option at all. The choice, as I see it, is between radical dualism and the weaker forms of dualism which merely deny any autonomy to the mental component of the psychophysical organism. As for idealism, the idea that mind alone exists, which is the only other monistic option, while it is logically unassailable, it is so fantastic that there are today few explicit idealists although, as we shall see, it underlies a good deal in current thinking especially where this concerns the interpretation of modern physics (75)."

Either radical or weak dualism could help explain some paranormal phenomena. Both at least acknowledge a consciousness separate from our purely physical bodies. Neither make much of an attempt to explain how a separation is possible, and certainly weak dualism seems to suggest a materialist reality with consciousness more an intangible illusion subverted by the physical over which it appears to have no power.

MONISM

Mono meaning one, this broad philosophy is also known as panpsychism, idealism or phenomenalism. Immaterial monism is the opposite of materialism. Instead it suggests that everything from a rock, to my stupid goldfish to my physical person all have some degree of subjective consciousness, at either an elementary or fundamental level. There are certainly different degrees of panpsychism, and not all adherents to the theory believe that everything has a mental state. They don't necessarily believe that a building or the number 2, for example, possess some type of mental consciousness, but that other fundamental physical entities do.

Whether or not a rock has a consciousness, monism espouses the idea that all matter possesses phenomenal properties. Phenomenal properties are properties that can be affected by subjective observation, for example finding the electron in the quadrant we chose to look in. With our subjective observation we have distinct power over the physical world, versus weak dualism where the shoe is distinctly on the other foot. Most panpsychists suggest that the human mind is uniquely sophisticated, complex or possesses a more highly refined, higher-order consciousness than other creatures.

This philosophy suggests that consciousness is a primary presence in the universe, and while most panpsychists don't attempt to explain it beyond positing that it exists, some do. Monism then takes it one step further, suggesting that not only does a universal consciousness or willful mindfulness exist, but that it in turns shapes all physical reality through subjective observation. In other words, we shape the reality in which we live by our conscious observation of it, it doesn't intrude upon our conscious mind and shape us. I can't help but visualize the movie *The Matrix* with this philosophy, not only does consciousness exist separate from the physical world, but it creates the physical world! Do you feel those probability waves crashing down around your head now?

The philosopher Georg Wilhelm Friedrich Hegel, who was not a panpsychist, nevertheless believed in a world soul, a cosmopsychism, believing that the entire world had a consciousness. This suggests a type of protoconsciousness whereby, while not all fundamental entities were conscious, all did possess some fundamental components of consciousness, or perhaps certain properties that acted as a precursor to consciousness. In a larger system collectively these fundamental entities could start to display evidence of consciousness, which again appears to mimic certain theories in quantum physics such as entanglement, nonlocality and the interconnectedness of certain particles. If such is true of the material universe, why not of living matter as well?

Monism certainly would go a long way toward explaining all types of paranormal phenomena. If consciousness resides outside the body, then a person could justifiably report having consciousness despite not having brain activity, thus making an NDE possible. In fact people who experience an NDE speak of having a heightened sense of consciousness, as if not being tied to the physical body allows them an unfettered consciousness not experienced within the confines of the five senses. Monism could also explain how a person could experience an Out of Body experience. If consciousness is nonlocal, then it would suggest that it need not be tethered to a body in order to perceive and experience the world at large. It would also argue quite strongly for the psi abilities such as telepathy or precognition. If all of the information were available in nonlocal space where our consciousness also resided it would argue favorably that we could tap into this information on occasion. We know that a purely materialistic approach is inadequate to explain the mind's control over the body. Again the demonstrated neuroplasticity of the brain argues against materialism. Also the documented experiences of organ recipients developing personality characteristics of their organ donors suggests that not all of our personality is stored or retrieved in the brain.

THE CASE FOR NON-LOCAL CONSCIOUSNESS

Dr. Pim van Lommel, a medical researcher and author of *Consciousness Beyond Life; The Science of Near Death Experience* suggests the next rather obvious and plausible next step in the consciousness debate. He suggests a "complete and endless consciousness with retrievable memories has its origins in a nonlocal space in the form of indestructible and not directly observable wave functions. These wave functions, which store all aspects of consciousness in the form of information, are always present in and around the body (nonlocality). The brain and the body merely function as a relay station, receiving part of the overall consciousness and part of our memories in our waking consciousness in the form of measurable and constantly changing electromagnetic fields. In this view, these electromagnetic fields of the brain are not the cause but rather the effect or consequence of endless consciousness."

The invention of the internet makes this theory more believable to me. I remember my friend trying to explain the internet to my stymied self sometime in the early 1990's. "All of the information in the world would be stored on supercomputers and you would be able to access it from your home computer via a dial-up internet connection." I think my only response was, "how in the hell is that possible?" Yes, young ones, this was before Wi-Fi was invented. I was writing my college papers on my parent's beloved Apple IIe, and thinking myself quite progressive. (We were the only family I knew that actually owned a computer.) Yet here was this idea that all of the knowledge of the world was stored and could be accessed from the privacy of your own home via a telephone line.

What if the great design of the universe superseded our discovery of the internet, but acts much like it. Information could be stored and immutable on "the cloud". Perhaps our minds and even the DNA of our cells act more as a computer, receiving and decoding the information that is readable via electromagnetic waves of information. Dr. Lommel suggests that such a conclusion has its basis in scientific and prospective studies on NDE in survivors of cardiac arrest.

> *"These patients describe an enhanced consciousness, with cognition, emotions, memories, and the possibility of perception out and above the lifeless body the very moment that the brain does not function anymore during cardiac arrest (74)."*

Certainly eastern philosophies and reincarnation are more conceivable considering the theory of nonlocality. And again, many of the paranormal anomalies such as NDE's, OBE's, ADC's, hauntings and psi abilities such as telepathy, precognition and clairvoyance could all conceivably be answered with such a theory. We would no longer have to simply ignore such mysteries as outside the realm of possibility. If consciousness existed in nonlocal space and was neither tethered to time, body or space then nearly everything mysterious could be answered.

CHAPTER 9: ANGELS AND DEMONS

"Beloved, do not believe every spirit, but test the spirits to see whether they are from God, for many false prophets have gone out into the world."
1 John 4:1

"Be sober-minded; be watchful. Your adversary the devil prowls around like a roaring lion, seeking someone to devour. Resist him, firm in your faith, knowing that the same kinds of suffering are being experienced by your brotherhood throughout the world."
1 Peter 5:8-9

DEMONIC SPIRITS

I f we are to consider the idea of human consciousness surviving death we should probably consider other forms of ethereal life forms as well. Certainly both Christianity and Islam speak of other life forms such as angels and demons (djinn for the Muslims) as existing, and actually pre-existing human life forms in the universal schema. Angels were made in the image of God, according to the Bible, and were to be the servants of God. Accordingly, when God created man the angels were told to act as the defenders of the human race. Some of the angels, namely Satan (Shaitan in the Islamic religion) could not abide by the edict to defend the lesser of God's creation, and was thus thrust down from heaven into hell, along with his host of defenders. Thus we acquired heaven and hell or the factions of good and evil. This is probably all very familiar for those who attended Christian bible school.

FROM THE BIBLE

"Now war arose in heaven, Michael and his angels fighting against the dragon. And the dragon and his angels fought back, but he was defeated, and there was no longer any place for them in heaven. And the great dragon was thrown down, that ancient serpent, who is called the devil and Satan, the deceiver of the whole world—he was thrown down to the earth, and his angels were thrown down with him." Revelation 12:7-9

ISLAMIC RELIGION

The Qur'an speaks of a similar situation happening amongst the djinn. In fact a powerful djinn by the name of Iblis was so infuriated at the idea that he refused to bend the knee, and suffered the same fate as the biblical Lucifer. For his arrogance, Iblis and his followers were exiled from Earth, banished to Hell until Judgment Day when they would hopefully have mended their ways. God did grant Iblis one boon, he gave Iblis permission to tempt mankind away from the teachings of God. Note this excerpt from the Qur'an:

> ...We bade the angels prostrate to Adam, and they prostrate; not so Iblis [Shaitan]; He refused to be of those who prostrate.

> Allah: "What prevented thee from prostrating when I commanded thee?"

> Iblis: "I am better than he [man]: Thou didst create me from fire, and him from clay."

> Allah: "Get thee down from this: it is not for thee to be arrogant here. Get out, for thou art of the meanest. Be thou among those who have respite.

> Iblis: "Because thou hast thrown me out of the way, lo? I will lie in wait for them on thy straight way. Then I will assault them from before them and behind them, from their right and their left. Nor wilt thou find, in most of them gratitude."

> Allah: "Get out from this, degraced and expelled. If any of them follow thee, Hell will I fill with you all. " Al-A'Raf, 11-18.

According to an Arabian story, after Iblis' descent, his name was changed to Shaitan which means literally adversary or enemy. Notice the similarities between Shaitan and Satan.

BUDDHISM

In the Buddhist tradition Mara is the devil, representing temptation, sin and eventual death. He is also identified with Namuche, a wicked demon from Indian mythology. Also called Papiyan the Wicked one or the Evil One, the Murderer or the Tempter or Varsavarti which literally means he who fulfills desires. Varsavarti or Mara is the personification of all wicked desires or the triple thirst which is the thirst for existence, pleasure and power. He is the king of the Heaven of sensual delight. The selfishness of man is the devil and the actual satisfaction of unhealthy desires is Hell.

In the Dhammapada (the Buddhist scriptures) Mara is less an actual character than a personification of unhealthy desires, such as sensuality, sin, and egotistical pleasures. Thus the passages:

> "He who lives looking for pleasures only, his senses uncontrolled..." (66)

> "...immoderate in his food, idle and weak, him Mara will certainly overthrow as the wind throws down a feeble tree." (66)

HINDUISM

The evil spirits or demons for the Hindus are the asuras. They are fallen minor gods (the Hindu equivalent of an angel –known as devas) Once fallen they lose their home in the higher astral plane, and are thrust down into the mental plane of existence which is a lower astral plane. Unlike other theologies, however, the Hindus believe that an asuras can rectify their sins by performing good deeds, as which time they are reincarnated as devas.

Looking just for obvious parallels we can see blatant similarities in the theologies. In all the stories, demons or "the demon" was a higher celestial being, but did something that led to his or their eventual fall. He (they) were literally cast out, thrown down or lowered to an earthly plane or a lower plane of existence. There he/they prey on the wicked and those with unhealthy desires, hoping to cause their eventual damnation.

I'm often asked, depending on the prevailing winds of the current television programing season, if a house is haunted by a "demon." When it comes to television ratings all hauntings, you must understand, become demonic. However, to forego the collective groan of all paranormal research groups with any integrity, I must admit that demonic hauntings are very rare. So rare in fact that I have spoken with other paranormal researchers who have been in the field for years and have never come across such a haunting.

That said, it would be remiss to not include the signs of a demonic haunting in a book about hauntings. If for no other reason, they are by far the most sinister and dangerous. Do remember that a human spirit can be pretty dreadful as well. Rapists, murderers, child molesters, certainly some people have a penchant for doing evil deeds, and becoming a spirit doesn't make them any nicer to be around. A human spirit may even try to appear demonic in order to create greater fear.

One should consider the degree of the activity when trying to make the determination as to whether a haunting is demonic or human. Demons are traditionally much more powerful than a human entity, and the terror they evoke much more visceral. For example, a human spirit may move the car keys, a demon may move the car.

Collin was a paranormal investigator with whom I worked for a couple of years. He was also a trained member of the medical field and worked for a number of years at the local hospital. He was a person whose integrity I respected. Thus when I casually asked him what got him into the field of paranormal research I never expected to hear a story about a demon. In Collin's own words here is was what happened to him one frightening night:

"[This was] my first encounter with the paranormal. Please understand that in the paranormal Investigative world we look for proof to substantiate the claim. I have none. What I'm about to share has no audio or video evidence to back up my story. Only my word. I only say my word because my best friend Brian (who also experienced it) passed away from cancer in 2003. As we investigators would say "It's just a personal experience." It was the summer of 1989. I was 20 years old. For me, that meant weekends playing video games with my best friends Chris and Brian. This particular weekend I was staying at my best friend Brian's house. It was a usual weekend. We played video games and boards games all day and most of the night. When bedtime came it was about 2 am. Brian's room had 2 twin beds. We chatted just before we went to bed about going to church in the morning. He set the alarm and we turned out our lamps. As soon as the lights went out I laid my head on the pillow. I closed my eyes and all of a sudden I saw a white flash."

In a subsequent phone interview, Collin said that the flash was like a camera flash in brightness and that it happened closer to his side of the door. In the interview he admitted that the white flash felt like "an angelic presence."

"After the flash came this feeling of oppressive, thick, and evil. It felt like it had blanketed the whole room. I yelled at Brian saying "Dude!" He immediately said "Yeah, I feel it too." We both immediately knew what it was--something evil. We knew it had to be demonic. We turned on our lamps and began to pray immediately. It was most definitely panic prayer because of not knowing what exactly this evil was and what exactly to pray for except for protection. For the next couple of hours we sat there and prayed and talked. There was a couple of times I thought I could see what looked like yellow eyes peering back at us from just outside the doorway. Brian got up and approached the doorway a few times and I would say "dude, get back from the door. They're right there."

Collin said that a couple of times he felt he saw yellow eyes peering in the door from the darkened hallway, but that it was hard to be sure as both young men had their lamps on. Brian, a fairly good sized 6 foot two inches, eventually made a couple of trips out into the hall and around the house but saw nothing.

"Then again, you really didn't need to see anything because the oppressive evil was so heavy that was evidence enough for me to realize there was evil around us. The heaviness eventually went away. We suspected that the evil was coming from Brian's brother. At the time Brian's brother was into Nazi occult stuff." The two young men did not get to sleep until 5:30 or 6 o'clock in the morning, when they finally felt the threat had passed.

WAYS TO AVOID A DEMONIC HAUNTING

The predominating literature suggests that if one wishes to avoid a demonic haunting one should first and foremost not invite it. Obviously practicing Satan worship or any such nonsense, even in jest, is never a sound idea. Most experts also caution against the use of Ouija boards (angel boards) and home séances. The prevailing wisdom being that the use of such opens a door to another realm. Just why Ouija boards and séances invite darker entities is never explained fully, beyond the fact that if one opens the door and invites whatever riffraff in, then one may get more than they bargained for.

 Then again other experts note that whenever you open the door of communication with the supernatural realm through an Ouija board session, séance or simply a paranormal investigation, you open the door to whatever comes walking in, unless you take precautions. It's very much like the time I knowingly invited the vacuum cleaner salesman into my house and had the next two hours of my day taken up with vacuuming demonstrations and hard core sales pitches. The moral of the story is don't open the door and invite the boogey man in, as the vast majority of us don't know how to get rid of him.

Most of what we know about demons comes from holy books such as the Bible or the Quran. With my own background in Christianity, throughout the rest of the text most of the terms I will use will be traditional Christian names as they're perhaps the most familiar to a western audience.

LOOK FOR THE FLAW

According to the demon lore, demons can mask their appearance as they so choose. If they appeared in their natural form they would look monstrous and grotesque. That is not how they were created by God, who made the angels in his image. But how they changed over time, their outward appearance reflecting their inward evil. They will try to trick human contacts by appearing in human or humanoid form. They may also appear as a recently departed loved one or friend. According to God's law, however, if they choose a deceptive appearance there must always be a flaw to give them away – at least to the wary. They may be missing a hand, or an eye for example. Their face may be grotesquely twisted. It is a defect, whether obvious or subtle, that the departed person did not possess. Therein lies the sign that they are not who they appear to be.

DEMONS CANNOT READ MINDS; BUT THEY ARE SMART

Just as their appearance may be deceptive so too their words. Not surprisingly, a demon will lie or twist the truth in order to trick a human being. They are extremely intelligent and they will use that intelligence to outsmart or out-think the wariest of humans. They cannot read a person's mind. They may, however, know your history, your past sins and transgressions, and will try to use such knowledge against you. Demons are also not privy to the future, although they are smart enough to calculate and predict likely outcomes, and they can rapidly calculate possible outcomes by sifting through a large number of possible courses of action. This is how they can appear to know the future. Think of them as card counters at a casino. They know what cards you have played in the past, thus what cards are likely to be played in the future.

The sole desire of demons, according to the Bible, is to trick humans or cajole humans into wanton sinfulness. Drugs, alcohol, sex, acts of violence, lying, cheating, stealing – any behavior that directs man from the path of righteousness and steers him or her toward damnation is their ultimate goal. Put in a less religious way, they desire to lead a human into an unhealthy and/or unstable lifestyle, one that would make them susceptible to mental or physical decay (65).

THE RULES OF ENGAGEMENT

Michael Cardinuto, director of Long Island Paranormal Investigators notes that the rules of engagement are directed by God and are designed to keep the balance between the universal forces (65). These rules keep the balance between the universal forces. We've covered several of them already, but simply to be clear we will reiterate here. Demons are hell bent on sweeping mankind in order to create havoc and destroy God's lesser creatures. The balance established by God protects the order.

While demons may appear deceptively as humans, or even as departed loved ones, there will always be some obvious deformity which is the warning sign to beware.

While they may appear to know the future, this is not a power they possess. They may appear to have an uncanny knowledge, but this is their ability to assess past events to predict future outcomes.

Demons also do not possess the ability to read your mind, although again they may appear to do so. Again, this is assessing probabilities, not certainties.

Demons must be invited in, either through direct invitation or negligence. Certain lifestyle choices such as addiction or violence, or mental predispositions carry a higher chance of attracting negative entities. Those with mental illness appear the most susceptible to demonic possession, perhaps because they are the least likely to be detected, and the most easily manipulated. That is not to say that all people who are mentally ill are possessed by demons, nor that those who are not mentally ill cannot be targeted for possession (**65**).

SIGNS OF A DEMONIC HAUNTING

And finally, the answer to the 1-million-dollar question is my haunting a demonic haunting... The following list is compiled from the common symptoms or signs that a haunting is demonic. Do recall, however that many of the symptoms are true of an intelligent haunting as well, and finally that demonic hauntings are extremely rare.

Demonic activity apparently begins rather benignly but then begins to escalate. The list is compiled as a progression from first signs to finish. These are simply guidelines as a demonic haunting may consist of only some of the listed phenomena or none of them (65).

Young children and household pet are often the first targeted. They tend to be the first to respond or detect a presence.

Children may report seeing someone or something in their bedrooms.

The child or children may claim that they are being visited by a nice man (sometimes a woman). They may attempt to befriend the child, and at first are non-threatening. Eventually the man or woman begin to become abusive, nasty and even threatening. The child starts to become scared.

Strong unpleasant or even foul odors may begin to be detected for no apparent reason. The smell of Sulphur (rotten eggs) or decaying flesh are commonly reported. They may be stronger in one part of the house, or one room of the house in particular.

Finally the adults in a residence begin to see things or detect things as well.

A figure may appear that looks human but has no eyes, or appears to have dark or black eyes, occasionally they may have reddish glowing eyes.

Children begin to awake at night screaming that someone is attempting to hurt them.

The adults may start to awake as well, either at night or in the morning, bearing unaccountable scratch marks.

Children and adults may begin to show signs of sudden and mysterious illnesses, such that defy medical diagnosis and often treatment.

Objects in the house, even very heavy pieces of furniture may begin to move on their own. And the objects that do move appear to move in directions contrary to how they would normally be expected to move, such as a door trying to open the wrong way. Objects may move in a counter-clockwise direction.

Extremely high electromagnetic field readings are present throughout the building which defy mechanical and/or electrical explanation.

Unexplainable events occur in sets of three; that is, in a short amount of time three unexplainable events will happen.

Most of the paranormal events happen at night between the hours of 9:00 pm to 6:00 am, with 3:00-3:30 am being the most active.

The non-human entity is highly responsive to words that are considered holy, such as words from the Bible. This is not specific to a certain type of religion.

Demonic hauntings usually occur in already troubled homes. Families who are experiencing drug or alcohol abuse, physical or psychological abuse or dysfunction, depression, mental illness, mental and emotional instability. All of these scenarios seem to create an environment that is conducive to a demonic or non-human entity. They appear to thrive on (or feed on) the greater emotions such as terror or rage.

If you feel that a haunting meets these criteria it is important to contact a member of the clergy or a reputable paranormal research team immediately. Under the proper conditions a demonic entity can be enticed to move on, but it's important to eject them before they become too entrenched.

ANGELS

"Do not neglect to show hospitality to strangers, for thereby some have entertained angels unawares." Hebrew 13:2

If one is to entertain the idea of the devil, then one should consider the existence of angels as well. As we saw in the literature previously, a balance is to be maintained between the forces of good and evil, and angels are, according to the Bible, God's foot soldiers in the fight. Again, the belief and existence of angels is found throughout many religions.

ELAINE'S BRUSH WITH AN ANGEL

I met Elaine, (the name has been changed for anonymity) a respected member of the healthcare some time ago. It is often the way of things when people find out that I'm "into that kind of stuff..." In this case Elaine pulled me aside one day and related a personal experience that was so astounding I remembered it and contacted her several years after. Here is the story in her own words.

Pennsylvania, 1970
It was the winter of 1970 that it happened. The snow was coming down that night for hours and there was a thick coating on the trees as well as the streets. It was the kind of snow that was magical; not only did it look beautiful but it created a sudden shift to silence. That's quite a feat in the hectic rim of Philadelphia. As a child, I didn't realize that this tranquility was related to the fact that the vehicles couldn't operate in the treacherous weather. I just knew that the storm was wonderful and brought special things with it.

That night, I fell asleep looking out the window thinking about the snow and the fun that it would bring the next day. I didn't know that I wouldn't have to until morning for an adventure.

Something woke me up. Opening my eyes, I saw that the room was filled with a brilliant light. Fearfully, I let my eyes wonder around the room without moving my head. A fraction of a second later, I saw her sitting on top of my older sister Deborah who lay sleeping unknowingly on the bottom trundle bed. My breath caught and I was immediately paralyzed. I was shocked that she didn't see me. How could she not notice me, as I was awake and looking right at her! I moved my little body ever so slowly into the corner of the bed where I had a better view of her. She was the most spectacular thing I had ever seen in my whole five years of life. I estimated her illuminated body to be about 9 feet tall and 3 feet wide. Her crimped golden hair was so long it reached the bed and it followed her flowing robes that were multicolored shades of golds. A thick braided cord was attached just below her waistline and was touching my sister's little body. I realized that she looked just like the ceramic angels my mother brought out during the holidays and planted everywhere throughout the house. Her face so flawless and delicate that it looked as if she was dipped in paraffin wax. It was her wings though that were breathtaking. They were absolutely enormous and could hardly fit into our tiny bedroom with our sloped ceiling. They were the color of light caramel with hundreds of layers of feathers. They fluttered ever so slightly the entire time I watched her.

Her eyes were cast downwards so it was difficult to read her disposition but I knew intuitively that she was not friendly. She did not move off of my sister nor did she alter her position as if she was standing alert and on guard. When I could remove my eyes off this angel, I realized that there was a second smaller angel in the opposite corner of the room but she was vague and almost imperceptible. I somehow knew that vague one was second in command and was considerably nicer than the amazon sitting on my sister. How I knew this, I cannot tell you; I just knew.

I was scared. I felt that I was somehow in danger. I needed to escape but I had to do it before the large angel took notice of me. I knew that she was somehow taking care of my sister but I didn't know how and I certainly didn't know why Deborah would need anyone looking after her. After all, she was 8 years old and very capable of taking care of herself. Deborah was the smartest and bravest sister ever and she was great at everything she did.

After careful consideration, I decided that I was going to make a run for it. I planned to run into my mother's bedroom knowing I risked her wrath. My mother was very clear that her children were forbidden to share their parent's bed. This was 1970 and my parents shared a simple full size bed and not the luxury king size beds typical for today's couples. At this point, I didn't care and was willing to take my chances. I couldn't stay in my room any longer or it would be the death of me. Counting to three, I tried to jump over the railing but found that I couldn't move; my body was literally frozen. Petrified. Confused by my body's betrayal I knew I had to try again. Finding a live 9-foot angel in my room was taking its toll on my little 40 pound body. I continued to look at the angel and she continued to keep watch on Deborah without any reaction whatsoever to my attempted motion. I thought to myself "It is now or never". Taking one last look at the angel and Deborah, I jumped over the railing and made a beeline for my mother's room.

With a huge sigh of relief, I quietly tapped on my mother's shoulder. I was a child that always followed the rules but this time, no matter what she said, I wasn't going back. She roused to find me standing at her bedside. My mother quietly asked why I was there and I anxiously told her the entire story. She quietly listened to every word I said and then opened the covers for me to enter into the forbidden bed. She held me close and rubbed my back speaking tender words to me to calm me down. I felt warm and safe as she whispered, "Hush now and go to sleep; that's what is called a nightmare. You just stay here with me tonight." I closed my eyes and let this new word play on my tongue. A "night mare"...even the word itself was frightening to my child's mind. I was worried about Deborah being left alone in that room with the angels but my mother assured me there was nothing to worry about. For the rest of my childhood years, I believed that the visit from the angel was exactly that. A nightmare. I was mistaken.

TAMPA 1990

I took a deep breath and inhaled the fresh balmy air into my lungs. I scanned the wide expanse of the bay that made up the coastal waterway between Saint Petersburg and Tampa Bay and took in the panoramic view of crystal clear water for as far as the eye could see. The deck of the watering hole where we were hanging out was actually 20 feet into the bay making it seem as if we were floating in the water during high tide. I sighed and looked at my newfound friends "I cannot believe that I am sitting here watching manatees swim by while the sun sets over the bay! This is amazing." Smiling, I turned and looked back at the scene "You have got to forgive me, but this is a little different than what I am use to!" My friends Jenny and Lisa laughed but added that within a year I was going to be like everyone else who moved to Florida and would soon take for granted the beauty that surrounded me. "Doubtful," I added.

As the night moved on, the crowd did too and we were left to have the deck to ourselves. As we sat outside, we shared wine and talked all night as girlfriends do but eventually this night the talk turned serious. My coworker and friend Jenny who was 15 years my senior, was having persistent depression issues and wasn't sure if she would be able to climb out of her hole. She brought up how even her tried and true belief in angels was failing her this time around.

Jenny's mention of the angels along with the atmosphere and the wine let down my guard to my treasured secret. I told Jenny and Lisa that I wanted to share a story with them that happened in my childhood. A story I hadn't shared with anyone. I told them about the visit from the angel when I was very young and added that my sister Deb in the story was diagnosed with a serious chronic illness as a young teenager. I told them how my mother mistakenly identified my experience as a nightmare and that I believed that it was in fact a nightmare for many years until I was old enough to know what a nightmare was. As I finished my story, I looked up to find both of my friends looking at me strangely so I quickly shrugged and explained that it was a silly story because the angels were almost the exact replicas of my mother's ceramic figures. Picking up my purse, I dismissively waived my hand saying "I mean how it could possibly be as real as I think if they looked like they were plucked right from Michelangelo's paintings.... right?" I desperately wanted to disappear as I was betraying myself and what I knew to be true.

Jenny grabbed my hand halting me in my tracks. She looked directly at me smiling and willing me to sit back down. "Honey, angels reveal themselves to people in the form that the person will understand them. Does that make sense to you?"

It took me a moment to comprehend Jenny's words. Finally, tears filled my eyes and I looked up at her "Yeah that makes sense. I didn't know that. All these years, I didn't know that." The tears fell. Tears of relief and tears of joy and celebration that I can own my angels. "I didn't want to tell anyone because the experience was so important to me that I didn't want to be ridiculed for something that was sacred to me. I kept it close to my heart where no one could reach it. I never brought it up to my mother again and I never even told my sister Deborah. That was going to change.

I looked at Jenny and I was having trouble containing my joy. "Thank you, Jenny. Do you know what you did for me tonight?"

Jenny looked at me "Yeah, I think so."

We wrapped things up that night and the world changed for me. My world was different. A new perspective. A paradigm shifts. The kind of world I wanted to believe in but was afraid to. A world where there is more than meets the eye. A world filled with love and hope and light and spirit and angels. I not only believe in these things, I am certain of them and this is the best gift a person can be granted. It was a moment for me when it was confirmed that we live among spirits and there is an afterlife. An enlightenment that changes a person to the core.

Pablo Picasso believed that all children are artist and that we forget our artistic creative talents as we grow older. He said it took him a lifetime to remember to learn to paint like a child. In line with Pablo Picasso's thinking, perhaps it will take me a lifetime to learn to see the angels sitting in the room with me. One can only hope.

I linked my arm in Jenny's as we walked out. Jenny turned to me and said she suddenly felt better. It seemed that her world suddenly had color in it again.

The funny thing is, Jenny and I were very good friends but only for a brief time. I left Tampa a few years later and didn't stay in touch with Jenny. She was the kind of friend I trusted immediately and could have an intimate discussion with. Almost like an angel sent to me to bring me a message and then leave. Perhaps, I am still sitting in the room with angels.

Most of the world's major religions either have an equivalent to the western angel, or belief in some type of celestial being that was created to help mankind.

BUDDHISTS

For the Buddhists, the equivalent to an angel is the devas, or celestial beings. In some sects of Buddhism, they are referred to as dharmapalas or dharma protectors. For Tibetan Buddhists devas are the emanations of the bodhisattvas or enlightened beings. There are many important devas in the Buddhist religion, and most predate modern Buddhism.

Devas are considered spiritual beings, thus not corporeal. They are usually described as creatures of light or pure energy. They are depicted in physical form, however, in the Tibetan Buddhist iconography.

The devas do not usually interfere in the affairs of humans, although the Lama Surya Das, the Buddhist teacher, noted that they could rejoice, applaud or rain flowers down upon a person for the doing of good deeds for humanity. In Thailand the devas are thought to harass those who do not meditate often enough, and of whose behavior they do not approve. The Kwan Yan is the bodhisattva of compassion in China, the Chenrezig the equivalent for Tibetans. The original Sanskrit name for the bodhisattva was Avolokiteshvara which translates to, "the hearer of ten-thousand cries" or she who perceives the suffering of all sentient beings. In some schools of teaching merely saying her name is believed to summon her to your aid. Oddly, the bodhisattva was originally male in the texts, but is represented as female in many Buddhist schools (67).

HINDUISM

While the Hindus do not have a specific angelic being, they do have many creatures of spirit who act in a similar capacity. Minor gods, again called devas, are literally "shining ones" who inhabit a higher astral plane than humans, and they can, in conjunction with ancestors, teachers and gods, help play a protective role for humans against the asuras or evil spirits (demons). They can inspire or destroy people, either aiding or hindering one's spiritual journey. Again while considered spiritual beings, thus not possessing a body, they are often depicted in physical form. Apsaras are represented as seductively beautiful, and devas are thought to be stately and handsome creatures of aristocratic bearing (67).

ISLAM

In the Islamic faith angels are beings of pure light created before man. Being creatures solely of light there are few pictures or symbolic representations in Islamic art. Despite this, they are believed to be beautiful winged creatures. They are literally different beings from Shaitan and his legion of demons (djinn) who are creatures created from smokeless flame. Unlike Christian beliefs in angels, Muslims believe that angels are mortal, although with a much longer lifespan than a mere mortal, angels will eventually suffer death. As such they are not considered divine or even semi-divine, but more as a different species from man or demons (68).

As in Christianity, there are thought to be different hierarchies within the legions of angels, and thus they have different sizes, status and value. While there are innumerable angels, mankind remains privy only to the names of four. The greatest of the angels is Gabriel. Mikal (Michael) is the angel of nature, Izrail (Azrael) is the angel of death and Israfil is the angel responsible for placing a soul in the body and who sounds the last judgment. The direct attendants to Allah are also among the top of the order as well (67).

As top dog, Gabriel acts as God's messenger to man, bringing God's word to his chosen (**68**).

> "Say: whoever is an enemy to Gabriel - for he brings down the (revelation) to your heart by God's will..." (Quran 2:97)

Angels were created from light before human beings were created, and thus their representation in Islamic art is rare. Despite this, angels do have the ability to present themselves in human form in order to converse with humans.

They are created from light, as 'Aa'ishah reported: "The Messenger of Allah said: 'The angels are created from light, just as the djinn are created from smokeless fire and mankind is created from what you have been told about.'" (**71**).

Being of spiritual makeup they do not desire food or drink, and they never grow tired of worshipping God.

> "They celebrate His praises night and day, nor do they ever slacken." (Quran 21:20)

While they may not partake in the everyday machinations of mankind they are thought to love the true followers of Islam, and will beseech Allah on their behalf in the forgiveness of sins.

Because they are not divine, they are not to be beseeched through prayer, nor are they to be worshipped.

CHRISTIAN BELIEF IN ANGELS IN THE U.S.

Strangely the belief in both angels and demons appears to be on the rise in the U.S. According to a 1994 Gallup poll 72% of Americans said they believed in angels. That number rose to 78% in a similar 2004 poll. Belief in Satan is also on the rise, markedly so.

In 1990 55% reported believing in Lucifer. By 2004, however, his poll numbers increased to 70%. Even accounting for polling error, this increase is rather remarkable (72).

The United States remains a singularly spiritual nation with polls indicating that only 56% of Canadians and 36% of Britons believe in angels and only 37% of Canadians and 29% of Britons believe in the devil (69). Why the increase at a time when Christianity appears to be under direct attack stymies the imagination. However, spirituality was under attack at the start of the spiritualist movement as well, when under the edict of positivism, science and the industrial revolution Americans and Britons alike began to search for something more and something deeper than pure materialism. I would posit perhaps something of the like is again happening in our age of empty realism and values.

The English word angel is merely a translation of an earlier Greek word meaning messenger. In many of the Bible verses I've so far perused that does appear to be much of what the angelic realm was thought to do, bring God's messages to his people. For example:

> "In the sixth month of Elizabeth's pregnancy, God sent the angel Gabriel to Nazareth, a town in Galilee, 27 to a virgin pledged to be married to a man named Joseph, a descendant of David. The virgin's name was Mary." Luke 1:26-27

However, angels were also assigned, according to Christian doctrine, as protectors of the people, and to bear judgment in God's name.

> "For he will command his angels concerning you, to guard you in all your ways." Psalm 91:11

> "Are not all angels ministering spirits sent to serve those who will inherit salvation?" Hebrews 1:14

> "So shall it be at the end of the world: the angels shall come forth, and sever the wicked from among the just." Matthew 13:49-50.

It is probably such verses as the Psalm 91:11 passage that has led to fervor among Christians to believe, or at least hope that one of the heavenly host has been assigned to every person as protector and guardian. One writer described it as a type of angel mania, a desire among Christians to believe that a specific guardian angel had been solely assigned to watch over and protect them specifically. No one passage in the Bible states this, and trying to interpret such appears to be splitting syntactical hairs.

In Christian iconography, angels are usually depicted as being human in appearance, though most theologians have argued that because angels have no physical body they cannot possibly resemble humans. They began to be depicted with wings in the 4th century, perhaps in order to express their ability to move quickly and to descend the realms of heaven and Earth. Seraphim, the highest order of angels are usually depicted as having six wings —two wrapped around their heads, two around their feet and two around their torso with which they actually fly. I find this counter to aerodynamics, thinking that that many wings would simply get in the way of things. But again, they didn't consult me.

Much like demons, angels are thought to be able to reason infinitely faster than humans, and to move instantly, merely upon a thought, which seems to parallel some theories of quantum physics, in particular entanglement and nonlocality. Theologians also suggest that angels act as intermediaries between humans and what would otherwise be conceived as natural forces of nature. Thus they can help with the rotation of planet and the motion of the stars, though how that really helps humans is beyond me. More important would be the ability to bring rain in time of draught, or stop rain in time of floods. Actually much of human existence is tied up with water, if you think about it. But that's me spit-ballin.

Angels also appear to possess the beatific vision, the unencumbered or undiluted vision and understanding of God. Again, the parallels to Islamic doctrine are striking. The Islamic vision of angels as never resting, and always worshipping God.

ANGEL NAMES

If you've never noticed most of the angel names we know to end in 'el suffix. Gabriel, Michael, and Ezekiel for example all end with the 'el suffix. This apparently is not a coincidence. In the Hebrew, the 'el literally means "similar to God." Thus the angels, in particular the Arch (over) angels are literally "from God," "for God," or "given of God."

If belief in Jesus and the apostolic church are the absolute tickets to winning admission into heaven, then anyone who does not acknowledge these beliefs are, of course, excluded. This is the power that the "Church" has always wielded over those who were none church goers.

However, the Gospel of Thomas, which is markedly not in the Bible - nor appears likely to be included, suggests faith as being more of a personal spiritual journey. The Gospel of Thomas is actually a listing of 114 sayings, in no particular order, many of which parallel the gospels in the Bible, but in a more primitive manner. There have only been two versions of the Thomas Gospel found, and one was only an impartial document. The best preserved, most complete version is a Coptic translation of an earlier Greek translation or Jesus' oral Aramaic sayings (logoi). In other words someone attempting to write down what Jesus actually said. Both versions date to the mid-first to second centuries.

"Jesus said: If your leaders say to you 'Look! The Kingdom is in the heavens!" Then the birds will be there before you are. If they say that the Kingdom is in the sea, then the fish will be there before you are. Rather, the Kingdom is within you and it is outside of you." (Gospel of Thomas 3a) **(73)**

Jesus said, "I am the light that is over all things. I am all: from me all came forth, and to me all attained.

Split a piece of wood; I am there.

Lift up the stone, and you will find me there." (Gospel of Thomas 77b) **(73)**

Words actually attributed to Stephen in Act 7:48 "The Most High does not dwell in houses made with hands."

The movie Stigmata said it more eloquently when it combined the Thomas Gospel 3a with 77b. Hence my favorite translation:

The kingdom of God is in you and all around you.

Not in a mansion of wood and stone

Split a piece of wood and I am there

Lift a stone and you will find me.

Was Jesus sent to teach us the correct way to live our lives, or to advocate for a strong, controlling church? Perhaps Emily Dickinson wasn't completely far off when she penned the words,

Some keep the Sabbath going to Church –

I keep it, staying at Home -

With a Bobolink for a Chorister –

And an Orchard, for a Dome-

So what are angels in all this? Perhaps they are divine creatures made by God. But perhaps some of them are Clarence- like, as in the movie, *It's a Wonderful Life.* Apparently Louis Charles of Angels&Ghosts.com has a similar view. With permission I reprint his theory on what many angels may actually be:

If Accurate, Jesus Told Us Who Angels Are

"For when the dead rise, they will neither marry nor be given in marriage. In this respect they will be like the angels in heaven." Matthew 22:30

The following Bible verse clearly states that we are angels. Jesus explained the metaphor by proclaiming this in Matthew 22:30: "For in the resurrection they (us) neither marry, nor are given in marriage, but are as angels in heaven."

Traditional Western religion might have you believe that this passage means that some of us will be only similar to the angels, but that's not what we see Jesus revealing. Jesus seems to [be] clarifying that we ARE the angels (other translations, especially of Luke 20:36, uses the words equal to the angels) who have lost our first estate, meaning, while earthbound, we do not know who we really are.

And they will never die again. In this respect they will be like angels. They are children of God and children of the resurrection. Luke 20:36

That would make the human race, in a sense, fallen angels. That could be why it was written that he said we will be like the angels (who are not fallen), one day; perhaps, Jesus was trying to help us comprehend an amazing truth: We are the fallen angels who have lost our way and will be restored. This restoration is the resurrection, which means a raising up from the dead.

Symbolically, the Bible states that one third of the angels lost their former place and fell from the heavens. The heavens would represent the higher realm or "spirit." The fall would be moving away from light and truth and unto darkness, or perhaps, the fall would be our temporary appearance in this physical plane. (Darkness always represents being "lost" or "lack of knowledge" in the bible.) If those of us in physical bodies are the third of angels that fell from the heavens, then two thirds remain in the light. Perhaps, these angels bring messages to us, daily, and are waiting for us to "re-join" them. We read of them having rank or hierarchies, but maybe this is indicative of their elevation: what degree of enlightenment (understanding) they possess.

Maybe, life is a journey that never ends - and that includes never-ending spiritual growth [through which] is ascension (or elevation of knowledge).

Now that you know many angel names end with el, it's clear that angels hold an elevated status within the Bible and within many religions. We read that in the Bible, Jesus was called, Immanuel (notice, again, the el) or God with us. Jesus' life had a simple yet hard (because it must be spiritually heard) to understand message; and it was not what religious institutions would teach you, today. This is why he was considered a radical in his day.

His message was that religion has helped to blind us from the truth of who we really are and that each of us has the ability to communicate with those on the other side who are in spirit. These messengers, or angels, of whom you are also, are guiding and assisting all of mankind in understanding the truth. Jesus stated it his way: "The Kingdom of God is within you." That would indicate that eternal Spirit (think energy) is within all of us, and all of us are a part of that sole, eternal Spirit.

Looking at that 'el' word, again, in the Bible's Old Testament, we are called, Elohim, meaning 'gods.' Elohim is often incorrectly translated as God in the Old Testament Bible; but it's clear that people are the Elohim, the messengers, angels or gods on either side of the veil. Walking around as humans in physical bodies, unaware that we are gods, is precisely what Jesus was trying to proclaim in John 10:33-34: "We are not stoning you for any of these, replied the Jews, but for blasphemy, because you, a mere man, claim to be God. Jesus answered them, "Is it not written in your Law (believed to be given by God), 'I have said you are gods'"

Jesus was quoting a passage from Psalm 82, where mankind is called gods. It is a passage that clearly shows all of us exist within God, or Spirit, as gods, but we do not know who we truly are and walk in darkness because of it: "Gods stand in the congregation of God; He governs among the gods, they know not, neither do they understand; they walk to and fro in darkness: All the foundations of the earth are shaken. I said, "You are gods, and all of you sons of the Most High. Nevertheless you shall die like men." - Psalm 82:1, 5-7

Angels who have fallen, all of mankind for that matter, will be resurrected unto understanding [of] who we are. We will be rejoined with loved ones, though they are not far away and are with us, even now. This is the great mystery of who we are and what may await us in life (**70**).

Certainly all this coincides with much Eastern religion. We live, we learn, we grow spiritually – we are all eventually moving toward Nirvana and beyond. The basic idea being that with each successive life we gain knowledge and wisdom and move toward a higher plane. Certainly Christianity does not teach this, but given in these contexts the similarities become outstanding. We live, we sin, we screw up...as we were destined to do. Eventually we are reborn to try it all over again. In the meantime we oversee the safety of those souls with which we are entangled. Suddenly our Western Christian religion isn't so far different than say Buddhism. Perhaps all of the world's major religions all have the same message but say it in different ways. There is one god, and one universe (at least for us) and perhaps we keep repeating our lives until we eventually get it right. While we're toiling away, mucking everything up, we have our spiritual guides who are merely souls with whom we are connected. Eventually we even swap spots with our spiritual guides and do it all over again until...we figure it out?

I found in my studies angel encounter stories all over the internet. Many of them deal with times of extreme distress, and they're often reported along with an NDE experience. But they also appear to happen at times when people are simply in a bind, and report a kindly man giving them the money for a tank of gas when they're broke and

100 miles from home. Many recollect a stranger giving them a hand at a bad moment.. What makes the stories interesting is that after the fact the nice stranger simply seems to disappear, with no one seeing him approach or leave. Later, only the person who experienced the encounter has any recollection of the "kind stranger." There often seems to be something slightly odd about the encounter. Perhaps the nice person won't give you their name, although they seem to know you quite well.

In some cases they appear to be rather unemotional, or appearing with a rather flat affect. I posit that not being familiar with a corporeal form, they are also unfamiliar with the proper facial gestures and display of emotions. Thus recall the angel described in Elaine's story seeming extremely frightening, perhaps without intentionally doing so.

Despite these oddities they often appear as completely solid – until they simply aren't there any longer. Still other accounts record that they may not be visible at all at the time of the encounter. There is one story, recounted by a mother, in which her son was crossing the street. What he hadn't seen was the car speeding up the road. Suddenly the mother reports the boy being hauled straight up by his backpack out of danger. The question we ask is why? Why, if we all have a guardian angel do angels appear to help during relatively mundane events, but fail to prevent tragedies? Then again, perhaps this is part of the balance between good and evil, suggested in the Bible.

PARANORMAL RESEARCH

There appears to be a fascination with demons and demonic hauntings in this country, mainly driven by the producers of television shows. And there are paranormal investigators out there, some members of the clergy, others that are not, that claim to specialize in this area. If demonic hauntings are rare one wonders how an investigator would gain such working knowledge. I've also met paranormal investigators that have investigated for years that claim never to have experienced anything demonic. That's because, let me emphasize one more time, demonic hauntings are exceedingly rare. That's not to say that you can't open the door and invite one in, as appears to be the case with the brother of Collin's friend. However, doing so would be extremely foolish.

Included in this section was literature on angels, not because as a paranormal researcher we investigate angels, but because I have received first-hand testimony by a reliable source of such events occurring, and second because I feel that angels get short shrift among all the literature and television shows about demons. Of course the difficulty with studying angels is that all the evidence is anecdotal. Like studying Near Death Experiences or After Death Communications the best a researcher can do is collect a heap of testimonials and then search for parallels in the material. The fact that the major religions I researched all have some form of angels and demons tells me that the idea of such celestial beings appears to be universal throughout mankind. Such universality makes one wonder; perhaps the ancients were on to something.

PARANORMAL RESEARCH

CHAPTER 10: RESOURCES, CREDITS & ACKNOWLEDGEMENTS

1. Wilson, Vince (2012). Ultimate Ghost Tech: The Science, History and Technology of Ghost Hunting. Cosmic Pantheon Press.

2. Melton, Gordon, Editor (2001). Encyclopedia of Occultism and Parapsychology; Fifth Edition. Gale Group, Inc. Farmington Hills, MI Volume 1 A-L pps 280-281.

3. Melton, Gordon, Editor (2001). Encyclopedia of Occultism and Parapsychology; Fifth Edition. Gale Group, Inc. Farmington Hills, MI Volume 1 A-L pps. 482-483.

4. Anonymous (2015). "Athenodorus Cananites." Wikipedia.org. Retrieved January 31, 2016 from https://en.wikipedia.org/wiki/Athenodorus_Cananites

5. Anonymous (2015). "Pliny the Younger." Livius.org. Retrieved January 31, 2016 from http://www.livius.org/articles/person/pliny-the-younger/

6. Zack Davisson (2013). "The Ghost of Oyuki." In Japanese Afterlife, Yūrei Stories. Hyakumonogatari Kaidankai. Retrieved January 31, 2016 from https://hyakumonogatari.com/2013/06/12/the-ghost-of-oyuki/

7. Hay, Jeffrey (2013). "Japanese Ghost Stories." Classic Japanese Literature: Folk Tales, Ghost Stories, Kenko and the Tale of 47 Loyal Assassins. Retrieved January 31, 2016 from http://factsanddetails.com/japan/cat20/sub128/item682.html#chapter-8

8. Mark, Joshua J. (2014). "Ghosts in the Ancient World." Ancient History Encyclopedia. Retrieved January 31, 2016 from http://www.ancient.eu/ghost/

9. Anonymous "Obon" Japan Guide.com Retrieved February 4, 2016 from http://www.japan-guide.com/e/e2286.html

10. Nardo, Don (2003). Exploring Cultural History: Living in Ancient Rome. Greenhaven Press. San Diego, CA.

11. Melton, Gordon, Editor (2001). Encyclopedia of Occultism and Parapsychology; Fifth Edition. Gale Group, Inc. Farmington Hills, MI Volume 1 A-L pps. 151-152.

12. Cheung, Theresa (2008). The Element Encyclopedia of Ghosts and Hauntings. Barnes and Noble, Inc. in cooperation with Harper Collins Publishers. pps. 45-46.

13. Walsh, Jane (2016). "The Scariest Monsters and Demons from Celtic Mythology." Irish Central.com Retrieved February 11, 2016 from http://www.irishcentral.com/culture/craic/the-scariest-monsters-and-demons-from-celtic-myth-67305337-237784881.html

14. McNamara-Wilson, Kim (2016). "Irish Fairy Folk of Today and Yesterday: The Slaugh." Irish Faerie Folk Series, Irish Mythology. Got Ireland? Retrieved February 11, 2016 from http://gotireland.com/2012/10/24/irish-faerie-folk-of-yore-and-yesterday-the-sluagh/

15. Ward, Christie (Gunnvôr Silfrahárr). (2016). "The Walking Dead: draugr and Aptrgangr in Old Norse Literature." The Viking Answer Lady. Retrieved February 13, 2016 from http://www.vikinganswerlady.com/ghosts.shtml

16. Fox, Denton, Translator, and Paisson, Herman, Translator (2001). Grettirs Saga. GoogleBooks.com. University of Toronto Press. pg. 37. Retrieved February 13, 2016 from https://books.google.com/books?

17. Lipka, Michael (2015). "18% of Americans say they've seen a ghost." Pew Research Center. Retrieved May 2, 2016 from http://www.pewresearch.org/fact-tank/2015/10/30/18-of-americans-say-theyve-seen-a-ghost/

18. Anonymous (2016). "Positivism." Wikipedia.com Retrieved on February 14, 2016 from https://en.wikipedia.org/wiki/Positivism

19. Wilson, Vince (2012). Ultimate Ghost Tech: The Science, History and Technology of Ghost Hunting. Cosmic Pantheon Press. pp. 11-12.

20. Cheung, Theresa (2008). The Element Encyclopedia of Ghosts and Hauntings. Barnes and Noble, Inc. in cooperation with Harper Collins Publishers. pp. 163-164.

21. Cheung, Theresa (2008). The Element Encyclopedia of Ghosts and Hauntings. Barnes and Noble, Inc. in cooperation with Harper Collins Publishers. pp. 211-214.

22. Melton, Gordon, Editor (2001). Encyclopedia of Occultism and Parapsychology; Fifth Edition. Gale Group, Inc. Farmington Hills, MI. Volume 1, A-L pp. 737-740.

23. Wilson, Vince (2012). Ultimate Ghost Tech: The Science, History and Technology of Ghost Hunting. Cosmic Pantheon Press. pp. 10-11.

24. Taylor, Troy (2003-2008). "The History and Mystery of Spiritualism." The Haunted Museum. American Hauntings and Dark Haven Entertainment. Retrieved February 21, 2016 from http://www.prairieghosts.com/spiritualism.html

25. Taylor, Troy (2008). "Eusapia Palladino; Psychic Wonder or Blatant Fraud." The Haunted Museum. American Hauntings and Dark Haven Entertainment. Retrieved February 21, 2016 from http://www.prairieghosts.com/spiritualism.html

26. Melton, Gordon, Editor (2001). Encyclopedia of Occultism and Parapsychology; Fifth Edition. Gale Group, Inc. Farmington Hills, MI. Volume 2, M-Z pp. 1214-1215.

27. Blum, Deborah (2006). Ghost Hunters: William James and the Search for Scientific Proof of Life after Death. Penguin Books. New York, NY. pp. 275-281.

28. Melton, Gordon, Editor (2001). Encyclopedia of Occultism and Parapsychology; Fifth Edition. Gale Group, Inc. Farmington Hills, MI. Volume 2, M-Z pp. 1428.

29. Tymn, Michael (2010). "Sir William Barrett." Biography. Legacy Division. Association for Communication and Evidence of Survival. Retrieved March 1, 2016 from http://www.aeces.info/Legacy-Section/Bios-1_Scientists/Barrett_W.pdf

30. Anonymous (2010). "*Eleanor Mildred Sidgwick.*" Retrieved August 6, 2010 from www.wikipedia.org/wiki/eleanor_mildred_Balfour

31. Anonymous (2010). "*Henry Sidgwick.*" Retrieved August 6, 2010 from www.wikipedia.org/wiki/Henry_Sidgwick

32. Taylor, Troy (2007). Ghosthunter's Guidebook; The Essential Guide to Investigating Ghost and Hauntings. Whitechapel Press Book. Dark Haven Entertainment Inc. Decatur, Illinois.

33. Gauld, Alan (2012). "Henry Sidgwick, Theism and Psychical Research." Retrieved March 18, 2016 from http://www.henrysidgwick.com/4th-paper.1st.congress.cat.eng.html

34. Targ, Russell (2014). "Human Personality and Its Survival of Bodily Death." Russell Targ website. Retrieved March 19, 2016 from http://www.espresearch.com/survival/

35. Gurney, Edmund, Myers F.W.H., Podmore, Frank (1886). Phantasms of the Living. Society for Psychical Research. TRÜBNER AND CO., Ludgate Hill, E.C., London, UK.

36. Balzano, Christopher. Weisberg, Tim (2012). Haunted Objects; Stories of Ghosts on Your Shelf. Krause Publications, Iola, WI.

37. Chestnut, Debbie (2011). Is Your House Haunted? Poltergeists, Ghosts or Bad Wiring. MJF Books. New York, New York.

38. Cheung, Theresa (2008). The Element Encyclopedia of Ghosts and Hauntings. Harper Collins Publishers in cooperation with Barnes and Noble. China.

39. Melton, J. G., Editor (2001). Encyclopedia of Occultism and Parapsychology. Fifth Edition, Vol. 2. Gale Group. New York.

40. La Grand, Louis E. PhD (1999). Messages and Miracles: Extraordinary Experiences of the Bereaved. Llewellyn Publications, St. Paul, Minnesota.

41. Offutt, Jason (2012). "The Lurking Shadow People." Mysterious Universe.org. Retrieved January 14, 2013 from http://mysteriousuniverse.org/2012/03/the-lurking-shadow-people/

42. Richford, Nannette (2007). Hauntings; What are Shadow People?" Retrieved January 14, 2013. Re-retrieved August 7, 2016 from StealthSkater.com http://www.stealthskater.com/Documents/Shadow_05.pdf

43. Russell, Shaan (2007). "Shadow People Phenomenon." Unexplained Mysteries. Retrieved January 14, 2013 from http://www.unexplained-mysteries.com/column.php?id=97317

44. van Lommel, Pim. M.D. (2010). Consciousness beyond Life: The Science of the Near Death Experience. Harper Collins Publishers. NY, NY.

45. **Special Thanks** to David Schumacher, Director of Anomalous Research Department, Paranormal Research Group and Jennifer Lauer, Co-Director of the Paranormal Research Group paranormalresearchgroup.com for their helpful insights and for pointing me towards other terrific sources of information.

46. Belanger, Michelle (2009). Haunting Experiences; Encounters with the Otherworldly. Llewellyn Publications. Woodbury, MN.

47. Belanger, Michelle (2009). The Ghost Hunters Survival Guide: Protection Techniques for Encounters with the Paranormal. Llewellen Worldwide. Woodbury, MN.

48. Grosset, Philip. "Alexandra David-Neel" Clerical Detectives. Retrieved April 30, 2016 from http://www.detecs.org/munpa.html

49. Gaizy, Bill (2012). "Tulpas – Creatures of the Mind, Mystery Files." Retrieved April 30, 2016 from http://hubpages.com/religion-philosophy/Tulpas-Creatures-of-the-Mind-Mystery-Files

50. Oreck, Alden (2016). "Modern Jewish History; The Golem." Jewish Virtual Library. Retrieved April 26, 2016 from https://www.jewishvirtuallibrary.org/jsource/Judaism/Golem.html

51. Twist, Elizabeth (2011). "Tulpa." Elizabeth Twist blogsite. Retrieved April 26, 2016 from http://elizabethtwist.blogspot.com/2011/04/tulpa.html

52. White, Charla (2006). "The Philip Experiment—A Study in Paranormal Research." Grimstone, Inc. Retrieved April 26, 2016 from http://www.grimstone-inc.com/News/e-news/grimstone2-7.pdf

53. Psalm 136:19 Bible Hub. Retrieved April 30, 2016 from http://biblehub.com/niv/psalms/139-16.htm

54. Beloff, John (1990). "Parapsychology and Radical Dualism." The Relentless Question. McFarland. Retrieved May 29, 2016 from http://www.newdualism.org/sites/moebius.psy.ed.ac.uk-dualism/papers/radical.html

55. La Grand, Louis. (Messages and Miracles: Extraordinary Experiences of the Bereaved. Llewellyn Publications, St. Paul Minnesota. 1999

56. Owen, Paula J. (2014). "After Death Communication Brings Solace to Many." Telegram.com. Worchester, Massachusetts.

57. van Lommel, Pim. M.D. (2010). Consciousness Beyond Life; The Science of Near-Death Experience. Harper Collins. New York, NY.

58. Guggenheim, Will (2016). "After Death Communication (ADC) Experiences." After-Death.com. Retrieved May 2, 2016 from http://www.after-death.com/Pages/About/ADC.aspx

59. Guggenheim Bill and Judy (1996). Hello from Heaven! Bantam Books. New York, New York.

60. Anonymous (2015). "Characteristics of a Near-Death Experience." International Association for Near-Death Studies Inc. (IANDS). Retrieved May 10, 2016 from http://iands.org/ndes/about-ndes/characteristics.html

61. Smed, Jouni A. (2015). "Introduction – Frequently Asked Questions." Out of Body Experience Research Foundation (OBERF). Retrieved June 5, 2016 from http://www.oberf.org/faq.html#Introduction

62. "Waves" Physics Classroom.com

63. van Lommel, Pim, M.D. (2010). Consciousness Beyond Life; The Science of the Near-Death Experience. Harper Collins. New York, NY.

64. Jones, Marie D. (2007). PSIence; How New Discoveries in Quantum Physics and New Science May Explain the Existence of Paranormal Phenomena. The Career Press Inc. Franklin Lakes, NJ.

65. Cardinuto, Michael (2013). "Symptoms/Characteristic of a Demonic Ghost Haunting" Long Island Paranormal Investigators. (L.I.P.I.) Retrieved on June 13, 2016 from http://liparanormalinvestigators.com/demonic.shtml

66. Carus, Paul (1900). "History of the Devil. Buddhism." Sacred-Texts.com Retrieved June 13, 2016 from http://www.sacred-texts.com/evil/hod/hod10.htm

67. Shoshan, Eran (2005-2013). "The Angels in Different Religions." Retrieved June 13, 2016 from http://guideangel.com/angels_in_religions.html

68. Mufti, Imam Kamil (2006). "The Six Pillars of Faith and other Islamic Beliefs; Belief in Angels." Islamic Religion .com Retrieved June 13, 2016 from http://www.islamreligion.com/articles/41/belief-in-angels/

69. Anonymous (2015). "Angels (Christianity)." ReligionFacts.com. Retrieved June 13, 2016 from www.religionfacts.com/angels/christianity

70. Charles, Louis. "What are Angels?" "Angels & Ghosts." AngelsGhosts.com. Retrieved June 19, 2016 from http://www.angelsghosts.com/angels_what_are_they

71. Sahih Muslim Book 7 Hadith 2996

72. Gallup (2016). "Most People Still Believe in God." Gallup Social Series. Retrieved August 7, 2016 from http://www.gallup.com/poll/193271/americans-believe-god.aspx

73. Lambdin, Thomas O., Translator. Gospel of Thomas Collection The Nag Hammadi Library. The Gnostic Society Library. Retrieved August 7, 2016 from http://gnosis.org/naghamm/gthlamb.html

74. van Lommel, Pim, M.D. (2016). Quote from private correspondence sent to author.

75. Beloff, John (1990). "Parapsychology and Radical Dualism." Originally published in the Relentless Question, McFarland (1990). Retrieved August 13, 2016 from http://www.newdualism.org/sites/moebius.psy.ed.ac.uk-dualism/papers/radical.html

76. Physics Classroom. Com "Definition of a wave." Retrieved August 13, 2016 from http://www.physicsclassroom.com/class/waves/Lesson-1/What-is-a-Wave

77. McCleod, Saul (2007). "Mind Body Debate." Retrieved August 13, 2016 from http://www.simplypsychology.org/mindbodydebate.html

78. Anonymous. Classroom notes. "Notes for Ontology I: Dualism and Behavioralism." http://philosophy.tamu.edu/~sdaniel/Notes/dualism.html

79. Myers, F.W.H. (1903) Human Personality and Its Survival of Bodily Death. Longmans, Green and Co. London, New York and Bombay.

80. Auerbach, Loyd (1986). ESP, Hauntings and Poltergeists: A Parapsychologist's Handbook. Warner Books. New York, NY.

81. Discovery Channel Series (1997). True Hauntings.

82. Bernstein, Adam (2005). "Psychology Expert Robert Baker; Unmasked Ghostly Apparitions." Washington Post. Obituary Section. Retrieved August 13, 2016 from http://www.washingtonpost.com/wp-dyn/content/article/2005/08/11/AR2005081102036.html

83. Redfern, Nick, Steiger, Brad (2014). The Zombie Book; the Encyclopedia of the Living Dead. Visible Ink Press. Pps. 92-95. Retrieved August 20, 2016 from https://books.google.com/books?id=64AsBQAAQBAJ&pg=PA93&lpg=PA93&dq=difference+between+a+haugbui+and+a+draugr&source=bl&ots=hnCYcdXmW4&sig=3DVynYupbBjT-lvRlfHXnGWam_Y&hl=en&sa=X&ved=0ahUKEwj2vsa_tdDOAhUG_R4KHV_2AroQ6AEIRDAH#v=onepage&q=difference%20between%20a%20haugbui%20and%20a%20draugr&f=false

84. Anonymous (2016) After Death Communications. "A Search for Life After Death." Retrieved August 30, 2016 from https://thesearchforlifeafterdeath.com/2016/05/07/after-death-communications-why-it-happens-why-it-doesnt-and-how-to-encourage-signs-from-loved-ones-in-spirit/

85. Lipka, Michael (2015). "18% of Americans say they have Seen a Ghost." Pew Research Center: FactTank. Retrieved August 30, 2016 from http://www.cbsnews.com/news/cbs-news-poll-contacted-by-the-dead/

86. CBS Interactive Inc. (2015). "CBS News Poll: Contacted by the Dead." Retrieved August 30, 2016 from http://www.cbsnews.com/news/cbs-news-poll-contacted-by-the-dead/

87. (2014) "Dr. Raymond Moody's Near Death Experience Research." Near Death Experiences and the Afterlife. Retrieved October 8, 2016 from Near-Death Experiences and the Afterlife

88. MacDonald, Fiona (2015) "There are seven types of near death experiences, according to research." Science Alert.com Retrieved October 8, 2016 from http://www.sciencealert.com/there-are-seven-types-of-near-death-experiences-according-to-new-research

89. Olson, Bob (2012) "Hello From Heaven; The 12 Types of After Death Communications with Bill Guggenehim." AfterlifeTV. Retrieved October 8, 2016 from http://www.afterlifetv.com/2012/08/22/hello-from-heaven-the-12-types-of-after-death-communication-with-bill-guggenheim/

90. Anonymous (2016) "The Twelve Most Frequent Types of After Death Communications." Near Death Experiences and the Afterlife. Near Death.com.

http://www.near-death.com/paranormal/synchronicity/introduction-to-synchronicity-and-adcs.html#a01

ART CREDITS

Artist Bubble Hermit. (2016). Wraith and Japanese Ghost with Crow. Original artwork created on commission and used with permission. Independent artist for DeviantArt.com.

Thompson, Edward, Photographer. "A Storm Approaching Pripyat, from The Red Forest" (2012). Shot on Kodak Aerochrome film. *The Unseen: An Atlas of Infrared Plates.* Schilt Publishing. Amsterdam, The Netherlands.

Photo Headers for Chapters 1,2,3,4,5,6,7,9 original photos by author.

SPECIAL THANKS

Maya Paveza for putting the book into its final format for no other reason than she wanted to help. Thank you sincerely for your hours of challenging work.

Vince Wilson for all his sage advice, generosity of spirit and for helping make sure that the publishing of this book wasn't simply a pipe dream.

Mr. Greg Pocha for letting me pick his brain, *repeatedly*, and for his patience with my inability to ever seem to get things *quite* right.

Dr. Pim van Lommell and Dr. Andrew Nichols for generously sharing their extensive research and knowledge.

To my husband and son for forgiving my hours of solitude and my grumbling acknowledgement to every inquiry being, "I can't talk to you now. I'm writing!"

And to my mother for laboriously reading through the manuscript even though she has absolutely no interest in the subject beyond the fact that her weird daughter decided to write a book on it.

ABOUT THE AUTHOR

Robin Strom-Mackey has been researching and investigating the paranormal for the better part of a decade. During that time, she has written extensively about ghosts for her blog *The Shore* at delawareparanormal.blogspot.com. She is the founder and director of Delaware Paranormal Research Group as well as being a medical professional, mother and wife. Formerly she was a teacher of English, Communications and broadcasting, and a television journalist for the U.S. Navy. Aside from video she is also an enthusiastic amateur photographer. She loves anything to do with the water, jogging, hiking, biking, drinking Bloody Mary's (Pina coladas being far too sweet) and getting caught in the rain. She lives in Delaware with husband, son, Uther the dog, Miss Scarlet the cat and a sugar glider named Hiccup.

CPSIA information can be obtained
at www.ICGtesting.com
Printed in the USA
BVOW08s2048041117
499557BV00001B/87/P